CASEBOOK SERIES

This book is to be returned on or before
the last date stamped below.

SHAKESPEARE: *Early Tragedies* Neil Taylor & Bryan Loughrey
SHAKESPEARE: *Hamlet* John Jump
SHAKESPEARE: *Henry IV Parts I and II* G.K. Hunter
SHAKESPEARE: *Henry V* Michael Quinn
SHAKESPEARE: *Julius Caesar* Peter Ure
SHAKESPEARE: *King Lear* Frank Kermode
SHAKESPEARE: *Macbeth* John Wain
SHAKESPEARE: *Measure for Measure* C. K. Stead
SHAKESPEARE: *The Merchant of Venice* John Wilders
SHAKESPEARE: *'Much Ado About Nothing' & 'As You Like It'* John Russell Brown
SHAKESPEARE: *Othello* John Wain
SHAKESPEARE: *Richard II* Nicholas Brooke
SHAKESPEARE: *The Sonnets* Peter Jones
SHAKESPEARE: *The Tempest* D. J. Palmer
SHAKESPEARE: *Troilus and Cressida* Priscilla Martin
SHAKESPEARE: *Twelfth Night* D. J. Palmer
SHAKESPEARE: *The Winter's Tale* Kenneth Muir
SPENSER: *The Faerie Queene* Peter Bayley
SHERIDAN: *Comedies* Peter Davison
STOPPARD: *'Rosencrantz and Guildenstern are Dead'*, *'Jumpers'* & *'Travesties'*
    T. Bareham
SWIFT: *Gulliver's Travels* Richard Gravil
SYNGE: *Four Plays* Ronald Ayling
TENNYSON: *In Memoriam* John Dixon Hunt
THACKERAY: *Vanity Fair* Arthur Pollard
TROLLOPE: *The Barsetshire Novels* T. Bareham
WEBSTER: *'The White Devil' & 'The Duchess of Malfi'* R. V. Holdsworth
WILDE: *Comedies* William Tydeman
VIRGINIA WOOLF: *To the Lighthouse* Morris Beja
WORDSWORTH: *Lyrical Ballads* Alun R. Jones & William Tydeman
WORDSWORTH: *The 1807 Poems* Alun R. Jones
WORDSWORTH: *The Prelude* W. J. Harvey & Richard Gravil
YEATS: *Poems 1919–35* Elizabeth Cullingford
YEATS: *Last Poems* Jon Stallworthy

Issues in Contemporary Critical Theory Peter Barry
Thirties Poets: 'The Auden Group' Ronald Carter
Tragedy: Developments in Criticism R.P. Draper
Epic Ronald Draper
Poetry Criticism and Practice: Developments since the Symbolists A.E. Dyson
Three Contemporary Poets: Gunn, Hughes, Thomas A.E. Dyson
Elizabethan Poetry: Lyrical & Narrative Gerald Hammond
The Metaphysical Poets Gerald Hammond
Medieval English Drama Peter Happé
The English Novel: Developments in Criticism since Henry James Stephen Hazell
Poetry of the First World War Dominic Hibberd
The Romantic Imagination John Spencer Hill
Drama Criticism: Developments since Ibsen Arnold P. Hinchliffe
Three Jacobean Revenge Tragedies R.V. Holdsworth
The Pastoral Mode Bryan Loughrey
The Language of Literature Norman Page
Comedy: Developments in Criticism D.J. Palmer
Studying Shakespeare John Russell Brown
The Gothic Novel Victor Sage
Pre-Romantic Poetry J.R. Watson

Pope

The Rape of the Lock

A CASEBOOK

EDITED BY

JOHN DIXON HUNT

MACMILLAN

First published 1968 by
THE MACMILLAN PRESS LTD
Houndmills, Basingstoke, Hampshire RG21 2XS
and London
Companies and representatives
throughout the world

ISBN 0–333–06995–1

A catalogue record for this book is available
from the British Library.

17 16 15 14 13 12 11 10
03 02 01 00 99 98 97 96 95

Printed in Hong Kong

CONTENTS

ACKNOWLEDGEMENTS

G. Wilson Knight, extract from *The Vital Flame* (Methuen & Co. Ltd); Geoffrey Tillotson, extract from *The Rape of the Lock and Other Poems* (Methuen & Co. Ltd, Yale University Press); 'The Case of Miss Arabella Fermor', from *The Well-Wrought Urn* (Dobson Books Ltd; Harcourt, Brace and World Inc.; © Cleanth Brooks 1947); *'The Rape of the Lock'*, from the Introduction to *The Augustans*, ed. Maynard Mack (Prentice-Hall Inc.); Hugo M. Reichard, 'The Love Affair in Pope's *Rape of the Lock*', from *Publications of the Modern Language Association of America*, LXIX, 1954 (The Modern Language Association of America); Reuben A. Brower, ' "Am'rous Causes" ', from *Alexander Pope: The Poetry of Allusion* (The Clarendon Press); Murray Krieger, 'The "Frail China Jar" and the Rude Hand of Chaos', from *Centennial Review of Arts and Sciences* (1961) pp. 176–94; 'The "Fall" of China and *The Rape of the Lock*', from *Philological Quarterly*, XLI (1962) (Mr Aubrey Williams and The University of Iowa); extract from *To The Palace of Wisdom* (Doubleday & Co. Inc.; © Martin Price 1964); J. S. Cunningham, Introduction to *The Rape of the Lock* (The Clarendon Press).

GENERAL EDITOR'S PREFACE

EACH of this series of Casebooks concerns either one well-known
and influential work of literature or two or three closely linked
works. The main section consists of critical readings, mostly
modern, brought together from journals and books. A selection
of reviews and comments by the author's contemporaries is also
included, and sometimes comments from the author himself.
The Editor's Introduction charts the reputation of the work from
its first appearance until the present time.

What is the purpose of such a collection? Chiefly, to assist
reading. Our first response to literature may be, or seem to be,
'personal'. Certain qualities of vigour, profundity, beauty or
'truth to experience' strike us, and the work gains a foothold in
our mind. Later, an isolated phrase or passage may return to
haunt or illuminate. Where did we hear that? we wonder – it
could scarcely be better put.

In these and similar ways appreciation begins, but major
literature prompts to very much more. There are certain facts
we need to know if we are to understand properly. Who were
the author's original readers, and what assumptions did he share
with them? What was his theory of literature? Was he committed
to a particular historical situation, or to a set of beliefs? We need
historians as well as critics to help us with this. But there are also
more purely literary factors to take account of: the work's
structure and rhetoric; its symbols and archetypes; its tone, genre
and texture; its use of language; the words on the page. In all
these matters critics can inform and enrich our individual responses by offering imaginative recreations of their own.

For the life of a book is not, after all, merely 'personal'; it is
more like a tripartite dialogue, between a writer living 'then', a

reader living 'now', and whatever forces of survival and honour link the two. Criticism is the public manifestation of this dialogue, a witness to the continuing power of literature to arouse and excite. It illuminates the possibilities and rewards of the dialogue, pushing 'interpretation' as far forward as it can go.

And here, indeed, is the rub: how far can it go? Where does 'interpretation' end and nonsense begin? Why is one interpretation superior to another, and why does each age need to interpret for itself? The critic knows that his insights have value only in so far as they serve the text, and that he must take account of views differing sharply from his own. He knows that his own writing will be judged as well as the work he writes about, so that he cannot simply assert inner illumination or a differing taste.

The critical forum is a place of vigorous conflict and disagreement, but there is nothing in this to cause dismay. What is attested is the complexity of human experience and the richness of literature, not any chaos or relativity of taste. A critic is better seen, no doubt, as an explorer than as an 'authority', but explorers ought to be, and usually are, well equipped. The effect of good criticism is to convince us of what C. S. Lewis called 'the enormous extension of our being which we owe to authors'. A Casebook will be justified only if it helps to promote the same end.

A single volume can represent no more than a small selection of critical opinions. Some critics have been excluded for reasons of space, and it is hoped that readers will follow up the further suggestions in the Select Bibliography. Other contributions have been severed from their original context, to which some readers may wish to return. Indeed, if they take a hint from the critics represented here, they certainly will.

A. E. DYSON

INTRODUCTION

SOME time during the summer of 1711 the circle of prominent Catholic families in the home counties was disturbed by the rash act of Robert, 7th Lord Petre, in removing part of her coiffure from a famous beauty, Arabella Fermor. As Pope himself told his first 'biographer', Joseph Spence,

The stealing of Miss Belle Fermor's hair was taken too seriously, and caused an estrangement between the two families, though they have lived long in great friendship before. A common acquaintance and well-wisher to both desired me to write a poem to make a jest of it, and laugh them together again. It was in this view that I wrote my *Rape of the Lock*, which was well received and had its effect in the two families.[1]

The first version of the poem in two cantos was written in less than a fortnight some time in the August or September of 1711. The well-wisher was Pope's intimate friend John Caryll, to whom the poem's invocation alludes. It is doubtful whether Pope personally knew any of the parties concerned, but the circulation among them of the manuscript, which the lady 'vouchsafe[d] to view' and which Lord Petre 'approve[d]', apparently succeeded in healing the breach between them. A later critic, Warburton, who knew Pope towards the end of his life, notes that Arabella Fermor even 'took it so well as to give about copies of it'.

We may fairly assume the lady did like the poem. As Thomas Parnell's complimentary poem on *The Rape of the Lock* explained,

---

[1] Spence's *Observations, Anecdotes and Characters of Books and Men*, ed. J. M. Osborn (Oxford, 1966) 1 43–4.

she had acquired almost unprecedented literary fame, whatever the social repercussions:

> How flame the glories of *Belinda's* Hair,
> Made by thy Muse the envy of the Fair?
> Less shone the tresses Ægypt's Princess wore,
> Which sweet Callimachus so sung before.

We have also a portrait of Arabella (see frontispiece to the Twickenham Edition of the poem) in which she wears the 'sparkling Cross' mentioned in the poem; Pope's couplet is inscribed on the canvas. There is some doubt as to the date of both the portrait and the addition of the lines, if they *were* added later; yet whatever the possibilities it seems fair to assume that the portrait must represent Arabella's pride or pleasure at her literary metamorphosis.

The anonymous publication in May 1712 of the two-canto version was also explained by Pope to Joseph Spence: 'copies of it got about, and 'twas like to be printed, on which I published the first draught of it (without the machinery), in a Miscellany of Tonson's . . .' (loc. cit.). Piracy in the book trade during the eighteenth century was notorious, and Pope doubtless wished to benefit himself from its publication (he received £7 for the first version, £15 for the second in 1714). In the dedication to the enlarged version, he states, with what justice we do not know, that Arabella Fermor herself authorised the original publication: 'But as it was communicated with the air of a Secret, it soon found its way into the world. An imperfect copy having been offer'd to a Bookseller, you had the good-nature for my sake to consent to the publication of one more correct . . .' But as Geoffrey Tillotson has explained in the Twickenham Edition of the poem, the danger of piracy meant that Arabella Fermor's only choice was between authorised or unauthorised publication, and that there is no reason to suppose she withheld permission. We know that Pope made quite certain that Miss Fermor as well as Lord Petre received 'advance copies' or 'offprints' of the poem, an unlikely gesture if he had gone ahead without the lady's authority. He represents her in *A Key to the Lock* as pleased with her part in the poem, taking up 'the character of *Belinda* with much Frankness and good Humour'.

But we have hints that some displeasure was incurred after the poem's first publication. In a letter of 8 November 1712 Pope writes: 'Sir Plume blusters, I hear; nay, the celebrated lady herself is offended, and, which is stranger, not at herself, but me . . .' Later he reported to Spence: 'Nobody but Sir George Brown was angry, and he was so a good deal and for a long time. He could not bear that Sir Plume should talk *nothing* but nonsense . . .' (loc. cit.).

Exactly why this belated offence was taken is unknown. Perhaps the poem offended by some of its indelicate innuendoes, perceived during more leisurely revisitings of the poem; but these are nothing compared to the normal strictures on ladies in periodical literature of the time. Certainly it is understandable how a closer reading and more consideration of Pope's satire might disturb all the parties concerned. But it is equally possible that the scandal had gone too far for Arabella, especially as the 'Baron', who might be supposed from internal literary evidence to be interested in marrying her, chose another bride just two months before the poem was issued. Whatever the cause and the nature of the offence taken, Pope seems to have been concerned to placate Sir George in *A Key to the Lock* by showing two men as possible candidates for the role of Sir Plume (see infra, p. 34). As for Arabella, Pope's dedication to the second and enlarged version of 1714 was contrived especially to give her favour, perhaps even to help her out of a rather silly or embarrassing position. Pope wrote to John Caryll on 9 January 1714:

As to the *Rape of the Lock*, I believe I have managed the dedication so nicely that it can neither hurt the lady, nor the author. I writ it very lately, and upon great deliberation; the young lady approves of it; and the best advice in the kingdom, of the men of sense has been made use of in it, even to the Treasurer's. A preface which salved the lady's honour, without affixing her name, was also prepared, but by herself superseded in favour of the dedication.

The rejected 'preface' is probably the verse epistle 'To Belinda
. . .' (see infra, p. 23).

The dedication to Arabella and the enlarged poem of 1714 take
us from the complicated and ultimately unimportant tangle of
social trivia into the subtle and permanent fabric of the poem's
creation. For of the original events which led to the poem, the
dedication stresses only the central one:

As to the following Cantos, all the Passages of them are as
Fabulous, as the Vision at the Beginning, or the Transformation
at the End; (except the Loss of your Hair, which I always name
with Reverence). The Human Persons are as Fictitious as the
Airy ones; and the Character of *Belinda*, as it is now manag'd,
resembles You in nothing but in Beauty.

Pope's concern, palpable beneath his careful courtesies, is now
for his art. He stresses his metamorphic, creative endeavours. The
reference to the lock, which might pass with the dedicatee as
social decorum, is a witty acknowledgement of the poet's gratitude
for such a superb subject. The last lines of the fifth canto confirm
this. They celebrate the lasting fame which poetry has granted
the ephemeral lock ('since Locks will turn to grey') and by implication which the lock offers poetry; in doing so they echo
Spenser's *Amoretti*, LXXV –

> Not so, (quod I) let baser things devize
>   to dy in dust, but you shall live by fame:
>   my verse your vertues rare shall eternize,
>   and in the hevens wryte your glorious name.

The reverence that Pope has for Belinda's lock is for the opportunity afforded him to transform the passing social event into
permanent relevance.

If the 1712 version sold poorly, Pope was completely gratified
by the reception of the 1714 poem, which sold 3000 copies within
four days. It was justly preferred to the earlier and shorter poem.
Despite Addison's advice to leave the first version as it was, Pope
expanded two cantos into five and introduced the domesticated
supernatural agents, including the Cave of Spleen, the scene at

Belinda's toilet and the game of Ombre. He told Spence in 1739 that the

machinery was added afterwards to make it look a little more considerable; and the scheme of adding it was much liked and approved of by several of my friends, and particularly by Dr. Garth, who, as he was one of the best-natured men in the world, was very fond of it. (loc. cit.)

(This Dr Garth is, of course, the author of *The Dispensary* of 1699, which served Pope as a model for his mock-epic.) The only other major addition or alterations came in 1717, when Pope decided to 'open more clearly the MORAL of the Poem' by adding Clarissa's speech in canto five; hitherto her role had been confined to handing the Baron the fatal scissors in the third canto. The poem was then included in the *Works* of that year, by which time the 1714 version had reached a fifth edition.

Ever since 1714 *The Rape of the Lock* has almost always enjoyed an enthusiastic and delighted reception, of which George (later Bishop) Berkeley's in a letter to its author is typical:

I have accidentally met with your Rape of the Lock here [in Leghorn!], having never seen it before. Style, painting, judgement, spirit, I had already admired in other of your writings; but in this I am charmed with the magic of your invention, with all those images, allusions, and inexplicable beauties, which you raise so surprisingly, and at the same time so naturally out of a trifle.[1]

When the poem did suffer censure for such 'faults' as its plagiarism of Garth and Boileau, it was usually a victim of the literary in-fighting and personality-conflicts of Pope's career, which have little to do with its poetic achievement. Addison's reserved comments in the *Spectator*, no. 523, probably have political origins, and Dennis's graceless *Remarks on Mr. Pope's Rape of the Lock* stem from personal animosity and professional rivalries which involved any modern poem like Pope's in the endless and

[1] Quoted R. K. Root, *The Poetical Career of Alexander Pope* (Princeton, 1938) p. 87.

often fruitless battle between the Ancients and Moderns. Dennis composed his *Remarks* in 1714, but withheld them for fourteen years until stung into publication by references to himself in *The Dunciad*. The *Remarks* contains much that is sheer bad-tempered blindness, though it displays some shrewdness on the moral purpose of the poem and on the machinery. Its main interest is as an example both of the distortions that personal conflicts produce in criticism and of that critical obtuseness and dullness which Pope and his friends, notably Swift, saw pervading the world of scholarship and taste and to combat which the Scriblerus Club was established. The most successful pieces which the Club stimulated are *Gulliver's Travels*, *The Dunciad* and the *Memoirs of Martinus Scriblerus*. But Pope's *Key to the Lock* also derives its satiric energies from that enterprise. Through the pedantic and injudicious mind of the apothecary Barnivelt it mocks the inept and tendentious criticism which can so belabour the fine subtleties of imagination.[1]

The first real adjustments in critical reaction to Pope begin in the second half of the century and are due mainly to new movements in taste and aesthetics. The most famous example of this complex of new ideas and attitudes and a book that accelerated their growth was Edmund Burke's *Philosophical Inquiry into the Origin and Nature of our Ideas of the Sublime and the Beautiful* (1756). That year also saw the first volume by another writer intimately connected with the new aesthetics, Joseph Warton's *Essay on the Genius and Writings of Pope*. It is here that the consequences of these fresh ideas for a reading of Pope become conspicuous. Although Warton still displays some eighteenth-century notions of how poetry should work, he is equally confident of new criteria which lead him to observe that Pope is more a 'Man of Wit' and a 'Man of Sense' than a 'True Poet'. He expresses his general position very clearly in a passage that is worth setting down in full:

There is nothing in so sublime a style as *The Bard* of Gray. This is a matter of *fact*, not of *reasoning*; and means to point out, what

[1] For a further account of the Scriblerus Club, see *Memoirs of Martinus Scriblerus*, ed. Charles Kerby-Miller (New Haven, 1950).

Pope *has actually done*, not what, if he had put out his full strength, he was *capable* of *doing*. No man can possibly think, or can hint, that the Author of *The Rape of the Lock*, and the *Eloisa*, wanted *imagination*, or *sensibility*, or *pathetic*; but he certainly did not so often indulge and exert those talents, nor give so many proofs of them, as he did of strong sense and judgement. This turn of mind led him to admire French models; he studied *Boileau* attentively; formed himself upon *him*, as Milton formed himself upon the Grecian and Italian Sons of *Fancy*. He stuck to describing *modern manners*; but these *manners*, because they are *familiar, uniform, artificial, and polished*, are, for these four reasons, in their very nature *unfit* for any lofty effort of the Muse. ... Whatever poetical enthusiasm he actually possessed, he with-held and suppressed. The perusal of him ... affects not our minds with such strong emotions as we feel from *Homer* or *Milton* so that no man, of a true poetical spirit, is master of himself while he reads them. Hence he is a writer fit for universal perusal, and of general utility; adapted to all ages and all stations; for the old and for the young; the man of business and the scholar. He who would think, and there are many such, the *Faerie Queene, Palamon and Arcite, The Tempest*, or *Comus*, childish and romantic, may relish Pope. Surely it is no narrow, nor individious, nor niggardly encomium to say, he is the great Poet of Reason; the *First* of *Ethical* Authors in Verse; which he was by choice, not necessity.

The consequences of this radically new response to Pope will be traced further in a moment. But it is important meanwhile to insist that Warton's ideas were not allowed to dominate at once. Samuel Johnson's *Life of Pope* reaffirms traditional views of his work as late as 1781, only one year before the issue of Warton's completed *Essay*. Johnson even suggested that the long delay in the appearance of the second volume was a result of Warton's inability to persuade the public of his qualified disapproval of Pope. Certainly it is Johnson's weighty pronouncements which are sustained by the authority of established criteria, while Warton's pioneer reading has to wait for general agreement.

But as far as the nineteenth century was concerned, it is

Warton's critique that triumphs. From him proceeds all the
doubts expressed about Pope's imagination, from Coleridge's
distaste for the 'logic of wit' in poetry to Arnold's apophthegm
in his essay on Gray:

The difference between genuine poetry and the poetry of Dryden
and Pope, and all their school, is briefly this: their poetry is conceived and composed in their wits, genuine poetry is conceived
and composed in the soul.

The examples of romantic criticism in this volume also betray the
pervasive effect of Warton's *Essay*. Partly because Johnson had
expressed a dislike for the 'Elegy to the Memory of an Unfortunate Lady', the opposing criticism tended to base such claims
as they wished to make for Pope on the 'romantic' group of poems
that included, besides the 'Elegy', *Eloisa to Abelard*; in those two
Pope could be shown to display a true taste for the pathetic and
the sublime. Although it cannot compete on those counts, *The
Rape of the Lock* continued to be a favourite for its wit and invention. Both Bowles and Hazlitt honour the poem's artificiality
(though the Romantics tend to exaggerate the artifice of eighteenth-century society), but they cannot equate poetic seriousness
with a satiric intention, nor do they seem to recognise that
serious poetry may use ephemeral trivialities as its subject-matter.
Even where Romantic criticism – as in the case of Campbell, an
enthusiastic defender of eighteenth-century poetry – tries to do
justice to Pope, it is hampered by severely limiting preconcep-
tions, and in the end only hedges its judgements. Thus Campbell
writes of *The Rape of the Lock* that 'There is no finer gem than
this poem in all the *lighter* treasures of English fancy' (his italics,
see infra, p. 87). Alone among the Romantics Byron admired
Pope for the right reasons.

   The criticism of Pope in the nineteenth century has really more
historical interest than intrinsic value. Leigh Hunt's account of
The Rape of the Lock ('the airiest wit that ever raised a joke') is
typical of the limited delight with which it was read; little has
changed since Warton's claim that it was the 'best SATIRE extant'.
It has been the responsibility of modern criticism to rescue

Pope as a serious writer and to justify satire as the vehicle of real imagination.

Modern readings of *The Rape of the Lock* in this volume have, not surprisingly, revised most Romantic ideas about the poem. Its moral seriousness and imaginative intelligence have been reasserted, its 'full richness and complexity' explored and established. The lightness and delicacy of its tone are still acknowledged, but this does not necessarily mean the poem dwindles into flimsy. More attention to the social details of Belinda's world have not diminished Pope's imaginative and witty manipulation of them, but the poem's artificiality has been revisited with some new sense of its contemporary context and the social *mores* out of which the poem comes. Above all, the modern approach rests upon the assumption that the texture of poetry can bear close examination, that we may usefully examine how, for example, wit works and how it enhances what G. Wilson Knight calls the 'imaginative solidity' of the poem.

This in its turn opens up for criticism an important area of the poem's existence: the fashion in which Pope uses allusions to other writing with something of the force of metaphor. John Dennis marshalled parallels with Homer and Virgil to prove how ludicrous Pope was for him; we now respect the extent to which the poetry depends upon such allusions and upon our participating as readers in a creative act which accommodates the appropriateness or inappropriateness of their reference into our sense of the whole poem. Both Reuben A. Brower and Earl R. Wasserman[1] are concerned to illuminate the poetry's allusive life in this way. Moreover, the density of allusion in such a poem as *The Rape of the Lock* has also put criticism on its guard against too simple notions of the mock-epic. The poem may mimic the heroic actions of Virgil's heroes or Homer's warriors, but it is also a flirtation with the sublime. It implies in its parody of the epic fresh possibilities for the heroic mode in an age that could be embarrassed by its own lack of heroic potential. A majority of the modern essays in this volume amplify our sense of the

[1] See Select Bibliography.

mock-epic *genre*, the mock-heroic stance which the poem adopts and the mythopoeic activities in which the poet engages.

All these modern inquiries encourage us to discover in the poem a moral seriousness that the Romantics would never attribute to such a satire. Above all, I think, many of these articles make us recognise that *The Rape of the Lock* owes its resonance to the accommodation within a delicate scheme and tone of dangerous, powerful motifs – sex and religion. The poet who is alert to the superficialities of his contemporary society and is witty and charming at its expense can yet *at the same time* appreciate the serious relevance of the human passions. Pope contrives from both his responses a poem that maintains what J. S. Cunningham calls a 'continuous doubleness of apprehension, by which the bathetic can yield poignancy, the mock-portentous can function genuinely, the trivial can seem significant'.

Finally, two articles collected here remind us of other works outside *The Rape of the Lock*. Martin Price looks forward to the 'more inclusive and morally significant visions of order' that inform Pope's *Moral Essays*, Horatian imitations and *The Dunciad*. Murray Krieger sees in *The Rape of the Lock* an infinitely precarious image of art's fragility that the chaotic and rude world of Dullness will threaten and finally overwhelm. Both are important reminders of what otherwise this collection would perhaps tend to ignore, that *The Rape of the Lock* should be set in the context of Pope's whole work and accorded proportionate praise.

JOHN DIXON HUNT

PART ONE

Four Contemporary
Documents
by Alexander Pope

Four documents by Pope will be useful for a reading of The Rape of the Lock. *The first, 'To Belinda on the Rape of the Lock', is undoubtedly the alternative dedication Pope offered to Miss Fermor, which she rejected in favour of the prose letter that mentioned her by name. The rejected poem was published anonymously by Pope in a miscellany of 1717 (for further details, see the Twickenham Edition of the poems, VI 108–9). The second is a witty recipe for epic poetry which Pope contributed as no.* LXXVIII *of the* Guardian, *for 10 June 1713; this is the text printed here. It was used by Pope, with the introductory paragraphs altered, as chapter 15 of* The Art of Sinking in Poetry *(1728). The third is Pope's own translation from the* Iliad *of Sarpedon's rousing battle speech, on which he modelled Clarissa's appeal for wise tolerance. It was first published in* Poetical Miscellanies: The Sixth Part *(1709), where it formed part of a larger translation called 'The Episode of Sarpedon'. The speech itself, later incorporated with some few changes into Pope's* Homer, *is here printed in the original version. The fourth is his mock-criticism,* A Key to the Lock, *published in April 1715.*

TO BELINDA ON THE RAPE OF THE LOCK

Pleas'd in these lines, *Belinda*, you may view
How things are priz'd, which once belong'd to you:
If on some meaner head this Lock had grown,
The nymph despis'd, the Rape had been unknown.
But what concerns the valient and fair,
The Muse asserts as her peculiar care.
Thus *Helen's* Rape and *Menalaus'* wrong
Became the Subject of great *Homer's* song;
And, lost in ancient times, the golden fleece
Was rais'd to fame by all the wits of *Greece*.

Had fate decreed, propitious to your pray'rs,
To give their utmost date to all your hairs;
This Lock, of which late ages now shall tell,
Had dropt like fruit, neglected, when it fell.
Nature to your undoing arms mankind
With strength of body, artifice of mind;
But gives your feeble sex, made up of fears,
No guard but virtue, no redress but tears.
Yet custom (seldom to your favour gain'd)
Absolves the virgin when by force constrain'd.
Thus *Lucrece* lives unblemish'd in her fame,
A bright example of young *Tarquin's* shame.
Such praise is yours – and such shall you possess,
Your virtue equal, tho' your loss be less.
Then smile Belinda at reproachful tongues,
Still warm our hearts, and still inspire our songs.
But would your charms to distant times extend,
Let *Jervas* paint them, and let *Pope* commend.
Who censure most, more precious hairs would lose,
To have the *Rape* recorded by his Muse.

(1714)

A RECEIT TO MAKE
AN EPICK POEM

Docebo
Unde parentur opes, quid alat, formetque Poetam. Hor.

Wednesday, June 10. 1713.

IT is no small Pleasure to me, who am zealous in the Interests of Learning, to think I may have the Honour of leading the Town into a very new and uncommon Road of Criticism. As that kind of Literature is at present carried on, it consists only in a Knowlege of Mechanick Rules, which contribute to the Structure of different sorts of Poetry, as the Receits of good Houswives do to the making Puddings of Flower, Oranges, Plumbs, or any other Ingredients. It would, methinks, make these my Instructions more easily intelligible to ordinary Readers, if I discoursed of these Matters in the Stile in which Ladies Learned in Œonomicks dictate to their Pupils for the Improvement of the Kitchin and Larder.

I shall begin with Epick Poetry, because the Criticks agree it is the greatest Work Human Nature is capable of. I know the *French* have already laid down many Mechanical Rules for Compositions of this Sort, but at the same time they cut off almost all Undertakers from the Possibility of ever performing them; for the first Qualification they unanimously require in a Poet, is a *Genius.* I shall here endeavour (for the Benefit of my Countrymen) to make it manifest, that Epick Poems may be made *without a Genius,* nay without Learning or much Reading. This must necessarily be of great Use to all those Poets who confess they never Read, and of whom the World is convinced they never Learn. What *Moliere* observes of making a Dinner, that any Man can do it *with Mony,* and if a profest Cook cannot *without,* he has his Art for nothing; the same may be said of making a Poem,

'tis easily brought about by him that *has* a Genius, but the Skill
lies in doing it without one. In pursuance of this End, I shall
present the Reader with a plain and certain *Recipe*, by which even
Sonneteers and Ladies may be qualified for this grand Performance.

I know it will be objected, that one of the chief Qualifications
of an Epick Poet, is to be knowing in all Arts and Sciences. But
this ought not to discourage those that have no Learning, as long
as Indexes and Dictionaries may be had, which are the Com-
pendium of all Knowledge. Besides, since it is an established Rule,
that none of the Terms of those Arts and Sciences are to be made
use of, one may venture to affirm, our Poet cannot impertinently
offend in this Point. The Learning which will be more particularly
necessary to him, is the ancient Geography of Towns, Mountains, and Rivers: For this let him take *Cluverius*, Value Four-
pence.

Another Quality required is a compleat Skill in Languages. To
this I answer, that it is notorious Persons of no Genius have been
oftentimes great Linguists. To instance in the *Greek*, of which
there are two Sorts; the Original *Greek*, and that from which our
Modern Authors translate. I should be unwilling to promise
Impossibilities, but modestly speaking, this may be learned in
about an Hour's time with Ease. I have known one, who became
a sudden Professor of *Greek*, immediately upon Application of
the Left-hand Page of the *Cambridge Homer* to his Eye. It is,
in these Days, with Authors as with other Men, the well bred
are familiarly acquainted with them at first Sight; and as it is
sufficient for a good General to have *survey'd* the Ground he is to
conquer, so it is enough for a good Poet to have *seen* the Author
he is to be Master of. But to proceed to the Purpose of this Paper.

A Receit to make an *Epick* Poem

For the *Fable.*

*Take out of any old Poem, History-books, Romance, or Legend,
(for instance* Geffry of Monmouth *or* Don Belianis of Greece)

those Parts of Story which afford most Scope for long Descriptions: Put these Pieces together, and throw all the Adventures you fancy into one Tale. Then take a Hero, whom you may chuse for the Sound of his Name, and put him into the midst of these Adventures: There let him work, *for twelve Books; at the end of which you may take him out, ready prepared to conquer or to marry; it being necessary that the Conclusion of an Epick Poem be fortunate.*

To make an Episode. *Take any remaining Adventure of your former Collection, in which you could no way involve your Hero; or any unfortunate Accident that was too good to be thrown away; and it will be of Use, applyed to any other Person; who may be lost and evaporate in the Course of the Work, without the least Damage to the Composition.*

For the Moral and Allegory. *These you may Extract out of the Fable afterwards at your Leisure: Be sure you strain them sufficiently.*

For the Manners.

For those of the Hero, take all the best Qualities you can find in all the best celebrated Heroes of Antiquity; if they will not be reduced to a Consistency, lay 'em all on a heap upon him. But be sure they are Qualities which your Patron *would be thought to have; and to prevent any Mistake which the World may be subject to, select from the Alphabet those Capital Letters that compose his Name, and set them at the Head of a Dedication before your Poem. However, do not absolutely observe the exact Quantity of these Virtues, it not being determined whether or no it be necessary for the Hero of a Poem to be an honest Man – For the* Under-Characters, *gather them from* Homer *and* Virgil, *and Change the Names as Occasion serves.*

For the Machines.

Take of Deities, Male and Female, as many as you can use. Separate them into two equal parts, and keep Jupiter *in the middle. Let* Juno *put him in a Ferment, and* Venus *mollifie him. Remember on all Occasions to make use of Volatile* Mercury. *If you have need of Devils, draw them out of* Milton's Paradise, *and extract your*

Spirits from Tasso. *The Use of these Machines is evident; for since no Epick Poem can possibly subsist without them, the wisest way is to reserve them for your greatest Necessities. When you cannot extricate your Hero by any Human Means, or your self by your own Wit, seek Relief from Heaven, and the Gods will do your Business very readily. This is according to the direct Prescription of* Horace *in his Art of Poetry.*

> Nec Deus intersit, nisi dignus vindice *Nodus*
> Inciderit ——

That is to say, a Poet should never call upon the Gods for their Assistance, but when he is in great Perplexity.

For the Descriptions.

For a Tempest. *Take* Eurus, Zephyr, Auster, *and* Boreas, *and cast them together in one Verse. Add to these of Rain, Lightning, and of Thunder (the loudest you can)* quantum sufficit. *Mix your Clouds and Billows well together till they foam, and thicken your Description here and there with a Quicksand. Brew your Tempest well in your Head, before you set it a blowing.*

For a Battel. *Pick a large Quantity of Images and Descriptions from* Homer's *Iliads, with a Spice or two of* Virgil, *and if there remain any Overplus you may lay them by for a* Skirmish. *Season it well with* Similes, *and it will make an* Excellent Battel.

For a Burning Town. *If such a Description be necessary, because it is certain there is one in* Virgil, *Old* Troy *is ready burnt to your Hands. But if you fear That would be thought* borrowed, *a Chapter or two of the Theory of the* Conflagration, *well circumstanced, and done into Verse, will be a good* Succedaneum.

As for Similes *and* Metaphors, *they may be found all over the Creation, the most ignorant may gather them, but the danger is in applying them. For this: advise with your Bookseller.*

For the Language.

(*I mean the* Diction). *Here it will do well to be an Imitator of* Milton, *for you'll find it easier to imitate him in this than any thing else.* Hebraisms *and* Grecisms *are to be found in him, without the trouble of Learning the Languages. I knew a Painter, who (like our Poet) had no* Genius, *make his Dawbings be thought* Originals *by setting them in the* Smoak: *You may in the same manner give the venerable Air of Antiquity to your Piece, by darkening it up and down with* Old English. *With this you may be easily furnished upon any Occasion, by the Dictionary commonly Printed at the end of* Chaucer.

I must not conclude, without cautioning all Writers without Genius in one material Point; which is, never to be afraid of having *too much Fire* in their Works. I should advise rather to take their warmest Thoughts, and spread them abroad upon Paper; for they are observed to cool before they are read.

(1713)

SARPEDON TO GLAUCUS

Why boast we, *Glaucus*, our extended Reign
Where *Xanthus*' Streams enrich the *Lycian* Plain?
Our num'rous Herds that range each fruitful Field,
And Hills where Vines their Purple Harvest yield?
Our foaming Bowls with gen'rous *Nectar* crown'd,
Our Feasts enhanc'd with Musick's sprightly Sound?
Why on these Shores are we with Joy survey'd,
Admir'd as Heroes, and as Gods obey'd?
Unless great Acts superior Merit prove,
And Vindicate the bounteous Pow'rs above:
'Tis ours, the Dignity They give, to grace;
The first in Valour, as the first in Place:
That while with wondring Eyes our Martial Bands
Behold our Deeds transcending our Commands,
Such, they may cry, deserve the Sov'reign State,
Whom those that Envy dare not Imitate!
Cou'd all our Care elude the greedy Grave,
Which claims no less the Fearful than the Brave,
For Lust of Fame I shou'd not vainly dare
In fighting Fields, nor urge thy Soul to War.
But since, alas, ignoble Age must come,
Disease, and Death's inexorable Doom;
The Life which others pay, let Us bestow,
And give to Fame what we to Nature owe;
Brave, tho' we fall; and honour'd, if we live;
Or let us Glory gain, or Glory give!

(1709)

A KEY TO THE LOCK

Or a Treatise proving, beyond all Contradiction,
the dangerous Tendency of a late Poem
entitled *The Rape of the Lock*
to Government and Religion
by Esdras Barnivelt, Apothecary*

THE EPISTLE DEDICATORY
TO MR *POPE*

THOUGH it may seem foreign to my Profession, which is that of
making up and dispensing salutary Medicines to his Majesty's
Subjects, (I might say my Fellow-Subjects, since I have had the
Advantage of being naturalised) yet cannot I think it unbecoming
me to furnish an Antidote against the Poyson which hath been
so artfully distilled through your Quill, and conveyed to the
World through the pleasing Vehicle of your Numbers. Nor is
my Profession as an Apothecary so abhorrent from yours as a
Poet, since the Ancients have thought fit to make the same God
the Patron of Both. I have, not without some Pleasure, observ'd
the mystical Arms of our Company, wherein is represented
Apollo killing the fell Monster *Python*; this in some measure ad-
monishes me of my Duty, to trample upon and destroy, as much
as in me lies, that Dragon, or baneful Serpent, *Popery*.

I must take leave to make you my Patient, whether you will
or no; though out of the Respect I have for you, I should rather
chuse to apply Lenitive than Corrosive Medicines, happy, if
they may prove an Emetic sufficient to make you cast up those
Errors, which you have imbibed in your Education, and which,
I hope, I shall never live to see this Nation digest.

Sir, I cannot but lament, that a Gentleman of your acute Wit,
rectified Understanding, and sublimated Imagination, should

* [Editor's note]. Barnivelt is, of course, Pope's pseudonym. This
amusing interpretation of the poem as an insidious political allegory
is printed here, partly because it is not easily available, partly because
it serves as a warning to the heavy-handed critic of the poem.

misapply those Talents to raise ill Humours in the Constitution of the Body Politick, of which your self are a Member, and upon the Health whereof your own Preservation depends. Give ne leave to say, such Principles as yours would again reduce us to the fatal Necessity of the Phlebotomy of War, or the Causticks of Persecution.

In order to inform you of this, I have sought your Acquaintance and Conversation with the utmost Diligence; for I hoped in Person to persuade you to a publick Confession of your Fault, and a Recantation of these dangerous Tenets. But finding all my Endeavours ineffectual, and being satisfied with the Conscience of having done all that became a Man of an honest Heart and honourable Intention; I could no longer omit my Duty in opening the Eyes of the World by the Publication of this Discourse. It was indeed written some Months since, but seems not the less proper at this Juncture, when I find so universal an Encouragement given by both Parties to the Author of a libellous Work that is designed equally to prejudice them both. The uncommon Sale of this Book (for above 6000 of 'em have been already vended) was also a farther Reason that call'd aloud upon me to put a stop to its further Progress, and to preserve his Majesty's Subjects, by exposing the whole Artifice of your Poem in Publick.

Sir, to address my self to so florid a Writer as you, without collecting all the Flowers of Rhetorick, would be an unpardonable *Indecorum*; but when I speak to the World, as I do in the following Treatise, I must use a simple Stile, since it would be absurd to prescribe an universal Medicine, or *Catholicon*, in a Language not universally understood.

As I have always professed to have a particular Esteem for Men of Learning, and more especially for your self, nothing but the Love of Truth should have engaged me in a Design of this Nature. *Amicus Plato, Amicus Socrates, sed magis Amica Veritas.* I am

> Your most Sincere Friend,
> and Humble Servant,
> *E. Barnivelt.*

A KEY TO THE *LOCK*

SINCE this unhappy Division of our Nation into Parties, it is not to be imagined how many Artifices have been made use of by Writers to obscure the Truth, and cover Designs, which may be detrimental to the Publick; in particular, it has been their Custom of late to vent their Political Spleen in Allegory and Fable. If an honest believing Nation is to be made a Jest of, we have a Story of *John Bull* and his Wife; if a Treasurer is to be glanced at, an *Ant* with a *white Straw* is introduced; if a Treaty of Commerce is to be ridiculed, 'tis immediately metamorphosed into a Tale of Count *Tariff*.

But if any of these Malevolents have never so small a Talent in Rhime, they principally delight to convey their Malice in that pleasing way, as it were, gilding the Pill, and concealing the Poyson under the Sweetness of Numbers. Who could imagine that an *Original Canto* of *Spencer* should contain a Satyr upon one Administration; or that *Yarhel's Kitchin*, or the *Dogs of Egypt*, should be a Sarcasm upon another.

It is the Duty of every well designing Subject to prevent, as far as in him lies, the ill Consequences of such pernicious Treatises; and I hold it mine to warn the Publick of the late Poem, entituled, the *Rape of the Lock*; which I shall demonstrate to be of this nature. Many of these sort of Books have been bought by honest and well-meaning People purely for their Diversion, who have in the end found themselves insensibly led into the Violence of Party Spirit, and many domestick Quarrels have been occasioned by the different Application of these Books. The Wife of an eminent Citizen grew very noisy upon reading *Bob Hush*; *John Bull*, upon *Change*, was thought not only to concern the State, but to affront the City; and the Poem we are now treating of, has not only dissolved an agreeable Assembly of Beaus and Belles, but (as I am told) has set Relations at as great a distance, as if they were married together.

It is a common and just Observation, that when the Meaning of any thing is dubious, one can no way better judge of the true

Intent of it, than by considering who is the Author, what is his Character in general, and his Disposition in particular.

Now that the Author of this Poem is professedly a *Papist*, is well known; and that a Genius so capable of doing Service to that Cause, may have been corrupted in the Course of his Education by *Jesuits* or others, is justly very much to be suspected; notwithstanding that seeming *Coolness* and *Moderation*, which he has been (perhaps artfully) reproached with, by those of his own Profession. They are sensible that this Nation is secured with good and wholesome Laws, to prevent all evil Practices of the Church of *Rome*; particularly the Publication of Books, that may in any sort propagate that Doctrine: Their Authors are therefore obliged to couch their Designs the deeper; and tho' I cannot averr that the Intention of this Gentleman was directly to spread Popish Doctrines, yet it comes to the same Point, if he touch the Government: For the Court of *Rome* knows very well, that the Church at this time is so firmly founded on the State, that the only way to shake the one is by attacking the other.

What confirms me in this Opinion, is an accidental Discovery I made of a very artful Piece of Management among his Popish Friends and Abettors, to hide this whole Design upon the Government, by taking all the Characters upon themselves.

Upon the Day that this Poem was published, it was my Fortune to step into the *Cocoa Tree*, where a certain Gentleman was railing very liberally at the Author, with a Passion extremely well counterfeited, for having (as he said) reflected upon him in the Character of *Sir Plume*. Upon his going out, I enquired who he was, and they told me, *a Roman Catholick Knight*.

I was the same Evening at *Will*'s, and saw a Circle round another Gentleman, who was railing in like manner, and shewing his Snuff-box and Cane, to prove he was satyrized in the same Character. I asked this Gentleman's Name, and was told, he was *a Roman Catholick Lord*.

A Day or two after I was sent for, upon a slight Indisposition, to the young Lady's to whom the Poem is dedicated. She also took up the Character of *Belinda* with much Frankness and good

Humour, tho' the Author has given us a Key in his* Dedication, that he meant something further. This Lady is also a *Roman Catholick.* At the same time others of the Characters were claim'd by some Persons in the Room; and all of them *Roman Catholicks.* But to proceed to the Work itself.

In all things which are intricate, as Allegories in their own Nature are, and especially those that are industriously made so, it is not to be expected we should find the Clue at first sight; but when once we have laid hold on that, we shall trace this our Author through all the Labyrinths, Doublings and Turnings of this intricate Composition.

First then let it be observed, that in the most demonstrative Sciences, some *Postulata* are to be granted, upon which the rest is naturally founded. I shall desire no more than one *Postulatum* to render this obvious to the meanest Capacity; which being granted me, I shall not only shew the Intent of this Work in general, but also explain the very *Names,* and expose all his fictitious *Characters* in their true Light; and we shall find, that even his *Spirits* were not meerly contrived for the sake of *Machinary.*

The only Concession which I desire to be made me, is, that by the *Lock* is meant

The BARRIER TREATY.

i. First then I shall discover, that BELINDA represents GREAT BRITAIN, or (which is the same thing) her late MAJESTY. This is plainly seen in his Description of her.

On her white Breast a sparkling Cross she bore.

Alluding to the antient Name of *Albion,* from her *white Cliffs,* and to the *Cross,* which is the Ensign of *England.*

ii. The BARON, who cuts off the Lock, or Barrier Treaty, is the E[arl] of O[xfor]d.

iii. CLARISSA, who lent the Scissars, my Lady M[ashe]m.

* *The Character of* Belinda (*as it is here manag'd*) *resembles you in nothing but in Beauty.* Dedication to the *Rape of the Lock.*

IV. THALESTRIS, who provokes *Belinda* to resent the Loss of the Lock or Treaty, the D[uches]s of *M*[*arlborou*]*gh*.

V. SIR PLUME, who is mov'd by *Thalestris* to redemand it of *Great Britain*, P[rin]ce *Eu*[*ge*]*ne*, who came hither for that purpose.

There are other inferior Characters, which we shall observe upon afterwards; but I shall first explain the foregoing.

The first Part of the *Baron*'s Character is his being *adventrous*, or enterprizing, which is the common Epithet given the E[arl] of *O*[*xfor*]*d* by his Enemies. The Prize he aspires to is the T[reasur]y, in order to which he offers a Sacrifice.

> ─────────────────────an Altar built
> Of twelve vast *French* Romances neatly gilt.

Our Author here takes occasion maliciously to insinuate this Statesman's *Love to France*; representing the Books he chiefly studies to be vast *French Romances*. These are the vast Prospects from the Friendship and Alliance of *France*, which he satyrically calls *Romances*, hinting thereby, that these Promises and Protestations were no more to be relied on than those idle Legends. Of these he is said to build an Altar; to intimate, that all the Foundation of his Schemes and Honours was fix'd upon the *French Romances* abovementioned.

> A Fan, a Garter, Half a Pair of Gloves.

One of the Things he sacrifices is a *Fan*, which both for its *gaudy Show* and *perpetual Flutt'ring*, has been made the Emblem of *Woman*. This points at the Change of the *Ladies* of the *Bedchamber*; the *Garter* alludes to the Honours he conferr'd on some of his Friends; and we may without straining the Sense, call the Half Pair of Gloves, a *Gauntlet*; the Token of those Military Employments, which he is said to have sacrificed to his Designs. The Prize, as I said before, means the T[reasur]y, which he makes it his Prayers *soon to obtain*, and *long to possess*.

> The Pow'rs gave ear, and granted half his Pray'r,
> The rest the Winds dispers'd in empty Air.

In the first of these Lines he gives him the T[reasur]y, and in the last suggests that he should not long possess that Honour.

That *Thalestris* is the D[uches]s of M[arlborou]gh, appears both by her Nearness to *Belinda*, and by this Author's malevolent Suggestion, that she is a Lover of War.

> To Arms, to Arms, the bold *Thalestris* cries.

But more particularly in several Passages in her Speech to *Belinda*, upon the cutting off the Lock, or Treaty. Among other Things she says, *Was it for this you bound your Locks in Paper Durance?* Was it for this so much Paper has been spent to secure the Barrier Treaty?

> Methinks already I your Tears survey,
> Already hear the horrid Things they say;
> Already see you a degraded Toast.

This describes the Aspersions under which that good Princess suffer'd, and the Repentance which must have followed the Dissolution of that Treaty, and particularly levels at the Refusal some People made to drink Her M[ajest]y's Health.

Sir Plume (a proper Name for a Soldier) has all the Circumstances that agree with P[rin]ce *Eu[ge]ne*.

> *Sir Plume* of Amber Snuff-box justly vain,
> And the nice Conduct of a clouded Cane,
> With earnest Eyes ———

'Tis remarkable, this General is a great Taker of Snuff as well as Towns; his Conduct of the clouded Cane gives him the Honour which is so justly his due, of an exact Conduct in Battle, which is figured by his Truncheon, the Ensign of a General. His earnest Eye, or the Vivacity of his Look, is so particularly remarkable in him, that this Character could be mistaken for no other, had not this Author purposely obscur'd it by the fictitious Circumstance of a *round, unthinking Face*.

Having now explained the chief Characters of his *Human Persons* (for there are some others that will hereafter fall in by the by, in the Sequel of this Discourse) I shall next take in pieces his

Machinary, wherein his Satyr is wholly confined to Ministers of State.

The Sylphs and Gnomes at first sight appeared to me to signify the two contending Parties of this Nation; for these being placed in the *Air*, and those on the *Earth*, I thought agreed very well with the common Denomination, High and Low. But as they are made to be the first Movers and Influencers of all that happens, 'tis plain they represent promiscuously the *Heads of Parties*, whom he makes to be the Authors of all those Changes in the State, which are generally imputed to the Levity and Instability of the *British* Nation.

> This erring Mortals Levity may call,
> Oh blind to Truth! The Sylphs contrive it all.

But of this he has given us a plain Demonstration; for speaking of these Spirits, he says in express Terms,

> —— The chief the Care of Nations own,
> And guard with Arms Divine the *British* Throne.

And here let it not seem odd, if in this mysterious way of Writing, we find the same Person, who has before been represented by the *Baron*, again described in the Character of *Ariel*; it being a common way with Authors, in this fabulous Manner, to take such a Liberty. As for instance, I have read in the *English St. Evremont*, that all the different Characters in *Petronius* are but *Nero* in so many different Appearances. And in the Key to the curious Romance of *Barclay*'s *Argenis*, that both *Poliarchus* and *Archombrotus* mean only the *King* of *Navarre*.

We observe in the very Beginning of the Poem, that *Ariel* is possess'd of the Ear of *Belinda*; therefore it is absolutely necessary that this Person must be the Minister who was nearest the Queen. But whoever would be further convinc'd, that he meant the late T[reasure]r, may know him by his Ensigns in the following Line.

> He rais'd his Azure Wand.——

His sitting on the Mast of a Vessel shows his presiding over the S[ou]th S[e]a Tr[a]de. When *Ariel* assigns to his *Sylphs* all the

Posts about *Belinda*, what is more clearly described, than the
Tr[easure]r's disposing all the Places of the Kingdom, and particularly about her M[ajest]y? But let us hear the Lines.

> —— Ye Spirits to your Charge repair,
> The flutt'ring Fan be *Zephyretta*'s Care;
> The Drops to thee, *Brillante*, we consign,
> And, *Momentilla*, let the Watch be thine:
> Do thou, *Crispissa*, tend her fav'rite Lock.

He has here particularized the Ladies and Women of the Bed-
Chamber, the Keeper of the Cabinet, and her M[ajest]y's Dresser,
and impudently given Nicknames to each.

To put this Matter beyond all Dispute, the *Sylphs* are said to
be *wond'rous fond of Place*, in the Canto following, where *Ariel*
is perched uppermost, and all the rest take their Places subor-
dinately under him.

Here again I cannot but observe, the excessive Malignity of
this Author, who could not leave this Character of *Ariel* without
the same invidious Stroke which he gave him in the Character
of the *Baron* before.

> Amaz'd, confus'd, he saw his Power expir'd,
> Resign'd to Fate, and with a Sigh retir'd.

Being another Prophecy that he should resign his Place, which
it is probable all Ministers do with a Sigh.

At the Head of the *Gnomes* he sets *Umbriel*, a dusky melancholy Spright, who makes it his Business to give *Belinda* the
Spleen; a vile and malicious Suggestion against some grave and
worthy Minister. The Vapours, Fantoms, Visions, and the like,
are the Jealousies, Fears, and Cries of Danger, that have so often
affrighted and alarm'd the Nation. Those who are described in
the House of Spleen, under those several fantastical Forms, are
the same whom their Ill-willers have so often called the *Whimsical*.

The two fore-going Spirits being the only considerable
Characters of the Machinary, I shall but just mention the *Sylph*
that is wounded with the Scissars at the Loss of the Lock, by
whom is undoubtedly understood my L[ord] *To[wnshen]d*, who

at that Time received a Wound in his Character for making the
Barrier Treaty, and was cut out of his Employment upon the
Dissolution of it: But that Spirit reunites, and receives no Harm;
to signify, that it came to nothing, and his L[o]rdsh[i]p had no
real Hurt by it.

But I must not conclude this Head of the Characters, without
observing, that our Author has run through every Stage of
Beings in search of Topicks for Detraction; and as he has charac-
teriz'd some Persons under Angels and Men, so he has others
under Animals, and Things inanimate. He has represented an
eminent Clergy-man as a Dog, and a noted Writer as a Tool.
Let us examine the former.

> —But *Shock*, who thought she slept too long,
> Leapt up, and wak'd his Mistress with his Tongue.
> 'Twas then, *Belinda*, if Report say true,
> Thy Eyes first open'd on a Billet-doux.

By this *Shock*, it is manifest he has most audaciously and pro-
fanely reflected on Dr. *Sach*[*evere*]*ll*, who leap'd up, that is, into
the Pulpit, and awaken'd *Great Britain* with his *Tongue*, that is,
with his *Sermon*, which made so much *Noise*; and for which he
has frequently been term'd by others of his Enemies, as well as
by this Author, a Dog: Or perhaps, by his *Tongue*, may be more
literally meant his *Speech* at his *Trial*, since immediately there-
upon, our Author says, her Eyes open'd on a *Billet-doux*;
Billets-doux being Addresses to Ladies from Lovers, may be aptly
interpreted those Addresses of Loving Subjects to her M[ajest]y,
which ensued that Trial.

The other Instance is at the End of the third Canto.

> Steel did the Labours of the Gods destroy,
> And strike to Dust th'Imperial Tow'rs of *Troy*.
> Steel could the Works of mortal Pride confound,
> And hew Triumphal Arches to the Ground.

Here he most impudently attributes the Demolition of *Dun-
kirk*, not to the Pleasure of her M[ajest]y, or her Ministry, but to
the frequent Instigations of his Friend Mr. *Steel*; a very artful
Pun to conceal his wicked Lampoonery!

Having now consider'd the general Intent and Scope of the Poem, and open'd the Characters, I shall next discover the Malice which is covered under the Episodes, and particular Passages of it.

The Game at *Ombre* is a mystical Representation of the late War, which is hinted by his making Spades the Trump; Spade in *Spanish* signifying a Sword, and being yet so painted in the Cards of that Nation; to which it is well known we owe the Original of our Cards. In this one Place indeed he has unawares paid a Compliment to the Queen, and her Success in the War; for *Belinda* gets the better of the two that play against her, the Kings of *France* and *Spain*.

I do not question but ev'ry particular Card has its Person and Character assign'd, which, no doubt, the Author has told his Friends in private; but I shall only instance in the Description of the Disgrace under which the D[uke] of M[arlborou]gh then suffer'd, which is so apparent in these Verses.

> Ev'n mighty *Pam*, that Kings and Queens o'erthrew,
> And mow'd down Armies in the Fights of *Lu*,
> Sad Chance of War! now destitute of Aid,
> Falls undistinguish'd——

That the Author here had an Eye to our modern Transactions, is very plain from an unguarded Stroke towards the End of this Game.

> And now, as oft in some *distemper'd State*,
> On *one nice Trick* depends the gen'ral Fate.

After the Conclusion of the War, the publick Rejoicings and *Thanksgivings* are ridiculed in the two following Lines.

> The Nymph exulting, fills with Shouts the Sky,
> The Walls, the Woods, and long Canals reply.

Immediately upon which there follows a malicious Insinuation, in the manner of a Prophecy, (which we have formerly observ'd this seditious Writer delights in) that the Peace should continue

but a short Time, and that the Day should afterwards be curst
which was then celebrated with so much Joy.

> Sudden these Honours shall be snatch'd away,
> And curst for ever this victorious Day.

As the Game at *Ombre* is a satyrical Representation of the late
War; so is the Tea-Table that ensues, of the Council-Table and
its Consultations after the Peace. By this he would hint, that all
the Advantages we have gain'd by our late extended Commerce,
are only Coffee and Tea, or Things of no greater Value. That he
thought of the Trade in this Place, appears by the Passage where
he represents the *Sylphs* particularly careful of the *rich Brocade*;
it having been a frequent Complaint of our Mercers, that *French
Brocades* were imported in too great Quantities. I will not say,
he means those Presents of rich Gold Stuff Suits, which were said
to be made her M[ajest]y by the K[ing] of *F[rance]*, tho' I cannot
but suspect, that he glances at it.

Here this Author, as well as the scandalous *John Dunton*,
represents the Mi[nist]ry in plain Terms taking frequent Cups.

> And frequent Cups prolong the rich Repast.

Upon the whole, it is manifest he meant something more than
common Coffee, by his calling it,

> Coffee that makes the *Politician* wise.

And by telling us, it was this Coffee, that

> Sent up in Vapours to the *Baron's* Brain
> New *Stratagems* ———

I shall only further observe, that 'twas at this Table the Lock
was cut off; for where but at the Council Board should the Barrier
Treaty be dissolved?

The ensuing Contentions of the Parties upon the Loss of that
Treaty, are described in the Squabbles following the Rape of the
Lock; and this he rashly expresses, without any disguise in the
Words.

> All side in *Parties* ———

Here first you have a Gentleman who sinks beside his Chair:
A plain Allusion to a Noble Lord, who lost his Chair of Pre[si-
de]nt of the Co[unci]l.

I come next to the *Bodkin*, so dreadful in the Hand of *Belinda*;
by which he intimates the *British Scepter*, so rever'd in the Hand
of our late August Princess. His own Note upon this Place tells
us he alludes to a Scepter and the Verses are so plain, they need
no Remark.

> The same (his ancient Personage to deck)
> Her great great Grandsire wore about his Neck
> In three Seal Rings, which, after melted down,
> Form'd a vast Buckle for his Widow's Gown;
> Her Infant Grandame's Whistle next it grew,
> The Bells she gingled, and the Whistle blew,
> Then in a Bodkin grac'd her Mother's Hairs,
> Which long she wore, and now *Belinda* wears.

An open Satyr upon *Hereditary Right*. The three Seal Rings
plainly allude to the three Kingdoms.

These are the chief Passages in the Battle, by which, as hath
before been said, he means the Squabble of Parties. Upon this
Occasion he could not end the Description of them, without
testifying his malignant Joy at those Dissentions, from which he
forms the Prospect that *both* should be disappointed, and cries
out with Triumph, as if it were already accomplished.

> Behold how oft ambitious Arms are crost,
> And Chiefs contend till all the Prize is lost.

The Lock at length is turn'd into a *Star*, or the Old Barrier
Treaty into a new and glorious *Peace*; this no doubt is what the
Author, at the time he printed his Poem, would have been
thought to mean, in hopes by that Complement to escape
Punishment for the rest of his Piece. It puts me in mind of a
Fellow, who concluded a bitter Lampoon upon the Prince and
Court of his Days, with these Lines.

> God save the King, the Commons, and the Peers,
> And grant the Author long may wear his Ears.

Whatever this Author may think of that Peace, I imagine it the most *extraordinary Star* that ever appear'd in our Hemisphere. A Star that is to bring us all the Wealth and Gold of the *Indies*; and from whose Influence, not Mr. *John Partridge* alone, (whose worthy Labours this Writer so ungenerously ridicules) but all true *Britains* may, with no less Authority than he, prognosticate the Fall of *Lewis*, in the Restraint of the exorbitant Power of *France*, and the Fate of *Rome* in the triumphant Condition of the Church of *England*.

We have now considered this Poem in its Political View, wherein we have shewn that it hath two different Walks of Satyr, the one in the Story itself, which is a Ridicule on the late Transactions in general; the other in the Machinary, which is a Satyr on the Ministers of State in particular. I shall now show that the same Poem, taken in another Light, has a Tendency to Popery, which is secretly insinuated through the whole.

In the first place, he has conveyed to us the Doctrine of Guardian Angels and Patron Saints in the Machinary of his *Sylphs*, which being a Piece of Popish Superstition that hath been endeavoured to be exploded ever since the Reformation, he would here revive under this Disguise. Here are all the Particulars which they believe of those Beings, which I shall sum up in a few Heads.

1*st.* The Spirits are made to concern themselves with all human Acts in general.

2*dly.* A distinct Guardian Spirit or Patron is assigned to each Person in particular.

> Of these am I, who thy Protection claim,
> A watchful Sprite ———

3*dly.* They are made directly to inspire Dreams, Visions, and Revelations.

> Her Guardian *Sylph* prolong'd her balmy Rest,
> 'Twas he had summon'd to her silent Bed
> The Morning Dream ———

4*thly*. They are made to be subordinate, in different degrees, some presiding over others. So *Ariel* hath his several Under-Officers at Command.

> Superior by the Head was *Ariel* plac'd.

5*thly*. They are employed in various Offices, and each hath his Office assigned him.

> Some in the Fields of purest Æther play,
> And bask and whiten in the Blaze of Day.
> Some guide the Course, &c.

6*thly*. He hath given his Spirits the Charge of the several Parts of Dress; intimating thereby, that the Saints preside over the several Parts of Human Bodies. They have one Saint to cure the Tooth-ach, another cures the Gripes, another the Gout, and so of all the rest.

> The flutt'ring Fan be *Zephyretta*'s Care,
> The Drops to thee, *Brillante*, we consign, &c.

7*thly*. They are represented to know the Thoughts of Men.

> As on the Nosegay in her Breast reclin'd,
> He watch'd th' Ideas rising in her Mind.

8*thly*. They are made Protectors even to Animals and irrational Beings.

> *Ariel* himself shall be the Guard of *Shock*.

So St. *Anthony* presides over Hogs, &c.

9*thly*. Others are made Patrons of whole Kingdoms and Provinces.

> Of these the chief the Care of Nations own.

So St. *George* is imagined by the *Papists* to defend *England*: St. *Patrick*, *Ireland*: St. *James*, *Spain*, &c. Now what is the Consequence of all this? By granting that they have this Power, we must be brought back again to pray to them.

The *Toilette* is an artful Recommendation of the *Mass*, and pompous Ceremonies of the *Church of Rome*. The *unveiling* of the *Altar*, the *Silver Vases* upon it, being *rob'd* in *White*, as the Priests are upon the chief Festivals, and the *Head uncover'd*, are manifest Marks of this.

> A heav'nly Image in the Glass appears,
> To that she bends ———

Plainly denotes *Image-Worship*.

The *Goddess*, who is deck'd with *Treasures*, *Jewels*, and the various *Offerings of the World*, manifestly alludes to the Lady of *Loretto*. You have Perfumes breathing from the *Incense Pot* in the following Line.

> And all *Arabia* breaths from yonder Box.

The Character of *Belinda*, as we take it in this third View, represents the Popish Religion, or the Whore of *Babylon*; who is described in the State this malevolent Author wishes for, coming forth in all her Glory upon the *Thames*, and overspreading the Nation with Ceremonies.

> Not with more Glories in th'ætherial Plain,
> The Sun first rises o'er the purple Main,
> Than issuing forth the Rival of his Beams,
> Launch'd on the Bosom of the Silver *Thames*.

She is dress'd with a *Cross* on her Breast, the Ensign of Popery, the *Adoration* of which is plainly recommended in the following Lines.

> On her white Breast a sparkling *Cross* she wore,
> Which Jews might *kiss*, and Infidels *adore*.

Next he represents her as the *Universal Church*, according to the Boasts of the Papists.

> And like the Sun she shines on all alike.

After which he tells us,

> If to her Share some Female Errors fall,
> Look on her Face, and you'll forget them all.

Tho' it should be granted some Errors fall to her Share, look on
the pompous Figure she makes throughout the World, and they
are not worth regarding. In the Sacrifice following soon after,
you have these two Lines.

> For this, e'er *Phœbus* rose, he had implor'd
> Propitious Heav'n, and ev'ry Pow'r ador'd.

In the first of them, he plainly hints at their *Matins*; in the
second, by adoring ev'ry Power, the *Invocation of Saints*.

Belinda's Visits are described with numerous *Waxlights*,
which are always used in the Ceremonial Parts of the *Romish*
Worship.

> —— Visits shall be paid on solemn Days,
> When num'rous Wax-lights in bright Order blaze.

The *Lunar Sphere* he mentions, opens to us their *Purgatory*,
which is seen in the following Line.

> Since all Things lost on Earth are treasur'd there.

It is a Popish Doctrine, that scarce any Person quits this World,
but he must touch at Purgatory in his Way to Heaven; and it is
here also represented as the *Treasury* of the *Romish Church*.
Nor is it much to be wonder'd at, that the *Moon* should be
Purgatory, when a Learn'd Divine hath in a late Treatise proved
Hell to be in the *Sun*.

I shall now before I conclude, desire the Reader to compare
this Key with those upon any other Pieces, which are supposed
to be secret Satyrs upon the State, either antient or modern; as
with those upon *Petronius Arbiter*, *Lucian's* true History, *Barclay's Argenis*, or *Rablais's Garagantua*; and I doubt not he will
do me the Justice to acknowledge, that the Explanations here
laid down, are deduced as naturally, and with as little Force,
both from the general Scope and Bent of the Work, and from the
several Particulars, and are every Way as consistent and un-
deniable as any of those; and ev'ry way as candid as any modern
Interpretations of either Party, on the mysterious State Treatises
of our Times.

To sum up my whole Charge against this Author in a few Words: He has ridiculed both the present Ministry and the last; abused great Statesmen and great Generals; nay the Treaties of whole Nations have not escaped him, nor has the Royal Dignity itself been omitted in the Progress of his Satyr; and all this he has done just at the Meeting of a new Parliament. I hope a proper Authority may be made use of to bring him to condign Punishment: In the mean while I doubt not, if the Persons most concern'd would but order Mr. *Bernard Lintott,* the Printer and Publisher of this dangerous Piece, to be taken into Custody, and examin'd; many further Discoveries might be made both of this Poet's and his Abettor's secret Designs, which are doubtless of the utmost Importance to the Government.

(1715)

PART TWO

Extracts from Earlier Critics

John Dennis

I

As nothing could be more ridiculous than the writing a full, an exact, and a regular Criticism upon so empty a Business as this trifling Poem; I will say but a Word or two concerning the *Incidents*, and so have done with what relates immediately to the *Design*. The Intention of the Author in writing this Poem, as we find in the Title-Page, is to raise the Mirth of the Reader; and we find by the Effects which *Hudibras* and the *Lutrin* produce in us, that *Butler* and *Boileau* wrote with the same Intention. Now you know very well, Sir, that in a Poem which is built upon an Action, Mirth is chiefly to be rais'd by the *Incidents*. For Laughter in *Comedy* is chiefly to be excited, like Terror and Compassion in Tragedy, by Surprise, when Things spring from one another against our Expectation. Now whereas there are *several* ridiculous Incidents in the *Lutrin*, as, The Owl in the Pulpit frighting the nocturnal Champions; The Prelate's giving his Benediction to his Adversary, by way of Revenge and Insult; The Battle in the Bookseller's Shop, *&c.* And whereas there are a thousand such in *Hudibras*; There is not so much as *one*, nor the *Shadow of one*, in the *Rape of the Lock*: Unless the Author's Friends will object here, That his *perpetual Gravity*, after the *Promise* of his Title, makes the whole Poem one continued *Jest*.

II

I come now to the *Characters* and the *Machines*. The Characters in the *Lutrin* are well mark'd. They are the true Resemblances of Men, of active Men, who pursue earnestly what they are about. But there is no such Thing as a Character in the *Rape of the Lock*. *Belinda*, who appears most in it, is a Chimera, and not a Character.

She is represented by the Author perfectly *beautiful* and *well-bred*, *modest* and *virtuous*. Let us now see how he sustains these Qualities in her, and then we shall discover what Taste he has of *Nature* and of *Decorum*.

First then he represents her perfectly *beautiful*:

> *Sol* thro' white Curtains did his Beams display,
> And op'd those Eyes which brighter shone than they.

And thus in the next Page the Sylphs accost her:

> Fairest of Mortals, thou distinguish'd Care
> Of thousand bright Inhabitants of Air.

And yet in the latter End of this very *Canto* he makes her owe the greater Part of her Beauty to her Toilette:

> Unnumber'd Treasures ope at once, and here
> The various Offerings of the World appear;
> From each she nicely culls with curious Toil,
> And decks the Goddess with the glitt'ring Spoil,
> This Casket *India*'s glowing Gems unlocks,
> And all *Arabia* breathes from yonder Box.
> Now awful Beauty puts on all its Arms,
> The Fair each Moment rises in her Charms,
> Repairs her Smiles, awakens every Grace,
> And calls forth all the Wonders of her Face,
> Sees by Degrees a purer Blush arise,
> And keener Lightnings quicken in her Eyes.

Nay, the very *favourite Lock*, which is made the Subject for so many Verses, is not shewn so desirable for its native Beauty, as for the constant Artifice employ'd about it. Witness what *Thalestris* says to *Belinda* just after she had lost it:

> Was it for this you took such constant Care
> The Bodkin, Comb, and Essence to prepare?
> For this your Locks in Paper Durance bound,
> For this with torturing Irons wreath'd around?
> For this with Fillets strain'd your tender Head,
> And bravely bore the double Loads of Lead?

Such Artifice must deface the Lustre of Locks which were naturally lovely; and the Toilette must of Necessity detract from perfect Beauty. The Toilette indeed may add to some who are call'd Beauties, or to some who would be thought such. A decay'd superannuated Beauty may receive Advantage from her Toilette, may *rise* in her Charms, and by the Help of *Spanish Red*, a *purer Blush may arise*. But her *counterfeit Charms* can please none who have a Taste of *Nature*. . . .

When God and Nature design a Face to please, the Fair-one, on whom they bestow it, can never add to Workmanship Divine. She may spoil it indeed by Industry, but can never improve it. They, who made it, alone know the certain Ways of going to the Heart of Man, and alone can give it those resistless inimitable Graces which Industry does but spoil, and which Artifice does but hide. . . .

And our Ladies who spend so much Time at their Toilettes would do well to consider, that, after all the Pains which they take in adorning themselves, they who are most charm'd with their Persons, endeavour to retrieve their natural Beauty in Imagination at least, by divesting them of their borrow'd Ornaments, and cloathing them in the Simplicity of the rural Habit, when in their Sonnets they transform them to Shepherdesses.

But the Author has not only shewn *Belinda* an accomplish'd *Beauty*; he represents her likewise a fine, modest, *well-bred* Lady:

> Favours to none, to all she Smiles extends.

And a little below,

> With graceful Ease and Sweetness, void of Pride.

And yet in the very next *Canto* she appears an arrant Ramp and a Tomrigg;

> The Nymph exulting fills with Shouts the Sky;
> The Walls, the Woods, and long Canals reply.

Must not this be the legitimate Offspring of *Stentor*, to make such a Noise as that? The Nymph was within Doors, and she must set

up her Throat at a hellish Rate, to make the Woods (where, by
the by, there are none) and the Canals reply to it. Let us turn to
the fifth *Canto*, and we shall see her there as loud with Anger, as
she is now with Joy:

> *Restore the Lock*, she cries, and all around
> *Restore the Lock* the vaulted Roofs rebound;
> Not fierce *Othello* in so loud a Strain
> Roar'd for the Handkerchief that caus'd his Pain.

Well, but his Friends will object here, that this is an *Hyperbole*;
and an Hyperbole is design'd to carry us beyond the Truth, only
that it may make us enter more justly into it: and that when *Virgil*
says of *Camilla*,

> Illa vel intactæ segetis per summa volaret
> Gramina, nec teneres cursu læsisset aristas;
> Vel mare per medium fluctu suspensa tu menti,
> Ferret iter, celeres nec tingeret æquore plantas; —

He means only that *Camilla* was exceeding swift of Foot: Why,
be it so. But then by the same Rule, must not the Author of the
Rape mean, that *Belinda shouted* and *roar'd* very loud; and that,
in short, she made a *diabolick Din*? Now is *Shouting* and *Roaring*
proper for a well-bred Lady? Are they not below the Modesty
and the Decency even of those *sonorous* Nymphs of the Flood,
who haunt the Banks of the vocal *Thames* between the *Bridge*
and the *Tower*?

Let us look once more upon the last *Canto*. Is she not a terrible
Termagant there, and the exact Resemblance of *Magnano*'s
Lady in *Hudibras*?

> See *fierce Belinda* on the Baron flies,
> With more than usual Lightning in her Eyes—
> Now meet thy Fate, th' *incens'd Virago* cry'd,
> And drew a deadly Bodkin from her Side.

But *Belinda* is not only shewn *beautiful* and *well-bred*, she is
represented *virtuous* too:

> Favours to none, to all she Smiles extends.

And yet in the latter End of the fourth *Canto* she talks like an errant *Suburbian*:

> Oh, hast thou, Cruel, been content to seize
> Hairs *less in Sight*, or *any* Hairs but these.

Thus, Sir, has this Author given his fine Lady *Beauty* and *good Breeding*, *Modesty* and *Virtue* in Words, but has in Reality and in Fact made her an *artificial dawbing Jilt*; a *Tomrig*, a *Virago*, and a *Lady of the Lake*. There is no other Character in this Poem worth taking Notice of. . . .

III

I am now to treat of the *Machines*; in the doing which I shall lie under a great Disadvantage: For before I come to those of the *Rape*, it is necessary to say something of *Machines* in general, of the *Reason* of introducing them, of the *Method* us'd by the antient Poets in employing them, and of the *Practice* of the greatest and best of the Moderns. . . .

The Reasons, that first oblig'd those Poets which are call'd Heroic to introduce *Machines* into their *Poems*, were,

First, To make their *Fable* and their *Action* more instructive. . . . By introducing Machines into their Fables, the Epic Poets shew'd two Things, 1. That the great Revolutions in human Affairs are influenc'd by a particular Providence. 2. That the Deity himself promotes the Success of an Action form'd by Virtue, and conducted by Prudence. But,

Secondly, The Heroic Poets introduc'd *Machines* into their Fables in order to make those Fables more *delightful*: For the employing *Machines* made the Actions of those Poems *wonderful*; now every Thing that is *wonderful* is of course *delightful*. . . .

I shall now come to the Practice of the antient Poets, and the Method which they made use of in introducing their *Machines*, in order to render their Poems more *instructive* and more *delightful*.

1. They took their *Machines* from the Religion of their

Country, upon which Account these *Machines* made the stronger
Impression, and made their Fables, and the Actions of them,
probable as well as *wonderful*; for nothing was more natural than
for those antient Heathens to believe that the Powers which they
ador'd were wont to intermeddle in human Affairs, and to promote the Success of those Designs which they favour'd; and
nothing could be more natural for them, than to believe that that
Design must prosper which was espous'd by *Jupiter*. But this
was not all; for the *Machines*, by making the Actions of their
Poems *probable*, made them *wonderful* to Men of Sense, who never
can admire any Thing in Humanity which *Reason* will not let
them believe. But,

2. The antient Poets made their *Machines* allegorical, as well
as their human Persons.

3. They oppos'd them to one another.

4. They shew'd a just Subordination among them, and a just
Proportion between their Functions. While one was employ'd
about the greatest and the sublimest Things, another was not
bullied about the most trifling and most contemptible.

5. They always made their *Machines* influence the Actions of
their Poems; and some of those *Machines* endeavour'd to *advance*
the Action of their respective Poem, and others of them endeavour'd to *retard* it.

6. They made them infinitely more powerful than the human
Persons.

But, Secondly, The Practice of the greatest modern Heroic
Poets is conformable to that of the antient.

1. They take their *Machines* from the Religion of their
Country; witness *Milton, Cowley, Tasso*.

2. They make them Allegorical.

3. They oppose them to one another.

4. They shew a just Subordination among them, and a just
Proportion between their Functions.

The Author of the *Rape* has run counter to this Practice both
of the Antients and Moderns. He has not taken his *Machines*

from the Religion of his Country, nor from any Religion, nor from Morality. His Machines contradict the Doctrines of the Christian Religion, contradict all sound Morality; there is no allegorical nor sensible Meaning in them; and for these Reasons they give no Instruction, make no Impression at all upon the Mind of a sensible Reader. Instead of making the Action wonderful and delightful, they render it extravagant, absurd, and incredible. They do not in the least influence that Action; they neither prevent the Danger of *Belinda*, nor promote it, nor retard it, unless, perhaps, it may be said, for one Moment, which is ridiculous. And if here it be objected, that the Author design'd only to *entertain* and *amuse*; To that I answer, That for that very Reason he ought to have taken the utmost Care to make his Poem *probable*, according to the important Precept of *Horace*.

Ficta voluptatis causa sint proxima veris

And that we may be satisfy'd that this Rule is founded in *Reason* and *Nature*, we find by constant Experience, that any thing that shocks *Probability* is most insufferable in Comedy.

There is no Opposition of the *Machines* to one another in this *Rape of the Lock*. *Umbriel* the *Gnome* is not introduc'd till the Action is over, and till *Ariel* and the Spirits under him, have quitted *Belinda*.

There is no just *Subordination* among these *Machines*, nor any just *Proportion* between their *Functions*. *Ariel* summons them together, and talks to them as if he were their Emperor.

> Ye *Sylphs* and *Sylphids*, to your Chief give ear,
> *Fays*, *Fairies*, *Genii*, *Elves*, and *Dæmons*, hear;
> Ye know the Spheres and various Tasks assign'd,
> By Laws eternal, to th' aerial Kind.
> Some in the Fields of purest *Æther* play,
> And bask and whiten in the Blaze of Day.
> Some guide the Course of wandring Orbs on high,
> Or roll the Planets thro' the boundless Sky—
> Or brew fierce Tempests on the watry Main,
> Or o'er the Glebe distil the kindly Rain.
> Others on Earth o'er human Race preside,

Watch all their Ways, and all their Actions guide:
Of these the Chief the Care of Nations own,
And guard with Arms Divine the *British* Throne.

Now, Sir, give me leave to ask you one Question: Did you ever
hear before that the Planets were roll'd by the aerial Kind? We
have heard indeed of Angels and Intelligences who have perform'd these Functions: But they are vast glorious Beings, of
Celestial Kind, and *Machines* of another System. Pray which of
the *aerial* Kind have these *sublime* Employments? For nothing
can be more ridiculous, or more contemptible, than the Employments of those whom he harangues

> To save the Powder from too rude a Gale,
> Nor let th' imprison'd Essences exhale.

There is a Difference almost infinite between these vile Functions and the former sublime ones, and therefore they can never
belong to Beings of the same Species. Which of the aerial Kinds
are the Movers of Orbs on high, or the Guardians of Empires
below; when he who calls himself their Chief, is only the Keeper
of a vile *Iseland Cur*, and has not so much as the Intendance of the
Lady's *Favourite Lock*, which is the Subject of the Poem? But
that is entrusted to an inferior Spirit, contrary to all manner of
Judgment and Decorum.

The *Machines* that appear in this Poem are infinitely less
considerable than the *human Persons*, which is without Prece-
dent. Nothing can be so contemptible as the *Persons*, or so
foolish as the *Understandings* of these *Hobgoblins. Ariel's* Speech,
for the first thirty Lines, is one continu'd Impertinence: For, if
what he says is true, he tells them nothing but what they knew
as well as himself before. And when he comes at length to the
Point, he is full as impertinent as he was in his *Ramble* before;
for after he has talk'd to them of *black Omens* and *dire Disasters*
that threaten his Heroine, these Bugbears dwindle to the breaking
a Piece of *China*, the staining a *Petticoat*, the losing a *Necklace*,
a *Fan*, or a Bottle of *Sal Volatile*. . . .

I shall mention but one or two more of the numerous Defects
which are to be found in the *Machines* of this Poem; the one is,

The Spirits, which he intends for *benign* ones, are *malignant*, and those, which he designs for *malignant*, are *beneficent* to Mankind. The *Gnomes* he intends for *malignant*, and the *Sylphs* for *beneficent* Spirits. Now the *Sylphs* in this Poem promote that *Female Vanity* which the *Gnomes* mortify. And Vanity is not only a great Defect in Human Nature, but the Mother of a thousand Errors, and a thousand Crimes, and the Cause of most of the Misfortunes which are incident to Humanity.

The last Defect that I shall take notice of, is, That the *Machines* in this Poem are not taken from *one System*, but are *double*, nay *treble* or *quadruple*. In the first *Canto* we hear of nothing but *Sylphs*, and *Gnomes*, and *Salamanders*, which are *Rosycrucian* Visions. In the second we meet with *Fairies*, *Genii*, and *Dæmons*, Beings which are unknown to those Fanatick Sophisters. In the fourth, *Spleen* and the *Phantoms* about, are deriv'd from the Powers of *Nature*, and are of a separate System. And *Fate* and *Jove*, which we find in the fifth *Canto*, belong to the Heathen Religion. . . .

IV

I have now shewn that there is no such Thing as a *Fable* or *Characters* in the Poem of the *Rape*, and that what he calls his *Machinery* is most extravagantly chosen. I now come to the *Sentiments*, which are more absurd than the rest, and of such an odd Composition, that they are at one and the same Time both *trivial* and *extravagant*.

The Absurdity of the *Sentiments* begins with the Book, and the Author stumbles at the Threshold.

> What dire Offence from amorous Causes springs,
> What mighty Quarrels rise from trivial Things,
> I sing—This Verse to C—— Muse is due.

Where in three Lines there are no less than two Errors in the *Sentiments*. For, in the first Place, tho' the Author has neither *Fable* nor *general Action*, yet he proposes to sing something *general*, rather than that *particular Action* which is the *Subject* of his Poem, and he begins as if he design'd to make the Reader

expect a *Treatise* of Love-Quarrels; which Proceeding is just
contrary to the Practice of *Homer*, and *Virgil*, and to the Dictates
of *right Reason*. *Homer* and *Virgil* had *accomplish'd Fables*, and
their *Actions* at the Bottom were *universal* and *allegorical*: Yet
they each of them propos'd to sing these *Actions*, as they had
particulariz'd them by the Imposition of Names. *Homer* begins
thus:

Muse, sing the baleful Fury of *Achilles*.

And *Virgil* thus:

Arma virumque cano, Trojæ qui primus ab oris
Italiam, fato profugus, Lavinaque venit
Littora.—

In the third Line he does not invoke the Muse to sing, but
proposes to do it himself: And tho' he names the Muse immediately afterwards, he does it, forsooth, to acquaint her, that
'tis not she, but *Belinda*, that is to inspire him:

—This Verse to C—— Muse is due,
This ev'n *Belinda* may vouchsafe to view:
Slight is the Subject, but not so the Praise,
If she inspire, and He approve my Lays.

So that he has desir'd no Assistance from the *Muse*, and none she
has afforded him.

The *Muse* indeed could not possibly assist him in this Case.
The *Muse* is a Machine like *Fate* and *Jove*, belonging originally to
the *Ethnic* System, and transferr'd sometimes to the Christian
Religion only allegorically; and the *Muse* cannot be suppos'd to
bring him acquainted with *Rosycrucian* Spirits, which would
destroy her own Divinity, either as Heathen or Christian, since
they are Beings utterly unknown, either to the *Ethnic* System,
or to the Christian Religion: So that 'tis *Belinda*, and not the
Muse, that is to inspire him. He introduces *her* into the Acquaintance of the *Sylphs* and *Sylphids* in his Epistle, and she is to bring
him acquainted with them in the Body of the Book. And now,
Sir, is not this very *ingeniously*, and very *judiciously* contriv'd? He
has desir'd no Assistance from the *Muse*, and, as I said before,

none he has had from her. The whole Poem seems to have been infus'd by a *Coquette*, and not inspir'd by a *Muse*. . . .

I have already shewn, in speaking of the *Characters*, how injudicious all that Passage is which relates to the Toilette: And as I do not pretend to shew all his Errors, but only some few which are very gross ones, I shall now pass to the second *Canto*; in which there is a Remark that cannot but be the Effect of very *wise* and very *deep* Observation:

> With hairy Springes we the Birds betray,
> Slight Lines of Hair surprize the finny Prey,
> Fair Tresses Man's imperial Race insnare,
> And Beauty draws us with a single Hair.

That is to say, *Birds* are caught by the *Heels*, and *Fish* by the *Jaws*, with *Horse-Hair*; and *Men* are hamper'd by the *Souls* with *Woman's Hair*. Tell me truly, Sir, is not this the Effect of very *wise* and very *deep* Observation? I have been so taken with these four Verses, that I could not forbear making the four following in Imitation of them.

> With jingling Bells Night-Fowlers Birds betray,
> With these Night-Anglers catch the finny Prey:
> Small Poets hamper Fools by jingling Rhimes,
> And Nonsense draws them by its senseless Chimes.

In this second *Canto* we have another Imitation of *Virgil*, and one ten times more unhappy than the former in the first *Canto*. The Passage of *Virgil* is in the second Book of the *Æneis*:

> Dolus, an virtus, quis in hoste requirit?

That is to say, If a Captain obtains a Victory, few enquire whether he ow'd it to Stratagem or open Force.

The Imitation is included in the following Lines:

> Th' adventurous Baron the bright Lock admir'd,
> He saw, he wish'd, and to the Prize aspir'd;
> Resolv'd to win, he meditates the Way
> By Force to ravish, or by Fraud betray:
> For when Success a Lover's Toil attends,
> Few ask, if Fraud or Force attain'd his Ends.

Now the Mischief of it is, that if a Lover obtains his Ends by
Force, the whole Country makes a very severe Enquiry into it,
by their Representative, a *petty Jury*; and if he happens to be
convicted of it, in that Case poor Culprit passes his Time but
scurvily. . . .

V

I am now come to the *Sentiments*, which are to be found in the
fourth and fifth *Cantos* of this notable Poem. I shall only take
notice of a very few, by which you and your Friends may judge
of the whole.

The first thing I shall take notice of, is the impertinent Journey
of *Umbriel* the *Gnome*, who

> Down to the central Earth, his proper Scene,
> Repairs to search the gloomy Cave of Spleen.

Now to what Purpose does this fantastick Being take this Journey? Why, to give *Belinda* the Spleen. In order to which, *Spleen*
equips him with a *Bottle* and a *Bag*, as a Country Dame does her
Plough-Jobber, to equip him for his Day's Work.

> A wondrous Bag with both her Hands she binds,
> Like that where once *Ulysses* held the Winds;
> There she collects the Force of female Lungs,
> Sighs, Sobs, and Passions, and the War of Tongues.
> A Viol next she fills with fainting Fears,
> Soft Sorrows, melting Griefs, and flowing Tears.

Now what could be more impertinent than this Journey of
Umbriel, or more vain and useless than this Gift of *Spleen*,
whether we look upon the *Bag* or the *Bottle*?

Umbriel descends to the *central Earth* to give *Belinda* the
Spleen. Now 'tis plain, that before his Descent he leaves her *mad*,
and upon his Return, finds her in a *Fit of the Mother*.

That before his Journey he leaves her *mad*, is I think pretty
plain, from

> Then flash'd the livid Lightning from her Eyes,
> And *Screams* of *Horror* rend th' *affrighted* Skies.
> Not *louder Shrieks* by Dames to Heaven are ·cast—

That upon his Return he finds her in a *Fit of the Mother*, is manifest from

> Sunk in *Thalestris'* Arms the Nymph he found,
> Her Eyes dejected, and her Hair unbound.

How absurd was it then for this *Ignis Fatuus* to take a Journey down to the *central Earth*, for no other Purpose than to give her the *Spleen*, whom he left and found in the Height of it? . . .

Thus, Sir, have I gone thro' several of the *Sentiments* upon the *Rape*, which are either *trifling*, or *false*. But there are a great many Lines, which have *no Sentiment* at all in them, that is, no *reasonable Meaning*. Such are the *Puns* which are every where spread throughout it. *Puns* bear the same Proportion to *Thought*, that *Bubbles* hold to *Bodies*, and may justly be compared to those gaudy Bladders which Children make with Soap; which, tho' they please their weak Capacities with a momentary Glittering, yet are but just beheld, and vanish into Air. Of this Nature is that Pun in the *5th Canto*.

> See fierce *Belinda* on the Baron flies,
> With more than usual Lightning in her Eyes,
> Nor fears the Chief th' unequal Fight to try,
> Who fought no more than *on* his Foe to die.

That is to say, *He wish'd for nothing more than to fight with her, because he desired nothing more than to lie with her*. Now what sensible Meaning can this have, unless he takes her for a *Russian*, who is to grow passionately fond of him by the extraordinary Gallantry of a lusty Bastinado? Such likewise is that *Quibble* in the following Page:

> Boast not my Fall, (he cry'd) Insulting Foe,
> Thou by some others shalt be laid as low.

Now we heard nothing before of the Baron's lying low. All that we heard is, that by a dextrous Toss of this *modest Virgin*, his Nostrils were fill'd with Snuff. So that he seems here to say the same thing to her, that *Nykin* says to *Cocky* in the *Old Batchelor*;

I have it in my Head, but you will have it in another Place. What
follows seems to be very extraordinary:

> Nor think to die dejects my lofty Mind,
> All that I dread is leaving you behind:
> Rather than so, ah! let me still survive,
> And burn in *Cupid*'s Flames, but burn alive.

Now, Sir, who ever heard of a dead Man that burnt in *Cupid*'s
Flames?

Of the same Nature are those numerous Banters in Rhyme,
which are to be found throughout this Poem, which are so uniform, and so much of a piece, that one would swear the Author
were giving a Receipt for dry Joking: For by placing something
important in the Beginning of a Period, and making something
very trifling follow it, he seems to take pains to bring *something*
into a Conjunction Copulative with *nothing*, in order to beget
nothing. Of this there are divers Instances in *Ariel*'s Speech in the
2d Canto;

> This Day black Omens threat the brightest Fair
> That e'er deserv'd the watchfull'st Spirit's Care;
> Some dire Disaster, or by Force or Sleight,
> But what, or where, the Fates have wrapt in Night:
> Whether the Nymph shall break *Diana*'s Law,
> Or some frail *China* Jar receive a Flaw,
> Or stain her Honour, or her new Brocade,
> Forget her Pray'rs, or miss a Masquerade,
> Or lose her Heart, or Necklace at a Ball,
> Or whether Heav'n has doom'd that *Shock* must fall.

Which, by the way, I suppose is design'd as a bitter Bob for the
Predestinarians. Raillery apart, we pretend not to deny, that the
very minutest Events are foredoom'd by eternal Prescience; but
that Heaven should give notice of the Death of a vile Dog, by
what he calls black Omens, is a great deal too strong. Heaven
could do no more for *Cæsar* himself, the very Top of the human
Creation, and the Foremost Man of the Universe.

But now, Sir, give me leave to ask you one Question: Is *Ariel*
in Jest or in Earnest, in haranguing the Spirits at this rate? Is he in

Earnest? Why then even *Robin Goodfellow* himself is not a more senseless insignificant Hobgoblin. Is he in Jest? Why then all this is a very grand Impertinence, since it does not so much as aim at any thing: For how can the Spirits be any ways influenced by these dry Jokes of their Leader?

Of the same Stamp and the same Contrivance are these Lines in the Beginning of the *3d Canto*:

> Here *Britain*'s Statesmen oft the Fall foredoom
> Of foreign Tyrants, and of Nymphs at home;
> Here Thou, great *Anna*, whom three Realms obey,
> Dost sometimes Council take, and sometimes Tea;—
> One speaks the Glory of the *British* Queen,
> And one describes a charming *Indian* Screen.

As I said above, Sir, is not here a Receipt for dry Joking? and can any thing be more easy than to be a Wit at this rate?

But so much for the *Sentiments* in this *Rape of the Lock*; I should now come to the *Expression*. But I have already transgress'd the Bounds I prescribed to myself, and 'tis Time to take Pity of myself and you. . . .

(from *Remarks on Mr Pope's Rape of the Lock. In Several Letters to a Friend,* 1728)

Samuel Johnson

N OT long after, he wrote the *Rape of the Lock*, the most airy, the most ingenious, and the most delightful of all his compositions, occasioned by a frolic of gallantry, rather too familiar, in which Lord Petre cut off a lock of Mrs Arabella Fermor's hair. This, whether stealth or violence, was so much resented, that the commerce of the two families, before very friendly, was interrupted. Mr Caryl, a gentleman who, being secretary to King James's Queen, had followed his mistress into France, and who, being the author of *Sir Solomon Single*, a comedy, and some translations, was entitled to the notice of a wit, solicited Pope to endeavour a reconciliation by a ludicrous poem, which might bring both the parties to a better temper. In compliance with Caryl's request, though his name was for a long time marked only by the first and last letter, C—l, a poem of two cantos was written, as is said, in a fortnight, and sent to the offended lady, who liked it well enough to show it; and, with the usual process of literary transactions, the author, dreading a surreptitious edition, was forced to publish it.

The event is said to have been such as was desired, the pacification and diversion of all to whom it related, except Sir George Brown, who complained with some bitterness, that, in the character of Sir Plume, he was made to talk nonsense. Whether all this be true I have some doubt; for at Paris a few years ago, a niece of Mrs Fermor, who presided in an English convent, mentioned Pope's work with very little gratitude, rather as an insult than an honour; and she may be supposed to have inherited the opinion of her family.

At its first appearance it was termed by Addison 'merum sal'. Pope, however, saw that it was capable of improvement; and, having luckily contrived to borrow his machinery from the Rosicrucians, imparted the scheme with which his head was teeming to Addison, who told him that his work, as it stood, was 'a delicious little thing', and gave him no encouragement to retouch it.

This has been too hastily considered as an instance of Addison's jealousy; for, as he could not guess the conduct of the new design, or the possibilities of pleasure comprised in a fiction of which there had been no examples, he might very reasonably and kindly persuade the author to acquiesce in his own prosperity, and forbear an attempt which he considered as an unnecessary hazard.

Addison's counsel was happily rejected. Pope foresaw the future efflorescence of imagery then budding in his mind, and resolved to spare no art, or industry of cultivation. The soft luxuriance of his fancy was already shooting, and all the gay varieties of diction were ready at his hand to colour and embellish it.

His attempt was justified by its success. The *Rape of the Lock* stands forward, in the classes of literature, as the most exquisite example of ludicrous poetry. Berkeley congratulated him upon the display of powers more truly poetical than he had shown before: with elegance of description and justness of precepts, he had now exhibited boundless fertility of invention.

He always considered the intermixture of the machinery with the action as his most successful exertion of poetical art. He indeed could never afterwards produce any thing of such unexampled excellence. Those performances, which strike with wonder, are combinations of skilful genius with happy casualty; and it is not likely that any felicity, like the discovery of a new race of preternatural agents, should happen twice to the same man.

Of this poem the author was, I think, allowed to enjoy the praise for a long time without disturbance. Many years afterwards, Dennis published some remarks upon it, with very little force, and with no effect; for the opinion of the public was already settled, and it was no longer at the mercy of criticism. . . .

To the praises which have been accumulated on the *Rape of the Lock*, by readers of every class, from the critic to the waiting maid, it is difficult to make any addition. Of that which is universally allowed to be the most attractive of all ludicrous compositions, let it rather be now inquired from what sources the power of pleasing is derived.

Dr Warburton, who excelled in critical perspicacity, has remarked, that the preternatural agents are very happily adapted to the purposes of the poem. The heathen deities can no longer gain attention: we should have turned away from a contest between Venus and Diana. The employment of allegorical persons always excites conviction of its own absurdity; they may produce effects, but cannot conduct actions: when the phantom is put in motion, it dissolves: thus *Discord* may raise a mutiny; but *Discord* cannot conduct a march, nor besiege a town. Pope brought in view a new race of beings, with powers and passions proportionate to their operation. The Sylphs and Gnomes act, at the toilet and the tea-table, what more terrific and more powerful phantoms perform on the stormy ocean, or the field of battle; they give their proper help, and do their proper mischief.

Pope is said, by an objector, not to have been the inventor of this petty nation; a charge which might with more justice have been brought against the author of the *Iliad*, who doubtless adopted the religious system of his country; for what is there, but the names of his agents, which Pope has not invented? Has he not assigned them characters and operations never heard of before? Has he not, at least, given them their first poetical existence? If this is not sufficient to denominate his work original, nothing original ever can be written.

In this work are exhibited, in a very high degree, the two most engaging powers of an author. New things are made familiar, and familiar things are made new. A race of aërial people, never heard of before, is presented to us in a manner so clear and easy, that the reader seeks for no further information, but immediately mingles with his new acquaintance, adopts their interests, and attends their pursuits, loves a Sylph, and detests a Gnome.

That familiar things are made new, every paragraph will prove. The subject of the poem is an event below the common incidents of common life; nothing real is introduced that is not seen so often as to be no longer regarded; yet the whole detail of a female day is here brought before us, invested with so much art of decoration, that, though nothing is disguised, every thing is striking, and we feel all the appetite of curiosity for that from which we have a thousand times turned fastidiously away.

The purpose of the poet is, as he tells us, to laugh at 'the little unguarded follies of the female sex'. It is therefore without justice that Dennis charges the *Rape of the Lock* with the want of a moral, and for that reason sets it below the *Lutrin*, which exposes the pride and discord of the clergy. Perhaps neither Pope nor Boileau has made the world much better than he found it: but, if they had both succeeded, it were easy to tell who would have deserved most from public gratitude. The freaks, and humours, and spleen, and vanity of women, as they embroil families in discord, and fill houses with disquiet, do more to obstruct the happiness of life in a year than the ambition of the clergy in many centuries. It has been well observed, that the misery of man proceeds not from any single crush of overwhelming evil, but from small vexations continually repeated.

It is remarked by Dennis likewise, that the machinery is superfluous; that by all the bustle of preternatural operation, the main event is neither hastened nor retarded. To this charge an efficacious answer is not easily made. The Sylphs cannot be said to help or to oppose; and it must be allowed to imply some want of art, that their power has not been sufficiently intermingled with the action. Other parts may likewise be charged with want of connection; the game at *ombre* might be spared; but, if the lady had lost her hair while she was intent upon her cards, it might have been inferred that those who are too fond of play will be in danger of neglecting more important interests. Those perhaps are faults; but what are such faults to so much excellence!

(from *The Life of Pope*, 1781)

Joseph Warton

The Rape of the Lock, now before us, is the fourth, and most excellent of the heroi-comic poems. The subject was a quarrel occasioned by a little piece of gallantry of lord Petre, who, in a party of pleasure, found means to cut off a favourite lock of Mrs Arabella Fermor's hair. Pope was desired to write it, in order to put an end to the quarrel it produced, by Mr Caryl, who had been secretary to queen Mary, author of *Sir Solomon Single*, a comedy, and of some translations in Dryden's *Miscellanies*. Pope was accustomed to say, 'What I wrote fastest always pleased most.' The first sketch of this exquisite piece, which Addison called Merum Sal, was written in less than a fortnight, in two cantos only: but it was so universally applauded, that, in the next year, our poet enriched it with the machinery of the sylphs, and extended it to five cantos; when it was printed with a letter to Mrs Fermor, far superior to any of Voiture. The insertion of the machinery of the sylphs in proper places, without the least appearance of its being awkwardly stitched in, is one of the happiest efforts of judgment and art. He took the idea of these invisible beings, so proper to be employed in a poem of this nature, from a little French book entitled, *Le Comte de Gabalis*, of which is given the following account, in an entertaining writer. 'The Abbé Villars, who came from Thoulouse to Paris, to make his fortune by preaching, is the author of this diverting work. The five dialogues of which it consists, are the result of those gay conversations, in which the Abbé was engaged, with a small circle of men, of fine wit and humour, like himself. When this book first appeared, it was universally read, as innocent and amusing. But at length, its consequences were perceived, and reckoned dangerous, at a time when this sort of curiosities began to gain credit. Our devout preacher was denied the chair, and his book forbidden to be read. It was not clear whether the äuthor intended to be ironical, or spoke all seriously. The second volume which he promised, would have decided the question: but the unfortunate Abbé was soon afterwards assassinated by ruffians, on the road to Lyons. The laughers gave out, that the gnomes and sylphs, disguised like ruffians, had shot him, as a punishment for revealing the secrets of the Cabala; a crime not to be pardoned by these jealous spirits, as Villars himself has declared in his book.'

It may not be improper to give a specimen of this author's manner, who has lately been well imitated in the way of mixing jest with earnest, in an elegant piece called *Hermippus Redivivus*. The Comte de Gabalis being about to initiate his pupil into the most profound mysteries of the Rosicrusian philosophy, advises him to consider seriously, whether or no he had courage and resolution sufficient to renounce all those obstacles, which might prevent his arising to that height, which the figure of his nativity promised. 'Le mot de renoncer, says the scholar, m'effraya, & je ne doutai point qu'il n'allât me proposer de renoncer au baptême ou au paradis. Ainsi ne sçachant comme me tirer de ce mauvais pas; Renoncer, lui dis-je, Monsieur quoi, faut-il renoncer à quelque chose? Vraiment, reprit-il, il le faut bien; & il le faut si nécessairement, qu'il faut commencer par-là. Je ne sçai si vous pourrez vous résoudre: mais je sçai bien que la sagesse n'habite point dans un corps sujet au péché, comme elle n'entre point dans une âme prévenue d'erreur ou de malice. Les sages ne vous admettront jamais à leur compagnie, si vous ne renoncez dès à présent à un chose qui ne peut compatir avec la sagesse. *Il faut*, ajoûta-t-il tout bas en se baissant à mon oreille, *il faut renoncer à tout commerce charnel avec les femmes*.' On a diligent perusal of this book, I cannot find that Pope has borrowed any particular circumstances relating to these spirits, but merely the general idea of their existence.

These machines are vastly superior to the allegorical personages of Boileau and Garth; not only on account of their novelty, but for the exquisite poetry, and oblique satire, which

they have given the poet an opportunity to display. The business
and petty concerns of a fine lady, receive an air of importance
from the notion of their being perpetually overlooked and conducted, by the interposition of celestial agents.

It is judicious to open the poem, by introducing the Guardian
Sylph, warning Belinda against some secret impending danger.
The account which Ariel gives of the nature, office, and employment of these inhabitants of air, is finely fancied: into which
several strokes of satire are thrown with great delicacy and address.

> Think what an equipage thou hast in air,
> And view with scorn two pages and a chair.

The transformation of women of different tempers into different
kinds of spirits, cannot be too much applauded.

> The sprites of fiery Termagants, in flame
> Mount up, and take a salamander's name.
> Soft yielding minds to water glide away,
> And sip with Nymphs, their elemental tea.
> The graver Prude sinks downward to a gnome,
> In search of mischief still on earth to roam.
> The light Coquettes in sylphs aloft repair,
> And sport and flutter in the fields of air.

The description of the toilette, which succeeds, is judiciously
given in such magnificent terms, as dignify the offices performed
at it. Belinda dressing is painted in as pompous a manner, as
Achilles arming. The canto ends with a circumstance, artfully
contrived to keep this beautiful machinery in the reader's eye: for
after the poet has said, that the fair heroine

> Repairs her smiles, awakens ev'ry grace,
> And calls forth all the wonders of her face,

He immediately subjoins,

> The busy sylphs surround their darling care,
> These set the head, and those divide the hair:
> Some fold the sleeve, whilst others plait the gown,
> And Betty's prais'd for labours not her own.

The mention of the Lock, on which the poem turns, is rightly reserved to the second canto. The sacrifice of the Baron to implore success to his undertaking, is another instance of our poet's judgment, in heightening the subject. The succeeding scene of sailing upon the Thames is most gay and delightful; and impresses very pleasing pictures upon the imagination. Here too the machinery is again introduced with much propriety. Ariel summons his denizens of air; who are thus painted with a rich exuberance of fancy.

> Some to the sun their insect wings unfold,
> Waft on the breeze, or sink in clouds of gold:
> Transparent forms, too thin for mortal sight,
> Their fluid bodies half dissolv'd in light.
> Loose to the wind their airy garments flew,
> Thin glitt'ring textures of the filmy dew,
> Dipt in the richest tincture of the skies,
> Where light disports in ever-mingling dyes;
> While every beam new transient colours flings,
> Colours, that change whene'er they wave their wings.

Ariel afterwards enumerates the functions and employments of the sylphs, in the following manner: where some are supposed to delight in more gross, and others in more refined occupation.

> Ye know the spheres and various tasks, assign'd
> By laws eternal to th' aerial kind.
> Some in the fields of purest æther play,
> And bask and brighten in the blaze of day;
> Some guide the course of wandring orbs on high,
> Or roll the planets through the boundless sky;
> Some, less refin'd, beneath the moon's pale light,
> Pursue the stars, that shoot across the night;
> Or suck the mists in grosser air below;
> Or dip their pinions in the painted bow:
> Or brew fierce tempests on the wintry main,
> Or o'er the glebe distil the kindly rain.

Those who are fond of tracing images and sentiments to their source, may perhaps be inclined to think, that the hint of ascribing tasks and offices to such imaginary beings, is taken from

the Fairies and the Ariel of Shakespeare: let the impartial critic
determine, which has the superiority of fancy. The employment
of Ariel in the *Tempest*, is said to be,

> — — — To tread the ooze
> Of the salt deep;
> To run upon the sharp wind of the north;
> To do — business in the veins of th' earth,
> When it is bak'd with frost;
> — — To dive into the fire; to ride
> On the curl'd clouds.

And again,

> — — In the deep nook, where once
> Thou call'd'st me up at midnight, to fetch dew
> From the still-vext Bermoothes. — — —

Nor must I omit that exquisite song, in which his favourite and
peculiar pastime is expressed.

> Where the bee sucks, there suck I,
> In a cowslip's bell I lie;
> There I couch when owls do cry.
> On the bat's back I do fly,
> After sun-set, merrily;
> Merrily, merrily, shall I live now,
> Under the blossom that hangs on the bough.

With what wildness of imagination, but yet, with what propriety,
are the amusements of the fairies pointed out, in the *Midsummer
Night's Dream*: amusements proper for none but fairies!

> — — 'Fore the third part of a minute, hence:
> Some to kill cankers in the musk-rose buds.
> Some war with rear-mice for their leathern wings,
> To make my small elves coats; and some keep back
> The clamorous owl, that nightly hoots, and wonders
> At our queint spirits. — — — — —

Shakespeare only could have thought of the following gratifica-
tions for Titania's lover; and they are fit only to be offered, to her
lover, by a fairy-queen.

Be kind, and courteous to this gentleman,
Hop in his walks, and gambol in his eyes;
Feed him with apricocks and dewberries,
With purple grapes, green figs, and mulberries.
The honey-bags steal from the humble bees,
And for night-tapers crop their waxen thighs,
And light them at the fiery glow-worm's eyes,
To have my love to bed, and to arise:
And pluck the wings from painted butterflies,
To fan the moon-beams from his sleeping eyes.

If it should be thought, that Shakespeare has the merit of being the first who assigned proper employments to imaginary persons, in the foregoing lines, yet it must be granted, that by the addition of the most delicate satire to the most lively fancy, Pope, in the following passage, has excelled any thing in Shakespeare, or perhaps in any other author.

Our humbler province is to tend the fair,
Not a less pleasing, though less glorious care;
To save the powder from too rough a gale,
Nor let th' imprison'd essences exhale;
To draw fresh colours from the vernal flow'rs,
To steal from rainbows, ere they drop in show'rs,
A brighter wash; to curl their waving hairs,
Assist their blushes, and inspire their airs;
Nay oft, in dreams invention we bestow,
To change a flounce or add a furbelow.

The seeming importance given to every part of female dress, each of which is committed to the care and protection of a different sylph, with all the solemnity of a general appointing the several posts in his army, renders the following passage admirable, on account of its politeness, poignancy, and poetry.

Haste then ye spirits, to your charge repair;
The fluttering fan be Zephyretta's care;
The drops to thee, Brillante, we consign;
And, Momentilla, let the watch be thine;
Do thou, Crispissa, tend the fav'rite lock;
Ariel himself shall be the guard of Shock.

The celebrated raillery of Addison on the hoop-petticoat, has nothing equal to the following circumstance; which marks the difficulty of guarding a part of dress of such high consequence.

> To fifty chosen sylphs, of special note,
> We trust th' important charge the PETTICOAT:
> Oft have we known that sevenfold fence to fail,
> Tho' stiff with hoops, and arm'd with ribs of mail:
> Form a strong line about the silver bound,
> And guard the wide circumference around.

Our poet still rises in the delicacy of his satire, where he employs, with the utmost judgment and elegance, all the implements and furniture of the toilette, as instruments of punishment to those spirits, who shall be careless of their charge: of punishment such as sylphs alone could undergo. Each of the delinquents,

> Shall feel sharp vengeance soon o'ertake his sins,
> Be stop'd in vials, or transfix'd with pins;
> Or plung'd in lakes of bitter washes lie;
> Or wedg'd whole ages in a bodkin's eye;
> Gums and pomatums shall his flight restrain,
> While clog'd he beats his silken wings in vain;
> Or allum-styptics with contracting pow'r,
> Shrink his thin essence like a shrivel'd flow'r;
> Or, as Ixion fix'd, the wretch shall feel
> The giddy motion of the whirling mill;
> In fumes of burning chocolate shall glow,
> And tremble at the sea that froths below.

If Virgil has merited such perpetual commendation for exalting his bees, by the majesty and magnificence of his diction, does not Pope deserve equal praises, for the pomp and lustre of his language, on so trivial a subject?

The same mastery of language, appears in the lively and elegant description of the game at Ombre; which is certainly imitated from the Scacchia of Vida, and as certainly equal to it, if not superior. Both of them have elevated and enlivened their subjects, by such similies as the epic poets use; but as Chess is a play of a far higher order than Ombre, Pope had a more difficult task than Vida, to raise this his inferior subject, into equal dignity and gracefulness. Here again our poet artfully introduces his machinery:

> Soon as she spreads her hand, th' aerial guard
> Descend, and sit on each important card;
> First Ariel perch'd upon a mattadore.

The majesty with which the kings of spades and clubs, and the knaves of diamonds and clubs are spoken of, is very amusing to the imagination: and the whole game is conducted with great art and judgment. I question whether Hoyle could have played it better than Belinda. It is finely contrived that she should be victorious; as it occasions a change of fortune in the dreadful loss she was speedily to undergo, and gives occasion to the poet to introduce a moral reflection from Virgil, which adds to the pleasantry of the story. . . .

To this scene succeeds the tea-table. It is, doubtless, as hard to make a coffee-pot shine in poetry as a plough: yet Pope has succeeded in giving elegance to so familiar an object, as well as Virgil. The guardian spirits are again active, and importantly employed;

> Strait hover round the fair her airy band;
> Some, as she sipp'd, the fuming liquor fann'd.

Then follows an instance of assiduity fancied with great delicacy;

> Some o'er her lap their careful plumes display'd,
> Trembling, and conscious of the rich brocade.

But nothing can excel the behaviour of the sylphs, and their wakeful solicitude for their charge, when the danger grows more imminent, and the catastrophe approaches.

> Swift to the Lock a thousand sprites repair.

The methods by which they endeavoured to preserve her from the intended mischief, are such only as could be executed by a sylph; and have therefore an admirable propriety, as well as the utmost elegance.

A thousand wings by turns blow back the hair.
And thrice they TWITCH'D the diamond in her ear,
Thrice she look'd back, and thrice the foe drew near.

Still farther to heighten the piece, and to preserve the characters
of his machines to the last, just when the fatal forfex was spread,

Ev'n then, before the fatal engine clos'd,
A wretched sylph too fondly interpos'd;——
Fate urg'd the sheers, and cut the sylph in twain,
(But airy substance soon unites again.)——

Which last line is an admirable parody on that passage of Milton,
which, perhaps oddly enough, describes Satan wounded:

The griding sword, with discontinuous wound,
Pass'd thro him; but th' etherial substance clos'd,
Not long divisible. —— —— —— ——

The parodies are some of the most exquisite parts of this poem.
That which follows from the 'Dum juga montis aper', of Virgil,
contains some of the most artful strokes of satire, and the most
poignant ridicule imaginable.

While fish in streams, or birds delight in air,
Or in a coach and six the British fair,
As long as Atalantis shall be read,
Or the small pillow grace a lady's bed,
While visits shall be paid on solemn days,
When numerous wax-lights in bright order blaze,
While nymphs take treats, or assignations give,
So long my honour, name, and praise, shall live.

The introduction of frequent parodies on serious and solemn
passages of Homer and Virgil, give much life and spirit to heroi-
comic poetry. 'Tu dors, Prelat? tu dors?' in Boileau, is the
'εὔδεις, 'Ατρέος υἰὲ' of Homer, and is full of humour. The
wife of the barber talks in the language of Dido in her expostula-
tions to her Æneas, at the beginning of the second canto of the
Lutrin. Pope's parodies of the speech of Sarpedon in Homer, and
of the description of Achilles's scepter, together with the scales
of Jupiter from Homer, Virgil, and Milton, are judiciously intro-

duced in their several places; are perhaps superior to those Boileau or Garth have used, and are worked up with peculiar pleasantry. The mind of the reader is engaged by novelty, when it so unexpectedly finds a thought or object it had been accustomed to survey in another form, suddenly arrayed in a ridiculous garb. A mixture of comic and ridiculous images, with serious and important ones, adds also no small beauty to this species of poetry. As in the following passages, where real and imaginary distress are coupled together.

> Not youthful kings in battle seiz'd alive,
> Not scornful virgins who their charms survive,
> Not ardent lovers robb'd of all their bliss,
> Not ancient ladies when refus'd a kiss,
> Not tyrants fierce that unrepenting die,

Nay, to carry the climax still higher,

> Not Cynthia when her manteau's pinn'd awry,
> E'er felt such rage, resentment, and despair.

This is much superior to a similar passage in the *Dispensary*, which Pope might have in his eye;

> At this the victors own such ecstacies
> As Memphian priests if their Osiris sneeze;
> Or champions with Olympic clangor fir'd,
> Or simp'ring prudes with spritely Nantz inspir'd,
> Or Sultans rais'd from dungeons to a crown,
> Or fasting zealots when the sermon's done.

These objects have no reference to Garth's subject, as almost all of Pope's have, in the passage in question, where some female foible is glanced at. In this same canto, the cave of Spleen, the pictures of her attendants, Ill-nature and Affectation, the effects of the vapour that hung over her palace, the imaginary diseases she occasions, the speech of Umbriel, a gnome, to this malignant deity, the vial of female sorrows, the speech of Thalestris to aggravate the misfortune, the breaking the vial with its direful effects, and the speech of the disconsolate Belinda; all these circumstances are poetically imagined, and are far superior to any of Boileau and Garth. How much in character is it for Belinda to mark a very dismal and solitary situation, by wishing to be conveyed,

> Where the gilt chariot never marks the way,
> Where none learn Ombre, none e'er taste Bohea!

Nothing is more common in the poets than to introduce omens as preceding some important and dreadful event. Virgil has strongly described those that preceded the death of Dido. The rape of Belinda's Lock must necessarily also be attended with alarming prodigies. With what exquisite satire are they enumerated!

> Thrice from my trembling hand the patch-box fell;
> The tottering china shook without a wind.

And still more to aggravate the direfulness of the impending evil,

> Nay Poll sate mute, and Shock was most unkind!

The chief subject of the fifth and last canto, is the battle that ensues, and the endeavours of the ladies to recover the hair. This battle is described, as it ought to be, in very lofty and pompous terms: a game of romps was never so well dignified before. The weapons made use of are the most proper imaginable: the lightning of the ladies eyes, intolerable frowns, a pinch of snuff, and a bodkin. The machinery is not forgot:

> Triumphant Umbriel on a sconce's height,
> Clapp'd his glad wings, and sate to view the fight,

Again, when the snuff is given to the Baron,

> The gnomes direct, to ev'ry atom just,
> The pungent grains of titillating dust.

Boileau and Garth have also each of them enlivened their pieces with a mock-fight. But Boileau has laid the scene of his action in a neighbouring bookseller's shop; where the combatants encounter each other by chance. This conduct is a little inartificial; but has given the satyrist an opportunity of indulging his ruling passion, the exposing the bad poets, with which France at that time abounded. Swift's *Battle of the Books*, at the end of the *Tale of a Tub*, is evidently taken from this battle of Boileau, which is excellent in its kind. The fight of the physicians, in the *Dispensary*, is one of its most shining parts. There is a vast deal of propriety, as well as pleasantry, in the weapons Garth has given to his warriours. They are armed, much in character, with caustics, emetics, and cathartics; with buckthorn, and steel-pills; with syringes, bed-pans, and urinals. The execution is exactly proportioned to the deadliness of such irresistible weapons; and the wounds inflicted, are suitable to the nature of each different instrument, said to inflict them.

We are now arrived at the grand catastrophe of the poem; the invaluable Lock which is so eagerly sought, is irrecoverably lost! And here our poet has made a judicious use of that celebrated fiction of Ariosto; that all things lost on earth are treasured in the moon. How such a fiction can properly have place in an epic poem, it becomes the defenders of this agreeably extravagant writer to justify; but in a comic poem, it appears with grace and consistency. . . .

The denouement, as a pedantic disciple of Bossu would call it, of this poem, is well conducted. What is become of this important Lock of Hair? It is made a constellation with that of Berenice, so celebrated by Callimachus. As it rises to heaven,

> The sylphs behold it kindling as it flies,
> And pleas'd pursue its progress through the skies.

One cannot sufficiently applaud the art of the poet, in constantly keeping in the reader's view, the machinery of the poem, to the very last. Even when the Lock is transformed, the sylphs, who had so carefully guarded it, are here once again artfully mentioned, as finally rejoicing in its honourable transformation.

In reading the *Lutrin*, I have always been struck with the impropriety of so serious a conclusion, as Boileau has given to so ludicrous a poem. Piety and Justice are beings rather too awful, to have any concern in the celebrated Desk. They appear as much out of place and season, as would the archbishop of Paris in his pontifical robes, in an harlequin entertainment.

Pope does not desert his favorite Lock, even after it becomes a constellation; and the uses he assigns to it are indeed admirable, and have a reference to the subject of the poem.

> This the beau monde shall from the Mall survey,
> And hail with music it's propitious ray;
> This the blest lover shall for *Venus* take,
> And send up prayers from Rosamunda's lake;
> This Partridge soon shall view in cloudless skies,
> When next he looks through Galileo's eyes;
> And hence th' egregious wizard shall foredoom,
> The fate of Louis, and the fall of Rome.

This is at once, *dulce loqui*, and *ridere decorum.*

Upon the whole, I hope it will not be thought an exaggerated panegyric to say, that the *Rape of the Lock*, is the best satire extant; that it contains the truest and liveliest picture of modern life; and that the subject is of a more elegant nature, as well as more artfully conducted, than that of any other heroi-comic poem. Pope here appears in the light of a man of gallantry, and of a thorough knowledge of the world; and indeed he had nothing, in his carriage and deportment, of that affected singularity, which has induced some men of genius to despise, and depart from, the established rules of politeness and civil life. For all poets have not practised the sober and rational advice of Boileau.

> Que les vers ne soient pas votre eternel emploi:
> Cultivez vos amis, soyez homme de soi.
> C'est peu d'etre agréeable et charmant dans un livre;
> Il fait savoir encore, et converser, et vivre.

If some of the most candid among the French critics, begin to acknowledge, that they have produced nothing in point of Sublimity and Majesty equal to the *Paradise Lost*, we may also venture to affirm, that in point of Delicacy, Elegance, and fine-turned Raillery, on which they have so much valued themselves, they have produced nothing equal to the *Rape of the Lock*. It is in this composition, Pope principally appears a Poet; in which he has displayed more imagination than in all his other works taken together. It should however be remembered, that he was not the first former and creator of those beautiful machines, the sylphs; on which his claim to imagination is chiefly founded. He found them existing ready to his hand, but has, indeed, employed them with singular judgment and artifice.

(from *An Essay on the Genius and Writings of Pope*, 1782)

Thomas Campbell

P OPE is naturally introduced as the successor of Dryden. His character is thus given by our lecturer.

In comparing and estimating different poets of the first class, we ought to observe something like mathematical accuracy, – we ought to weigh the whole aggregate of their respective merits. In making comparative estimates, with this justice to Pope, we should find in him so many, and so apparently incompatible excellences, that we should deem the possible and eternal privation of his works as great a single loss as could happen to the republic of letters. Of what a melancholy and irreparable chasm, among the poetical ornaments of England, would feeling hearts be sensible, if the Abelard to Eloisa could be lost! This poem is quite unrivalled in the ancient and modern world: it consists of three hundred and sixty lines, and every line is superlatively elegant, harmonious, and pathetic. This observation is not applicable to any other poem of such a length; but this is not its only glorious singularity. The hopes, the fears, the wishes, the raptures and the agonies of love, were never so naturally and forcibly impressed on the soul by any other eloquence, if we except Rousseau.

Pope is an excellent poet; but this is not a way to lecture on his merits. This is the common-place language, which every miss at a boarding-school could utter, if she had the boldness to acknowledge having read *Eloisa to Abelard*. Yet we have sought in vain for a more rational and discriminate eulogy on the favourite poet of the last century. The poem of Eloisa does indeed glow with the finer fires of passion and of feeling. It is his great work; but he is much indebted to Ovid for many of its beauties. There is much in Sappho to Phaon of which Eloisa's warmest and most enchanting passages remind us. Had Mr Stockdale told us, that *Eloisa to Abelard* is the finest of English love-epistles, we should not make any exception to the expression; had he called it the finest of all epistles antient or modern, we should have at least understood him; but what he means by saying, it is absolutely unrivalled in antient or modern times, is by no means so easily comprehended. Is it superior to the fourth book of Virgil's *Æneid?* is it superior to every thing of every kind in the poetical treasures of Greece and Rome? Were a parallel started between this epistle and some of the finest passages in antiquity, we have no doubt that Mr Stockdale would decide with as little hesitation, and probably with as much justice, as he devotes Homer to contempt, and all his pedantic admirers. But a modest man is slow in giving, and a reasonable man in believing, these decisions on comparison of old and new writings, especially against the antients. We shall not therefore believe, either that Homer is inferior to Milton, or that Pope's *Eloisa* is superior to every thing antient, merely on Mr Stockdale's assertion, till we ascertain with better certainty that he is competent to draw the comparison. To estimate Pope's value as a poet, by 'the melancholy chasm, of which feeling hearts would be sensible, if Eloisa's epistle were lost', we confess, exceeds our computing faculty. Our lecturer may have clearer notions on the subject; but there is something in the supposition which perplexes and confuses us. If the feeling hearts recollected the poem, then, it could not be lost; and if it was totally lost and forgotten, then they could not be aware that there was any thing so good to lament for.

We are told that Pope unites those excellences which are apparently incompatible. Now, superlative terms should always be used with caution, but above all when speaking of such a poet as Pope. He is one to be measured by no mean standard. What is good in his poetical character, is greatly good; so that, to match one acknowledged quality, that which we bring to prove his uniting with it another great quality, should be striking indeed. Our lecturer has, as usual, left those apparently incompatible excellences undefined. Correctness, which distinguishes Pope as one great excellence, is united with his shrewdness, his wit, and his common sense. There is nothing in these qualities apparently incompatible with correctness. The poetical quality,

which we should least expect to see united with correctness, is
that daring luxuriance of fancy or association which distinguishes
Spencer or Shakespeare, and which is found even in Dryden in
no scanty degree. But neither this romantic fancy, nor extreme
pathos, nor sublimity of the very first order, are discoverable in
Pope.

In the midst of this chapter, however unwilling we may be to
submit to the universal authority of Dr Johnson, yet it is quite
refreshing to meet with passages of his better sense and more dis-
passionate decisions, which our author quotes. The sentences of
Johnson stand indeed with peculiar advantage in this insulated
situation; and Mr Stockdale is entitled to the same sort of
gratitude which we feel to a dull landlord who has invited us to
dine with an interesting visitor. In fact, after the one has be-
wildered us, the other puts us right. It is not easy to add to what
Johnson has said; still less should we presume to take away from
the truly admirable summary of Pope's character which he has
drawn. But when we assent to the opinions of a superior mind, we
generally find its utterance so conveyed, that we can assent in a
qualified manner, where assent is, on the whole, due, and yet find
room for some partial distinction of our own. 'If Pope is not a
poet, (says Johnson), where is poetry to be found?' This is
certainly true; for though the forte of Pope be neither pathos,
sublimity, nor daring originality, yet that he moves the affections,
approaches to majesty of thought, and possesses much of his own
creation, who shall deny? The indiscriminate praise of our author
is, that Pope united apparently inconsistent excellences. Dr
Johnson touches off his picture more rationally, by saying, that
he had, in proportions very nicely suited to each other, all the
qualities which constitute genius. The excellences of Pope were
adjusted by proportion to each other, and not incompatible
qualities. 'He had invention, (Dr Johnson continues), by which
new trains of ideas are formed, and new scenes of imagery displayed, as in the *Rape of the Lock*; or extrinsic embellishments and
illustrations are connected with a known subject, as in the *Essay
on Criticism.*' The adaptation of his Rosicrucian machinery in the
Rape of the Lock, is indeed an inventive and happy creation, in

the limited sense of the word, to which all poetical creation must be restricted. There is no finer gem than this poem in all the *lighter* treasures of English fancy. Compared with any other mock-heroic in our language, it shines in pure supremacy for elegance, completeness, point and playfulness. It is an epic poem in that delightful miniature which diverts us by its mimicry of greatness, and yet astonishes by the beauty of its parts, and the fairy brightness of its ornaments. In its kind, it is matchless; but still it is but mock-heroic, and depends, in some measure, for effect on a ludicrous reference in our own minds to the veritable heroics whose solemnity it so wittily affects. His aerial puppets of divinity, – his sylphs and gnomes, and his puppet heroes and heroines, – the beaux and belles of high life, required rather a subtle than a strong hand to guide them through the mazes of poetry. Among inventive poets, this single poem will place him high. But if our language contains any true heroic creations of fancy, the agents of Spencer's and Milton's machinery will always claim a superior dignity to their Lilliputian counterfeits.

'He had imagination', Johnson observes, 'which enables him to convey to the reader the various forms of nature, incidents of life, and energies of passion, as in his *Eloisa*, his *Windsor Forest*, and his Ethic Epistles.' It is true that Pope's imagination could convey the forms of nature, yet many poets have looked upon nature much less through a medium than Pope, and have seen her and painted her in less artificial circumstances. The landscapes of Pope are either such as the tourist would sketch within ten miles of London; or, if he attempts more enchanting scenery, he gives, by his vague and general epithets, only the picture of a picture; he writes more by rote than by conception, like a man who saw nature through the medium of the classics, and not with the naked eye. In vain we shall search his *Pastorals*, or *Windsor Forest*, for such a landscape as surrounds the Castle of Indolence, the Bower of Eden, or the inimitable Hermitage of Beattie.

Without defining the picturesque, we all feel that it is a charm in poetry seldom applicable to Pope. In the knowledge and description of refined life, Pope is the mirror of his times. He saw through human character as it rose in the living manners of his age, with the eye of a judge and a satyrist; and he must be fond of exceptions, who should say that such a satyrist did not understand human nature. Yet, when we use the trite phrase of Shakespeare understanding human nature, we mean something greatly more extensive than when we apply the same praise to Pope. From the writings of the former, we learn the secrets of the human heart, as it subsists in all ages, independent of the form and pressure of the times. From Pope we learn its foibles and peculiarities in the eighteenth century. We have men and women described by Shakespeare; by Pope we have the ladies and gentlemen of England. Whatever distinctions of mental expression and physiognomy the latter delineates, we see those distinctions, whether leaning to vice or virtue, originate partly in nature, but still more in the artificial state of society. The standard of his ridicule and morality, is for ever connected with fashion and polite life. Amidst all his wit, it has been the feeling of many in reading him, that we miss the venerable simplicity of the poet, in the smartness of the gentleman. To this effect, the tune of his versification certainly contributes. Without entering into an inquiry whether his practice of invariably closing up the sense completely within the couplet is right or wrong, it is clear that Pope has made the melody of his general measure as perfect as it can be made by exactness: whether a slight return to negligence, might not be preferable to the very acme of smoothness which he has chosen, is a subject which, interesting as it is, we will not now encroach on the reader's patience by examining.

(from a review of Stockdale's *Lectures on Eminent Poets*, in *Edinburgh Review*, 1808)

William Hazlitt

DRYDEN and Pope are the great masters of the artificial style of
poetry in our language, as the poets of whom I have already
treated, Chaucer, Spenser, Shakspeare, and Milton, were of the
natural; and though this artificial style is generally and very
justly acknowledged to be inferior to the other, yet those who
stand at the head of that class, ought, perhaps, to rank higher than
those who occupy an inferior place in a superior class. They
have a clear and independent claim upon our gratitude, as having
produced a kind and degree of excellence which existed equally
nowhere else. What has been done well by some later writers of
the highest style of poetry, is included in, and obscured by a
greater degree of power and genius in those before them: what
has been done best by poets of an entirely distinct turn of mind,
stands by itself, and tells for its whole amount. Young, for
instance, Gray, or Akenside, only follow in the train of Milton
and Shakspeare: Pope and Dryden walk by their side, though of
an unequal stature, and are entitled to a first place in the lists of
fame. This seems to be not only the reason of the thing, but the
common sense of mankind, who, without any regular process of
reflection, judge of the merit of a work, not more by its inherent
and absolute worth, than by its originality and capacity of grati-
fying a different faculty of the mind, or a different class of readers;
for it should be recollected, that there may be readers (as well as
poets) not of the highest class, though very good sort of people,
and not altogether to be despised.

The question, whether Pope was a poet, has hardly yet been
settled, and is hardly worth settling; for if he was not a great poet,
he must have been a great prose-writer, that is, he was a great
writer of some sort. He was a man of exquisite faculties, and of the

most refined taste; and as he chose verse (the most obvious distinction of poetry) as the vehicle to express his ideas, he has
generally passed for a poet, and a good one. If, indeed, by a great
poet, we mean one who gives the utmost grandeur to our conceptions of nature, or the utmost force to the passions of the
heart, Pope was not in this sense a great poet; for the bent, the
characteristic power of his mind, lay the clean contrary way;
namely, in representing things as they appear to the indifferent
observer, stripped of prejudice and passion, as in his Critical
Essays; or in representing them in the most contemptible and
insignificant point of view, as in his Satires; or in clothing the
little with mock-dignity, as in his poems of Fancy; or in adorning
the trivial incidents and familiar relations of life with the utmost
elegance of expression, and all the flattering illusions of friendship
or self-love, as in his Epistles. He was not then distinguished as a
poet of lofty enthusiasm, of strong imagination, with a passionate
sense of the beauties of nature, or a deep insight into the workings
of the heart; but he was a wit, and a critic, a man of sense, of
observation, and the world, with a keen relish for the elegances
of art, or of nature when embellished by art, a quick tact for
propriety of thought and manners as established by the forms and
customs of society, a refined sympathy with the sentiments and
habitudes of human life, as he felt them within the little circle of
his family and friends. He was, in a word, the poet, not of nature,
but of art; and the distinction between the two, as well as I can
make it out, is this – The poet of nature is one who, from the
elements of beauty, of power, and of passion in his own breast,
sympathises with whatever is beautiful, and grand, and impas-
sioned in nature, in its simple majesty, in its immediate appeal to
the senses, to the thoughts and hearts of all men; so that the poet
of nature, by the truth, and depth, and harmony of his mind, may
be said to hold communion with the very soul of nature; to be
identified with and to foreknow and to record the feelings of all
men at all times and places, as they are liable to the same impressions; and to exert the same power over the minds of his
readers, that nature does. He sees things in their eternal beauty,
for he sees them as they are; he feels them in their universal

interest, for he feels them as they affect the first principles of his and our common nature. Such was Homer, such was Shakspeare, whose works will last as long as nature, because they are a copy of the indestructible forms and everlasting impulses of nature, welling out from the bosom as from a perennial spring, or stamped upon the senses by the hand of their maker. The power of the imagination in them, is the representative power of all nature. It has its centre in the human soul, and makes the circuit of the universe.

Pope was not assuredly a poet of this class, or in the first rank of it. He saw nature only dressed by art; he judged of beauty by fashion; he sought for truth in the opinions of the world; he judged of the feelings of others by his own. The capacious soul of Shakspeare had an intuitive and mighty sympathy with whatever could enter into the heart of man in all possible circumstances: Pope had an exact knowledge of all that he himself loved or hated, wished or wanted. Milton has winged his daring flight from heaven to earth, through Chaos and old Night. Pope's Muse never wandered with safety, but from his library to his grotto, or from his grotto into his library back again. His mind dwelt with greater pleasure on his own garden, than on the garden of Eden; he could describe the faultless whole-length mirror that reflected his own person, better than the smooth surface of the lake that reflects the face of heaven – a piece of cut glass or a pair of paste buckles with more brilliance and effect, than a thousand dew-drops glittering in the sun. He would be more delighted with a patent lamp, than with 'the pale reflex of Cynthia's brow', that fills the skies with its soft silent lustre, that trembles through the cottage window, and cheers the watchful mariner on the lonely wave. In short, he was the poet of personality and of polished life. That which was nearest to him, was the greatest; the fashion of the day bore sway in his mind over the immutable laws of nature. He preferred the artificial to the natural in external objects, because he had a stronger fellow-feeling with the self-love of the maker or proprietor of a gewgaw, than admiration of that which was interesting to all mankind. He preferred the artificial to the natural in passion, because the

involuntary and uncalculating impulses of the one hurried him
away with a force and vehemence with which he could not
grapple; while he could trifle with the conventional and superficial modifications of mere sentiment at will, laugh at or admire,
put them on or off like a masquerade-dress, make much or little
of them, indulge them for a longer or a shorter time, as he
pleased; and because while they amused his fancy and exercised
his ingenuity, they never once disturbed his vanity, his levity,
or indifference. His mind was the antithesis of strength and
grandeur; its power was the power of indifference. He had none
of the enthusiasm of poetry; he was in poetry what the sceptic is
in religion.

It cannot be denied, that his chief excellence lay more in
diminishing, than in aggrandising objects; in checking, not in
encouraging our enthusiasm; in sneering at the extravagances of
fancy or passion, instead of giving a loose to them; in describing
a row of pins and needles, rather than the embattled spears of
Greeks and Trojans; in penning a lampoon or a compliment, and
in praising Martha Blount.

Shakspeare says,

> ————In Fortune's ray and brightness
> The herd hath more annoyance by the brize
> Than by the tyger: but when the splitting wind
> Makes flexible the knees of knotted oaks,
> And flies fled under shade, why then
> The thing of courage,
> As roused with rage, with rage doth sympathise;
> And with an accent tuned in the self-same key,
> Replies to chiding Fortune.

There is none of this rough work in Pope. His Muse was on a
peace-establishment, and grew somewhat effeminate by long ease
and indulgence. He lived in the smiles of fortune, and basked in
the favour of the great. In his smooth and polished verse we meet
with no prodigies of nature, but with miracles of wit; the thunders
of his pen are whispered flatteries; its forked lightnings pointed
sarcasms; for 'the gnarled oak', he gives us 'the soft myrtle'; for

rocks, and seas, and mountains, artificial grass-plats, gravel-walks, and tinkling rills; for earthquakes and tempests, the breaking of a flower-pot, or the fall of a china jar; for the tug and war of the elements, or the deadly strife of the passions, we have

> Calm contemplation and poetic ease.

Yet within this retired and narrow circle how much, and that how exquisite, was contained! What discrimination, what wit, what delicacy, what fancy, what lurking spleen, what elegance of thought, what pampered refinement of sentiment! It is like looking at the world through a microscope, where every thing assumes a new character and a new consequence, where things are seen in their minutest circumstances and slightest shades of difference; where the little becomes gigantic, the deformed beautiful, and the beautiful deformed. The wrong end of the magnifier is, to be sure, held to every thing, but still the exhibition is highly curious, and we know not whether to be most pleased or surprised. Such, at least, is the best account I am able to give of this extraordinary man, without doing injustice to him or others. It is time to refer to particular instances in his works. – *The Rape of the Lock* is the best or most ingenious of these. It is the most exquisite specimen of *fillagree* work ever invented. It is admirable in proportion as it is made of nothing.

> More subtle web Arachne cannot spin,
> Nor the fine nets, which oft we woven see
> Of scorched dew, do not in th' air more lightly flee.

It is made of gauze and silver spangles. The most glittering appearance is given to every thing, to paste, pomatum, billet-doux, and patches. Airs, languid airs, breathe around; – the atmosphere is perfumed with affectation. A toilette is described with the solemnity of an altar raised to the Goddess of vanity, and the history of a silver bodkin is given with all the pomp of heraldry. No pains are spared, no profusion of ornament, no splendour of poetic diction, to set off the meanest things. The balance between the concealed irony and the assumed gravity is as nicely trimmed as the balance of power in Europe. The little is made great, and the great little. You hardly know whether to laugh or weep. It is the triumph of insignificance, the apotheosis of foppery and folly. It is the perfection of the mock-heroic!

(from *Lectures on the English Poets*, IV (1818–19))

W. L. Bowles

I PRESUME it will readily be granted, that 'all images drawn from what is beautiful or sublime in the works of Nature, are more beautiful and sublime than any images drawn from Art'; and that they are therefore, *per se*, more poetical.

In like manner, those *Passions* of the human heart, which belong to Nature in general, are, *per se*, more adapted to the *higher species* of Poetry, than those which are derived from *incidental* and *transient* Manners. A description of a Forest is more *poetical*, than a description of a cultivated Garden: and the *Passions* which are pourtrayed in the Epistle of an Eloisa, render such a Poem more *poetical* (whatever might be the difference of merit in point of execution), *intrinsically* more *poetical*, than a Poem founded on the characters, incidents, and modes of *artificial life*; for instance, the *Rape of the Lock*.

If this be admitted, the rule by which we would estimate Pope's general poetical character would be obvious.

Let me not, however, be considered as thinking that the *subject alone* constitutes poetical excellency. – The *execution* is to be taken into consideration at the same time; for, with Lord Harvey, we might fall asleep over the '*Creation*' of Blackmore, but be alive to the touches of animation and satire in Boileau. (By *execution*, I mean not only the colours of expression, but the design, the contrast of light and shade, the masterly management, the judicious disposition, and, in short, every thing that gives to a great subject relief, interest, and animation.)

The *subject*, and the *execution*, therefore, are equally to be considered; – the one respecting the *Poetry*, – the other, the *art* and *powers* of the *Poet*. The *poetical subject*, and the *art* and *talents* of the Poet, should always be kept in mind; and I imagine it is for want of observing this rule, that so much has been said, and so little understood, of the real ground of Pope's character as a Poet.

If you say he is not one of the first Poets that England, and the polished literature of a polished æra can boast,

> Recte necne crocos floresque perambulat Atti
> Fabula si dubitem, clamant periisse pudorem
> Cuncti pene patres.

If you say, that he stands *poetically* pre-eminent, in the highest sense, you must deny the principles of Criticism, which I imagine will be acknowledged by all.

In speaking of the *poetical subject*, and the *powers of execution*; with regard to the *first*, Pope cannot be classed among the highest orders of Poets; with regard to the *second*, none ever was his *superior*. It is futile to affect to judge of *one* composition by the rules of *another*. To say that Pope, in this sense, is not a Poet, is to say that a *didactic Poem* is not a *Tragedy*, and that a *Satire* is not an *Ode*. Pope must be judged according to the rank in which he stands, among those of the French school, not the Italian; among those whose delineations are taken more from manners, than from Nature. When I say that this is his *predominant* character, I must be insensible to every thing exquisite in Poetry, if I did not except, *instanter*, the Epistle of Eloisa: but this can only be considered according to its class; and if I say that it seems to me superior to any other of the kind, to which it might fairly be compared; such as the Epistles of Ovid, Propertius, Tibullus (I will not mention Drayton, and Pope's numerous subsequent Imitations); but when this transcendent Poem is compared with those which will bear the *comparison*, I shall not be deemed as giving reluctant praise, when I declare my conviction of its being infinitely superior to every thing of the kind, ancient or modern.

In this Poem, therefore, Pope appears on the high ground of the Poet of Nature; but this certainly is not his *general* character. In the particular instance of this poem, how distinguished and superior does he stand! It is sufficient, that nothing of the kind has ever been produced equal to it for pathos, painting, and melody.

From this exquisite performance, which seems to stand as the boundary between the Poetry derived from the great and primary feelings of Nature, and that derived from Art, to Satire, whose subject wholly concerns existing manners, the transition is easy, but the idea painful. Nevertheless, as Pope has chosen to write Satires and Epistles, they must be compared, not as Warton has, I think, injudiciously done, with pieces of genuine Poetry, but only with things *of the same kind*. To say that the beginning of one of Pope's Satires is *not poetical*; to say that you cannot find in it, if the words are transposed, the '*disjecti membra poetæ*', – is not criticism. The province of Satire is totally wide; its career is in *artificial life*; and therefore, to say that Satire is not Poetry, is to say an Epigram is not an Elegy. Pope has written Satires; that is, confined himself chiefly, as a Poet, to those subjects with which, as it has been seen, he was most conversant; subjects taken from living man, from *habits* and *manners*, more than from *principles* and *passions*.

The career, therefore, which he opened to himself was in the second order in Poetry; but it was a line pursued by Horace, Juvenal, Dryden, Boileau; and if in that line he stands the *highest*; upon these grounds we might fairly say, with Johnson, 'it is superfluous to ask whether Pope were a Poet'.

From the Poetry, which, while it deals in local manners, exhibits also, as far as the subject would admit, the most exquisite embellishments of fancy, such as the machinery of the *Rape of the Lock*, we may proceed to those subjects which concern 'living man'. . . .

But how different, how minute is his description, when he describes what he is master of: for instance, the game of Ombre, in the *Rape of the Lock?* This is from *artificial life*; and with artificial life, from his infirmities, he must have been chiefly conversant: But if he had been gifted with the same powers of observing outward Nature, I have no doubt he would have evinced as much accuracy in describing the appropriate and peculiar beauties, such as Nature exhibits in the Forest where he lived, as he was able to describe, in a manner so novel, and with colours so vivid, a Game of Cards.

It is for this reason that his *Windsor Forest*, and his *Pastorals*, must ever appear so defective to a lover of Nature.

Pope, therefore, wisely left this part of his art, which Thomson, and many other Poets since his time, have cultivated with so much more success, and turned to what he calls the 'Moral' of the Song.

I need not go regularly over his Works; but I think they may be generally divided under the heads I have mentioned; – Pathetic, Sublime, Descriptive, Moral, and Satirical.

In the Pathetic, *poetically* considered, he stands highest; in the Sublime, he is deficient; in descriptions from Nature, for reasons given, still more so. He therefore pursued that path in Poetry, which was more congenial to his powers, and in which he has shone without a rival.

We regret that we have little more, truly pathetic, from his pen, than the Epistle of Eloisa, the 'Elegy to the unfortunate Lady'; and let me not forget one of the sweetest and most melodious of his pathetic effusions, the Address to Lord Oxford:

Such were the notes thy once-lov'd Poet sung.

With the exception of these, and the Prologue to *Cato*, there are few things in Pope, of the order I have mentioned, to which the recollection recurs with particular tenderness and delight.

When he left these regions, to unite the most exquisite machinery of fancy with the descriptions of *artificial life*, the *Rape of the Lock* will, first and last, present itself; – a composition, as Johnson justly observes, the 'most elegant, the most airy', of all his Works; a composition, to which it will be in vain to compare any thing of the kind. He stands alone, unrivalled, and possibly never to be rivalled. All Pope's successful labours of correct and musical versification, all his talents of accurate description, though in an inferior province of Poetry, are here consummately displayed; and as far as artificial life, that is, Manners, not Passions, are capable of being rendered poetical, they are here rendered so, by the fancy, the propriety, the elegance, and the poetic beauty of the Sylphic machinery.

This 'delightful' Poem, as I have said, appears to stand conspicuous and beautiful, in that medium where Poetry begins to leave Nature, and *approximates* to *local manners*. The Muse has, indeed, no longer her great characteristic attributes, pathos or sublimity; but she appears so interesting, that we almost doubt whether the garb of elegant refinement is not as captivating, as the most beautiful appearances of Nature.

(from 'Concluding Observations on the Poetic Character of Pope', 1821)

Lord Byron[1]

I HAVE always admired him [i.e. Pope] sincerely – much more indeed than you[2] yourself in all probability, for *I* do not think him inferior to Milton – although to state such an opinion publicly in the present day would be equivalent to saying that I do not think Shakespeare without the grossest of faults, which is another heterodox notion of my entertainment. Indeed I look upon a proper appreciation of Pope as a touchstone of taste, and the present question as not only whether Pope is or is not in the first rank of our literature, but whether *that* literature shall or shall not relapse into the Barbarism from which it has scarcely emerged for above a century and a half. . . .

You will see that I have taken up the *Pope* question (in prose) with a high hand, and *you* . . . must help me. You know how often, under the Mira elms, and by the Adriatic on the Lido, we have discussed that question, and lamented the villainous cant which at present would decry him. It is my intention to give battle to the blackguards and try if the 'little Nightingale' can't be heard again . . .

With regard to poetry in general, I am convinced, the more I think of it, that he and *all* of us – Scott, Southey, Wordsworth, Moore, Campbell, I, – are all in the wrong, one as much as another; that we are upon a wrong revolutionary poetical system, or systems, not worth a damn in itself, and from which none but Rogers and Crabbe are free; and that the present and next generations will finally be of this opinion. I am the more confirmed in this by having lately gone over some of our classics, particularly *Pope*, whom I tried in this way, – I took Moore's poems and my own and some others, and went over them side by side with Pope's, and I was really astonished (I ought not to have been so) and mortified at the ineffable distance in point of sense, harmony, effect, and even *Imagination*, passion, and *Invention*, between the little Queen Anne's man, and us of the Lower Empire. . . . I have no patience with such cursed humbug and bad taste; your whole generation are not worth a canto of *The Rape of the Lock*, or the *Essay on Man*, or the *Dunciad*, or 'anything that is his'. . . . To the question, 'whether the description of a game of cards be as poetical, supposing the execution of the artist equal, as a description of a walk in the forest?'[3] it may be answered, that the *materials* are certainly not equal; but that 'the artist', who has rendered the 'game of cards poetical', is *by far the greater* of the two. . . .

Away, then, with this cant about nature, and 'invariable principles of poetry'. A great artist will make a block of stone as sublime as a mountain, and a good poet can imbue a pack of cards with more poetry than inhabits the forests of America. . . .

The depreciation of Pope is partly founded upon a false idea of the dignity of his order of poetry, to which he has partly contributed by the ingenuous boast,

> That not in fancy's maze he wander'd long,
> But *stoop'd* to truth, and moralized his song.

He should have written '*rose* to truth'. In my mind the highest of all poetry is ethical poetry, as the highest of all earthly objects must be moral truth. . . .

Whether I have made out the case for Pope, I know not; but I am very sure that I have been zealous in the attempt. If it comes to the proofs, we shall beat the Blackguards. I will show more *imagery* in twenty lines of Pope than in any equal length of quotation in English poesy, and that in places where they least expect it: for instance, in his lines on *Sporus*,[4] – now, do just *read* them over – the subject is of no consequence (whether it be Satire or Epic) – we are talking of *poetry* and *imagery* from *Nature* and *Art*.

(Observations selected from various writings)

NOTES

1. These selections are designed to show how one Romantic at least continued to look squarely at Pope without the distorting ideas of Warton. Partly because Byron was concerned to defend Pope fully and properly he does not have much specifically about the *Rape*. These extracts are culled from his famous *Letter to John Murray, on the Rev. W. L. Bowles' Strictures on the Life and Writings of Pope* (1821) and from other correspondence in *Byron: A Self-Portrait. Letters and Diaries, 1798 to 1824*, ed. Peter Quennell, 2 vols (1950).

2. Byron was writing to Octavius Gilchrist, a poetical grocer of Stamford, who had attempted to rescue Pope 'from the rancorous persecution' of Bowles.

3. The questions are from Bowles's remarks on Pope's poetry.

4. See *Epistle to Arbuthnot. Prologue to the Satires*, lines 305 ff.

PART THREE

Recent Studies

G. Wilson Knight

DRAMA AND EPIC IN
THE RAPE OF THE LOCK (1955)*

SHAKESPEARE gives us drama and Milton epic, and Pope
builds from both in *The Rape of the Lock* (1712–14). The poem
has Lyly's feeling for the delightfully evanescent, the poignant
attractiveness of a brilliant society. Yet Lyly offered no strong
action, and against this subtlest of poetic problems Pope very
early pits his genius, preserving the essence of heroic poetry on
condition of a semi-humorous treatment. Attempts to idealise
the crown in Dryden's *Absalom and Achitophel* are weak, and in
Windsor Forest the national fervour barely, if at all, carries off
the more royalistic idealism. But, by full acceptance of a changed
mental horizon, we may regain an integrity comparable with
Shakespeare's:

> Here thou, great Anna! whom three realms obey,
> Dost sometimes counsel take – and sometimes tea.
>
> (III 7)

The compliment is made possible and even powerful by the joke.
And by just such humour Pope integrates his whole poem into
the heroic and religious traditions, religious tonings taking their
place beside those royalistic and heroic, under similar semi-
humorous conditions. The poem is not iconoclastic, but holds a
warm humanism as surely as the somewhat similar *Love's
Labour's Lost*. It is written not from a scorn but from a love. The
whole is a flirtation with the sublime.

By seeing Belinda's toilet preparations as a ritual the poet
channels reverend associations that build his scene and its action
into both a more convincing and a more memorable impression-
istic whole than would otherwise be possible. Nor is this merely

* This essay was first published in 1939, and revised in 1955.

a technical fancy, since the religion of post-Renaissance literature is, fundamentally, an Eros cult. So, in blending religious tonings with feminine vanity, Pope makes a synthesis of the Christianity-Eros conflict on a comparatively superficial, but delightfully human, plane, the rich humour being both the measure of a relation and the resolving of a conflict. Here it is:

And now, unveil'd, the Toilet stands display'd,
Each silver Vase in mystic order laid.
First, rob'd in white, the Nymph intent adores,
With head uncover'd, the Cosmetic pow'rs.
A heav'nly image in the glass appears,
To that she bends, to that her eyes she rears;
Th' inferior Priestess, at her altar's side,
Trembling begins the sacred rites of Pride.
Unnumber'd treasures ope at once, and here
The various off'rings of the world appear;
From each she nicely culls with curious toil,
And decks the Goddess with the glitt'ring spoil.
This casket India's glowing gems unlocks,
And all Arabia breathes from yonder box.
The Tortoise here and Elephant unite,
Transform'd to combs, the speckled, and the white.
Her files of pins extend their shining rows . . .   (I 121)

He goes on to imagine a 'purer blush' suffusing her face, and 'keener lightnings' starting from her eyes. The delicate fun is obvious, but certain other significances may too easily be neglected. There is the same sense of wealth which we found in *Windsor Forest*: the poet feels his own corner of life interlocking with a vast whole of human co-operation. The use of perfumes is noteworthy: Pope consistently relies on them to establish his impressions. The whole passage is, to use the fine term applied by A. C. Bradley to the poetry of Keats, 'dense'. There is nothing visually flat. Pope is not a pre-eminently visual poet; rather he tells facts, names concrete objects, attaches needed epithets. But his reserve attains great richness, and his epithets modify with precision and force, as in the adjective 'mystic', both helping the main analogy and underlining the maid's professional care to serve a realistic purpose. The sacramental associations concretise, and give depth to, the whole business: objects are made alive, till they breathe out significant energy. Pope twice elsewhere in the poem uses such ritualistic colourings. There is the altar made of four French romances, and its offerings of love, in a passage to be quoted later, and here is a pretty description of coffee-making:

> On shining Altars of Japan they raise
> The silver lamp; the fiery spirits blaze:
> From silver spouts the grateful liquors glide,
> While China's earth receives the smoking tide.
>
> (III 107)

This is symbolism in a very valuable sense of the word: dynamic associations are used to realise, seriously or humorously, some whole event or scene, objects and atmosphere, facts and implications, together. Here the ordinary and trivial spring to sudden life, a hidden magic released.

Warfare, so continual in heroic, and, given a more psychological significance, in dramatic, poetry, is likewise used twice, the one instance forming a neat forecast of the other. First, there is the card-game. The emotionally heroic treatment of it is not illogical. Games are civilised substitutes for physical rivalry, and the kings and queens in chess or cards symbolise existent meanings, an age of settled culture, as Castiglione knew, needing an outlet for its warrior instincts. So phrases such as 'now move to war her sable Matadores' (III 47) and 'th' imperial consort of the crown of Spades' (III 68) reflect a truth. People *do* take their games seriously; they *have* been known to lose their tempers at bridge. Remembering this, ask whether the following lines overload their context, and if the rich humour is not dependent, as finest humour should be, on the holding up of a mirror to nature:

> And now (as oft in some distemper'd State)
> On one nice Trick depends the gen'ral fate.
> An Ace of Hearts steps forth: the King unseen
> Lurk'd in her hand, and mourn'd his captive Queen:
> He springs to Vengeance with an eager pace,

> And falls like thunder on the prostrate Ace.
> The nymph exulting fills with shouts the sky;
> The wells, the woods, and long canals reply.   (III 93)

The ordinary word 'thunder', without any attempt at original phrase-coining, starts from its context with crashing impact; next, the movement curves over to the quiet end of a completed whole, the usual Shakespearian technique in the organizing of speech, scene, or play. The rich humour is proportional to our recognition not of a distortion, but of a truth, depending, indeed, on a central, Shakespearian humility before the simple and the vast in human instincts. It is a quality which tends to elude the puritanical consciousness.

Our other war-incident is the general mêlée in Canto v. Though feminine dignity may be for a while lost as 'whalebones crack' (v 40), it is often cleverly preserved in delightfully mock-heroic terms, as when Thalestris 'scatters death around from both her eyes' (v 58), or Belinda scores a victory with a charge of snuff thrown at the Baron till 'the high dome re-echoes to his nose' (v 86). There is, too, the Shakespearian realisation of personal dignity where you least expect it, in the brainless aristocrat Sir Plume, with 'earnest eyes and round unthinking face', who has nevertheless also the mystery of his own precise individuality, and therefore his own causes of pride:

> Sir Plume of amber snuff-box justly vain,
> And the nice conduct of a clouded cane.   (IV 123)

The persons, it is true, are not strongly individualised except for this exquisite vignette of Sir Plume and his cleverly characterised words, but the presentation of people in general has a warmth, conviction, and sympathy that might well, at another time, have created drama on a wider scale. The fun is not derisive but cathartic.

Pope's use of his supernatural 'machinery' is clever. These 'light Militia of the lower sky' (I 42; observe the skilful 'i'-sounds) increase dramatic suspense, and therefore story-depth, since they foreknow and warn of the central disaster; help to universalise semi-humorously the whole action, used neatly as the binding symbolism of the little drama; are related to certain paradisal and, in Umbriel's journey, hellish colourings touching Dante, Shakespeare, and Milton; and finally reflect the implied belief of poetic art-forms in general that humanity and its sensible world do not exhaust the total of a comprehensive statement. They are of a race that lives in the pure upper light, that guides 'orbs' in heaven, like the child-spirit in Shelley's *Prometheus Unbound*, and follows shooting stars by moonlight. They are variously associated with rainbow, mists, tempests, earth, and the guardianship of the British throne (II 77–90). They are explicitly related to traditional beliefs, both trivial and profound:

> Fairest of mortals, thou distinguish'd care
> Of thousand bright Inhabitants of Air!
> If e'er one vision touch'd thy infant thought,
> Of all the Nurse and all the Priest have taught;
> Of airy elves by moonlight shadows seen,
> The silver token, and the circled green,
> Or virgins visited by Angel-pow'rs,
> With golden crowns and wreaths of heav'nly flow'rs . . .
>
> (I 27)

They are also spirits of the dead, now acting as guardian angels to the living (I 47–66). They are in part quite seriously imagined, and exquisitely realised, with names delicately composed to suit their peculiar charges; Zephyretta, Brillante, Momentilla, Crispissa corresponding to fan, drops, watch, and lock. Nowhere is Pope's artistry in vowel-colour more evident than in the description of Belinda's setting out on the Thames by sunlight with sylphs invisibly attending. The passage is introduced by three lines of light 'i'-sounds, followed by weightier though soft vowellings to match the expansive peace:

> But now secure the painted vessel glides,
> The sun-beams trembling on the floating tides:
> While melting music steals upon the sky,
> And soften'd sounds along the waters die;
> Smooth flow the waves, the Zephyrs gently play,
> Belinda smiled, and all the world was gay.
>
> (II 47)

Soon after, the Sylphs' introduction is accompanied by a growing
accumulation of 'i' vowels, steadily increasing in clustered force
for eight lines, before giving place to heavier sounds:

> Some to the sun their insect-wings unfold,
> Waft on the breeze, or sink in clouds of gold;
> Transparent forms, too fine for mortal sight,
> Their fluid bodies half dissolv'd in light,
> Loose to the wind their airy garments flew,
> Thin glitt'ring textures of the filmy dew,
> Dipt in the richest tincture of the skies,
> Where light disports in ever-mingling dyes,
> While ev'ry beam new transient colours flings,
> Colours that change whene'er they wave their wings.
> Amid the circle, on the gilded mast,
> Superior by the head, was Ariel plac'd;
> His purple pinions op'ning to the sun,
> He rais'd his azure wand, and thus begun . . .   (II 59)

In the couplet starting 'While every . . .' heavy and light sounds
interpenetrate to match the formation of deep colours from out
aerial brilliance.[1] Continual change and motion are cleverly expressed in a various dance of evanescent impressions very different from Milton's more static, or at the best solemn, appeals. The
final lines grow thicker with vowel-weight to establish a mock-
heroic grandeur and cause the little speaker to swell out in close-
up significance. So delicately rich and substantial an impres-
sionism cannot be exhausted by categories of social satire: you
could seriously compare this river-and-lady sun-piece with
Shakespeare's Cleopatra on Cydnus. The description, as 'insect-
wings' implies, depends on a close observation of nature. Pope's
sympathy with small life-forms is continual, and leads here to an
exquisite apprehension of a sylph's (or fly's) punishment:

> Gums and pomatums shall his flight restrain,
> While clogg'd he beats his silken wings in vain.
>   (II 129)

Heavy vowels oppose light ones. Later (II 135) there is the horror
and rounded sounds of 'fumes of burning Chocolate'. Trium-

phant Umbriel – another exquisite name – is shown mischievously clapping his wings 'on a sconce's height' during the mêlée (v 54), and the sombre effects of his descent to Hell, with comic description of the objects there, are done with a glorious sense of the trivial sublimated to heroic stature. The dark and light tonings throughout expand far beyond 'mockery'; rather the humour is the condition of poetic achievement.

The poem has imaginative solidity, which is not the same as the imaginings of solids in separation, presenting perceptual density and a close-packed unity. I have noticed the perceptual quality of Belinda's toilet, but, whatever is handled, the Lock itself, the guarded petticoat, Sir Plume's 'amber snuff-box' and 'clouded cane', bodkins, sconces, coffee-pots, all are rounded and convincing, and cohere together in their particular world. There is a heavy stress on bright substances, which are here peculiarly fitting. Silver is a persistent impression: 'The press'd watch return'd a silver sound' (I 18), a 'silver token' (I 32), 'each silver vase' (I 122), the 'silver Thames' (II 4), the petticoat's 'silver bound' (II 121), the 'silver lamp' and 'silver spouts' of coffee-pots (III 108–9). There is gold too: angels with 'golden crowns' (I 34), 'golden scales' (v 71), 'liquid gold' (IV 45) in the Cave of Spleen, 'clouds of gold' (II 60). It may take the form of gilt: 'gilded chariots' (I 55), the 'gilded mast' (II 69), the French romances 'neatly gilt' (II 38). But these rich solids – there are jewels too – blend naturally into the silvery glinting wings of sylphs in sunlight, the recurrent 'i'-sounds, the 'lightning' of Belinda's sparkling eyes (I 144), the glitter of poetic wit. Belinda dreams of 'a youth more glitt'ring than a birth-night beau' (I 23), her jewellery is a 'glitt'ring spoil' (I 132), the scissors to cut the lock a 'glitt'ring forfex' (III 147). Over all is raised the Lock, itself finally carried with a 'radiant trail' of light (v 128) to 'bespangle' the heavens. These impressions are gained almost entirely by naming appropriate objects; there is no over-plastering of descriptive imagery; nor is the aggregate result itself metallic, but rather warm with human contact, the prevailing impression being one of softness. Moreover, that most poignant method of bodying out the subtly atmospheric into poetic solidity, the use of smell, assists in 'Arabia' breathing from a box (I 134), the 'imprison'd essences' (II 94), and the 'fragrant steams' (III 134) of coffee. A profoundly sensuous nature is creating.

Though the humour is never bitterly satiric, Pope does sometimes appear as an amused grown-up writing of children; but then each of us is a grown-up, and the rest all children, where romantic emotions are concerned. So we get a delicate treatment of girls' amours with suggestion that the Gnomes

> Teach Infant-cheeks a bidden blush to know,
> And little hearts to flutter at a Beau.   (I 89)

A strangely purified sexuality is attained by this blend of child-innocence and desire, as in Byron's *Don Juan*. There is, as it were, a love for the object's very littleness, recalling the larks of *Windsor Forest* and the creation of the Sylphs themselves. The Sylphs protect young ladies from unchastity, by keeping their attention on the move:

> When Florio speaks what virgin could withstand,
> If gentle Damon did not squeeze her hand?
> With varying vanities, from ev'ry part,
> They shift the moving Toyshop of their heart.
>   (I 97)

Though lightly, a deep enough human truth is hinted. The gentle mockery may be yet deeper, as in

> What guards the purity of melting Maids,
> In courtly balls, and midnight masquerades,
> Safe from the treach'rous friend, the daring spark,
> The glance by day, the whisper in the dark,
> When kind occasion prompts their warm desires,
> When music softens, and when dancing fires?   (I 71)

It is the Sylphs who mysteriously save them, functioning as does the Attendant Spirit of *Comus*, and corresponding to what psychologists, who may not believe in such spirits, call 'inhibitions'. Notice especially the warm, sensuous creation here, the exquisite subtlety of verbal tone, consonants and vowels variously inter-shading.

In this last passage we may observe the central pauses in lines 2, 3, 4 and 6, and their comparative absence in lines 1 and 5. Such significant interplay is constant throughout Pope and should be carefully watched and followed in reading. Often contrasts are neatly balanced within one line. Here is another good example, where the antithesis of lines 1 and 2 with no internal pauses speeds up to internal antithesis in 3 and 4, gathers into the tripartite formation of line 5, and ends with a falling, run-on, pauseless unit in line 6:

> Whether the nymph shall break Diana's law,
> Or some frail China jar receive a flaw;
> Or stain her honour, / or her new brocade;
> Forget her pray'rs, / or miss a masquerade;
> Or lose her heart, / or necklace, / at a ball;
> Or whether Heav'n has doom'd that Shock must fall.

> > (II 105)

The contrasts of the important and the trivial are vitally organic, one at least definitely balancing flirtation and religion, playing on the usual conflict. The use of caesura is interesting: often you have in reading to change your vocal colour, and even pace, in mid-line. Here pauses hold up the speed for couplet after couplet, with a final swift release, and run-on. You find something similar in Virgil, and my understanding has been assisted by my brother's study of Virgilian verse-groups,[2] from which I take the term 'release'. Other variations are employed. You can discover them by reading aloud, often altering the pace and vocal colour in mid-line, with close attention to the stops, commas especially, which are carefully placed. Striking subtleties will reveal themselves. You must, however, never ignore the couplet basis and its rhymes, since only in close reference to these do the variations hold their value.

The love-feeling, the erotic warmth, is at once soft and burning, while the poetic medium attains a perfect poise of relaxation and control. The society Pope writes of is felt as eminently desirable.

We may be amused at the Baron who builds an altar to love of
'twelve vast French romances neatly gilt' and lays on it

> . . . three garters, half a pair of gloves;
> And all the trophies of his former loves.   (II 39)

Yet when Belinda's toilet is seen as a 'holy ritual' and her lock
called 'sacred', it is not all comedy. She presides over the poem,
with an especially spirited attraction:

> Her lively looks a sprightly mind disclose,
> Quick as her eyes, and as unfix'd as those:
> Favours to none, to all she smiles extends;
> Oft she rejects, but never once offends.   (II 9)

Such is the vital centre of Pope's inspiration: Shakespeare's
Rosalind might be so described, or Portia; they, too, are felt
as all but divine, without losing humanity. Pope writes from a
half-feminine gentleness, and can create sunshine feminine vitality
from loving admiration. His light, humorous touch continually
blends, as Milton, except once in Eden, cannot or must not,
romantic and religious emotions; and so, in terms precisely suited
to this glittering world, he sets on his heroine's 'white breast' a
'sparkling cross' (II 7).

The manipulation of the action as a whole is dramatic rather
than epic; and here, if we remember the comparative failure of
long narrative in *The Faery Queen* and *Paradise Lost*, we may
consider Pope's judgment sound. The excitement may be of a
sort often found in epic, as at the vividly presented climax:

> Swift to the Lock a thousand Sprites repair,
> A thousand wings, by turns, blow back the hair;
> And thrice they twitch'd the diamond in her ear;
> Thrice she look'd back, and thrice the foe drew near . . .
>   (III 135)

But this rises from a dramatically conceived whole, with Shakespearian forewarnings and fears. After the central event, the
held-up suspense finds violent release in discordant passions and
Umbriel's visit to the Cave of Spleen, as though a glittering

outside had been shattered to disclose gloom; but there is a return to sympathy, dignity, and an almost tragic pathos. The poem is close knit, with a dominating central climax and a curve over, more like a Shakespearian play than any epic, and it concludes on a note of quiet power.

A deeper note is struck towards the end. Clarissa urges that women should be gentle, not angry, else 'why Angels call'd and Angel-like adored?' (v 12). The thought recalls similar speeches at the conclusions of *The Taming of the Shrew* and *Love's Labour's Lost*, where ill moods and superficial glitter are respectively reminded of the tragic undertones of human existence. She continues:

> Oh! if to dance all night, and dress all day,
> Charm'd the small-pox, or chas'd old age away . . .
> (v 19)

– then, she says, gaiety alone might be our guiding star:

> But since, alas! frail beauty must decay,
> Curl'd or uncurl'd, since Locks will turn to grey . . .
> (v 25)

Read the last line slowly, dwelling on the vowels and wistfully stressing 'will'. Pope's profound treatment of superficiality is to be rigidly distinguished from the more facile, and more usual, brilliance of a superficial treatment of human profundities. No poem ever had a more exquisitely sensitive introduction than that addressed to Miss Arabella Fermor, nor any ended with so sure and sweet a pathos that, in placing the heroine's beauty in a context of ultimate defeat, somehow crowns it with an immortal lustre. The poet imagines the Lock lifted as a starry constellation, which is also the constellation of his poem, glittering through the centuries:

> Not all the tresses that fair head can boast
> Shall draw such envy as the Lock you lost.
> For, after all the murders of your eye,
> When, after millions slain, yourself shall die:
> When those fair suns shall set, as set they must,

> And all those tresses shall be laid in dust,
> The Lock the Muse shall consecrate to fame,
> And 'midst the stars inscribe Belinda's name.   (v 143)

'Consecrate': notice again the sacred and ritualistic colouring. Reading, let the commas hold up the movement with positionally varied pauses, changing your vocal colour deeply for 'as set they must', till in line 6 there is a quick release; then let the last couplet go with stately, measured emphasis. Again, notice the verbal statement and the concrete nouns. Though there is deepest sympathy, emotion never overspills the control; you read from a height, with sense of a unit completed at each instant, though each couplet is also organic to the paragraph whole. His 'holistic' instinct is at the back of Pope's allegiance to the couplet.

NOTES

1. In her 'Notes on Pope's Poetry', Edith Sitwell has commented on the 'texture' of this passage. She regards lines 59–68 as a crystal-lisation of the poem's unique quality – *Alexander Pope* (1930) pp. 272–3.
2. W. F. Jackson Knight, *Accentual Symmetry in Virgil* (Oxford, 1939).

Geoffrey Tillotson

THE RAPE OF THE LOCK:
AN INTRODUCTION (1940)

I

THE epic, along with tragedy, has always been considered the most serious of poetic forms, but from the earliest times it has been skirted, or even intruded upon, by the comic. Homer, or someone else, had written the *Margites*, which, said Aristotle, stood in the same relation to comedies as the *Iliad* and *Odyssey* to tragedies. And the *Battle of the Frogs and Mice* remains to show a trivial subject comically exalted by the epic manner, or, conversely, an exalted manner comically degraded by a trivial subject. Even in his 'serious' epics Homer did not seem entirely serious. He impaired the sacredness of his celestials, degrading gods into men at the same time that he elevated men into gods. The epic continued to be regarded as comic as well as serious, sometimes by the same poet. There is the *Æneid* and, set against it, the avowedly mock-heroic *Culex* and the mock-heroic dignifying of the bees in *Georgic* IV. Set against Vida's *Christiad*, in the sixteenth century, there is his *Scacchia Ludus* with its

> effigiem belli, simulataque veris
> Prœlia, buxo acies fictas, et ludicra regna.

Paradise Lost, in the next century, coexists with a number of comic poems which imitate the methods of the epic and so contribute to deflate its dignity. And along with mockery of the epic goes mockery of the romance, which had never been wholly separate from epic, except in the work of Lucan and Tasso.[1] 'Sir Thopas' leads to 'Nymphidia' and *Hudibras*, and in prose there had been *Don Quixote*. During the seventeenth and early eighteenth centuries, when so much reverence was being paid to the

serious epic by poet and critic, the best method of mimicking it
was perfected. This process culminates in the *Rape of the Lock*.
The epic, a dying mammoth, lives long enough to see its perfected self-criticism in Pope's poem.

But the triumph of the mock-heroic is not its mockery of a
literary form. The mock-heroic poets laugh at the epic form but
also at men. This is the reason why Addison's 'Prœlium inter
Pygmæos et Grues Commissum'[2] cannot be considered in the
line of development. Addison is back again at the *Battle of the
Frogs and Mice* where the mockery, if it touches life at all, only
touches life as it is lived in epics. It is as if the *Rape of the Lock*
consisted solely of its sylphs. The best mock-heroic poets mock
at the literary form for carrying the contemporary 'low' human
material, but they mock more severely at the material for being
so unworthy of the form. For though the mock-heroic poet
adopts a different angle from the epic poet, he is standing on the
same ground. Both are serious, morally interested, and in earnest.
The seventeenth and eighteenth centuries considered the moral
element in the epics their first glory, and they did not mock at
that as they mocked at the machinery. Indeed, the literary mockery, like the gilded carriages of the time, was intended to get
you somewhere worth getting to.

II

The literary mockery was found in practice to lead to complica-
tions. Boileau distinguished two bold methods: *Le Lutrin* was

un burlesque nouveau . . . car, au lieu que dans l'autre burlesque
Didon et Enée parloient comme des harengères et des croche-
teurs, dans celui-ci une horlogère et un horloger parlent comme
Didon et Enée.[3]

James Beattie called these two methods the burlesque and the
mock-heroic respectively.[4] Burlesque can be quickly dismissed. It
had been exploited in Scarron's *Virgile Travesti* (1648) and in the
work of his French and English imitators. The degradation of

the epic was complete when Dido spoke like a fishwife. It was, however, too complete: Scarron's long joke was as tediously insensitive as a schoolboy's. Boileau discredited burlesque by precept in the *Art Poétique*, and by practice in *Le Lutrin*; and after him Dryden, Garth, and Pope find the mock-heroic to be the only method worthy of the serious attention of a poet. But, though burlesque is inferior as a single method, it is found handy as a complication of mock-heroic. In Tassoni's *Secchia Rapita* (1622), for instance, the human characters are 'low' – citizens of Modena and Bologna warring over the theft of a bucket – but they act in the guise of epic heroes. This is the mock-heroic. But Tassoni brings in the epic gods to preside over his human action, and provides burlesque by degrading them to the level of men at their most unheavenly: Saturn, for example, has a bad cold, and Juno cannot attend an assembly of the gods because she is having her hair cut. But elsewhere Tassoni mixes the two kinds simultaneously. His low heroes, raised to epic stature, are often found breaking out into crude Italian dialects instead of grand epic speech. A similar complication exists in the *Rape of the Lock*. Clarissa and Thalestris, unlike Dido, are mere modern characters, but they are made to appear wholly heroic – indeed Clarissa's speech in Canto v minutely follows Sarpedon's speech to Glaucus in *Iliad* xii. But Sir Plume's heroics last no longer than his silence. He becomes burlesque when he bursts out into the appalling slang of 1712. In the *Rape of the Lock* the mock-heroic is established but not rigidly. The epical Belinda has hysterics, the Hector-like Baron sneezes: low figures which have been advanced into sublimity are suddenly dropped again, and dropped not only into Queen Anne courtiers, but into mere human beings at the mercy of their comic bodies. They begin as ordinary people – Belinda is asleep, the Baron has risen early – they are exalted by their epic context, and their fall is the sillier because it is from so high a perch. Pope makes much of both kinds in combination. But, unlike Tassoni, he does not go the whole hog and use full burlesque. His sylphs do not have colds, his gods are not blasphemed.

III

Le Lutrin is the first modern poem to mock the whole epic form
by the most ingenious means, those of diminution. Its epic is about
as long as a single 'book' of an epic poem. The mockery of the
complete epic form was seen to be essential to mock-heroic since
the comparatively fixed structure of an epic was the most obvious
thing about it, warranting the attention of Aristotle and many a
later critic.[5] Principal among the latest was Le Bossu, 'the best
of modern critics',[6] whose *Traité du Poëme Epique* appeared in
1675. The way the seventeenth-century critic looks at the epic
decrees the way he looks at the mock-epic. The epic is seen first
as a didactic poem, its chief end being the formation of the
manners. Technically speaking, it must consist of a single 'fable',
or action, which has its beginning, middle, and end and which
covers a long time in comparison with the twenty-four hours
allotted to a tragedy. The epic must arouse the motion of
wonder, particularly through its machinery (this machinery may
be theological – designed to show the nature of God; or physical
– representing external nature; or moral – representing virtues
and vices). There are also the obvious minor elements: armies,
fights, journeys by land and sea, a visit to the underworld, the
arming of heroes, harangues, the manner of conducting the
narration with its 'proposition' and 'invocation', its commentary
on the action, its passages of historical or 'scientific' disquisition.[7]
Then again the action of an epic should belong to the poet's own
nation: 'One design of the *Epick Poets* before [the transgressing
Davenant] was to adorn their own Countrey, there finding their
Heroes and patterns of Virtue',[8] and it was objected that Fénelon's
Télémaque (1699) had no relation to France.

    As Boileau saw it, or came to see it, the mock-epic included as
many of these epic ingredients as possible. It included them in one
of two ways: either by taking them as they stood or by inverting
them for comic purposes. The epic moral, for instance, is not
mocked at in *Le Lutrin*. Indeed its seriousness is deepened.
Seventeenth-century critics saw, of course, far more moral in
epic than was ever intended, and it may have been because of Le

Bossu that Boileau added the explicitly moral ending to *Le Lutrin*. The first four Chants appeared in 1674 and were followed in 1683 by two more, the fifth continuing the general mock-heroics of i–iv and the sixth ending the poem with full moral statement like that of the *Epîtres*. This last Chant has little of the mock-heroic about it, but its moral and poetic grandeur are not felt to be altogether an intrusion. For all the comedy of the poem, it is, throughout its six Chants, profoundly serious, even grave. Some of the incidents may suggest Fielding's boisterousness in 'comic epic', but Boileau's farce, like Fielding's, is weighty with moral concern. The world of *Le Lutrin*, that is, is almost the world of *Hudibras*. Le Bossu, however, may have been partly responsible for the length and directness of the moral statement in *Le Lutrin*, and Pope thinks the moral of the *Rape of the Lock* important enough to 'open [it] more clearly' in the speech of Clarissa that he added in 1717.

This moral element is transferred from the epic unchanged. In the same way, Boileau's machinery might almost be that of the later Latin epic. Like Lucan, he employs allegorical figures instead of gods, treating them seriously since they are the machinery of his moral as well as of his fable. These epic elements – including the native derivation of the fable, its singleness, its beginning, middle, and end – go unchanged into the mock-epic. The mockery lies elsewhere: in the diminution of size and time, in the meanness of the facts (instead of Tassoni's 'Elena transformarsi in una secchia' there is 'fait d'un vain pupitre un second Ilion'), in the low modernity of the characters and in the incongruity of the epic manner for its narration.

IV

Boileau's achievement is not the final one for the mock-heroic since Pope sees and takes the chance of going one better. *Le Lutrin* is a brief dictionary of epic gesture and phrase, and Pope only needed to put Boileau's method to further use. Like Boileau, he provides the epic opening of 'proposition' and 'invocation', the parody of actual epic speeches, the epic simile, the supernatural agent appearing in a dream, the allegorical figures given their appropriate setting, the battle, the learned survey of a tract of knowledge – in *Le Lutrin* it is the history of Christianity, in the *Rape of the Lock* the pre-existence and cosmology of the sylphs. There are, moreover, elements that have nothing to do with epic but belong rightly to mock-epic, which, being more 'literary' than epic (parody implies sophistication), allows the contemporary scene to intensify into actual names. Boileau names some of the books that are sent flying in his 'battle of the books', and Pope slights *Atalantis* by name;[9] Boileau hits at personal enemies – Ribou, Hainault, Barbin – and Pope at Partridge.

Pope is further indebted to Boileau for his adaptation of the epic dénouement of strategy in war. The Greeks had had their wooden horse as a last and successful resort. When, in *Le Lutrin*, the battle is on the point of ending disastrously for the *trésorier*, Boileau, perhaps remembering Tassoni, makes him forestall the vantages of victory by lifting his sacred hand to bless the victors, to disable them by forcing them to their knees; the *chantre* attempts flight but the 'doigts saintement allongés' pursue him till he, too, must kneel. This is the 'source' of Belinda's trick with the snuff:

> But this bold Lord, with manly Strength indu'd,
> She with one Finger and a Thumb subdu'd.

Nothing could excel the blessing in *Le Lutrin*: it seals the moral satire of the poem. Equally, nothing could excel Belinda's snuff in the *Rape of the Lock*: the contemporary reference is perfect. But the mock-heroic reference in Pope, accidentally as it were, improves on Boileau since the likeness between the blessing and the wooden horse is more difficult to trace than that between the *trésorier's* fingers and Belinda's finger and thumb. A comparison with Garth enforces Pope's superiority. In the *Dispensary*, just when the victorious physician is about to stab his opponent, Apollo interposes 'in form of Fee'. This imitation of Homeric stratagem is good, but neglects to go one better in parody by improving on a particular stratagem.

Pope improves on Boileau as to fable. He makes his more homo-
geneous and shapely, shortens its duration to half a day, and
refines its texture. This was no inevitable next step, since the
English translators and adaptors of *Le Lutrin* – Crowne, Old-
ham, N[icholas] O[kes] – made it more gross in matter and less
fine in manner. Nor had Garth taken his opportunity.

Garth is the most important poet connecting the mock-heroics
of Boileau and Pope. Pope early became his friend and took particular interest in the successive revisions of the *Dispensary*.
Garth failed to improve on Boileau himself, but he helps Pope to
improve on him. The *Dispensary*, which first appeared in 1699,
derives its theme from the dispute which arose between the
College of Physicians and the Company of Apothecaries when
the latter were ordered to dispense drugs *gratis* to the poor.
Garth lacks the control necessary for fine mockery either of
people or of a literary form. He has too many incidents. Indeed
his poem is almost an *Endymion*, so delighted is its author to pass
among 'gay gilded Meteors' and 'nimble Corruscations' in flying
to the Fortunate Isles, or to travel underground among coloured
ores 'glimm'ring in their dawning Beds'. Alternatively, his poem
sometimes reads like a satire or epistle of Boileau or Pope: at one
point he even adapts a passage from Boileau's *Art Poétique* and
puts it into the mouth of the Fury Disease. Far from providing
the mock-heroic with its perfect form, Garth unmakes it. The
charming elements jostle as in Tassoni; the less-than-perfect
form of Boileau's Chant vi is made the excuse for formlessness.
But one or two of Garth's original elements find their place in the
Rape of the Lock. Garth employed for his descriptions the method
of laying down parallel stripes of the beautiful and the sordid,
of enforcing his scale of values by pretending not to have one.
This method was more subtle than Tassoni's (familiar to English
readers in *Don Juan*) of dropping flat into bathos. Garth writes:

> With that, a Glance from mild *Aurora*'s Eyes
> Shoots thro' the Chrystal Kingdoms of the Skies;
> The Savage Kind in Forests cease to roam,

And Sots o'ercharg'd with nauseous Loads reel home.
Light's chearful Smiles o'er th' Azure Waste are spread,
And Miss from Inns o' Court bolt out unpaid.

This is one of the descriptive-satiric methods in the *Rape of the Lock* – see, e.g., III 19 ff. It is also the key to more concentrated effects:

> To stain her Honour, or her new Brocade . . .

or to that line which has troubled so many readers:

> Puffs, Powders, Patches, Bibles, Billet-doux.

Pope is indebted to Garth for these and other figures. But the real virtue of Garth in the history of mock-heroic lies in fragments of his material. Among the medical lumber of his poem are satiric references to the 'beau monde' (the phrase of the time) that provide Pope with hints and materials. Science in the *Dispensary*, among more serious concerns, seeks to understand

> Why paler Looks impetuous Rage proclaim,
> And why chill Virgins redden into Flame.
> Why Envy oft transforms with wan Disguise,
> And why gay Mirth sits smiling in the Eyes.
> All Ice why *Lucrece*, or *Sempronia*, Fire . . .

And Horoscope has his opinion sought by Iris, among others, who

> his Cosmetick *Wash* would try,
> To make her Bloom revive, and Lovers die . . .

There are other passages, some of them more medically outspoken.[10] And Garth's underworld has, like Virgil's, its 'Mansion of disastrous Love', but it is Virgil's with a difference:

> *Olivia* here in Solitude he found,
> Her down-cast Eyes fix'd on the silent Ground:
> Her Dress neglected, and unbound her Hair,
> She seem'd the mournful Image of Despair.
> How lately did this celebrated *Thing*
> Blaze in the Box, and sparkle in the Ring . . .

Two of these lines with little change go into the *Rape of the Lock* and the spirit and material of them are Pope's, too.[11]

Like most other elements in the *Dispensary*, these amusing, exquisite, or poignant glimpses of the 'beau monde' lose their value in the general chaos of the poem. The same fate befalls the 'beauty' in Garth's poem, and here again Pope takes, and makes significant, what in Garth was only half valued. The description of the Fortunate Isles, or of the gradual conversational collapse of the god of sloth –

> More had he spoke, but sudden Vapours rise,
> And with their silken Cords tie down his Eyes

– in such descriptions Garth manipulates silken cords of his own. The trouble is, however, that they are tangled in the litter of the poem, and in a medical satire in mock-heroics should not be there at all.

VI

When Pope came to write his poem he had little left to invent. The abstract form of his poem was already three-quarters ready in *Le Lutrin*. Like Boileau, he had been given his theme, and this theme entailed a fashionable setting that had been accidentally but memorably touched on by Garth – and, outside the mock-heroic, had been brilliantly recreated by Waller and fifty other poets, by Addison and Steele and the periodical writers, and was soon to furnish the material for Gay's *Fan*.[12] In creating the unified form of the mock-epic Pope had mainly to attend to the ending.

The characteristic ending for an epic is the work of a *deus ex machina*. In Boileau it had been Piété and Thémis, who sought out de Lamoignon. In Garth it had been Harvey, who was to be found plucking simples in the Elysian Fields. The quarrels of both their poems had been readily terminable by a return to a modified status quo. There was no such solution possible in Pope's poem since the fatal scissors had severed the lock 'From the fair Head, for ever and for ever!' Boileau had brought de Lamoignon into his poem as mediator, and Pope could have brought in Caryll whose role in the genesis of the poem had been similar. But he does not choose to end his poem in this way. What happened to the lock in Lord Petre's hands remains unknown. But, in the poem, it was as much an offence against poetic justice for him to keep it as it was futile for Belinda to take it back. The solution for Pope's difficulty needed to be one resembling as closely as possible the dénouement of some actual epic poem. Pope remembered a poem that had been a favourite since childhood. Ovid had ended his *Metamorphoses* by transforming the soul of Julius Caesar into a star. Callimachus had so transformed the locks of Berenice. Pope combines the two.[13] In adapting a metamorphosis from Ovid he is still in touch with epic. Ovid's poem borders on the epic, and similar metamorphoses are found in pure epic: Le Bossu had commented on them in his *Traité*.

Pope had been given his theme, complete with its setting, and seized it as an opportunity to sharpen the mock-heroic references to their final point. It was not a difficult task to intensify the mock-heroic references in number, for the simple reason that Pope followed rather than led. He used all the kinds of references used by Boileau and Garth and added to them (as Garth had added to those of Boileau)[14] by providing a voyage, Jove-like threats of torture, the genealogy of the bodkin, and so on. But the intensifying of the mock-heroic references in sharpness is the most brilliant and original thing about the *Rape of the Lock*. What Pope does is mainly to continue the process of diminution. He makes most things smaller in size and more femininely exquisite in quality, which better fulfilled the demands of mockery. He makes his hero a woman, and not simply any woman, but Belinda herself. In the old epics the heroes were god-like Hectors, in earlier mock-epics the heroes were common men: Pope completes the mockery in the mock-heroics by widening the gulf between Hector and the fat *trésorier* or Horoscope until it stretches between Hector and Belinda. From this beginning everything else follows. Instead of the rape of Helen, there was Tassoni's bucket, Boileau's pulpit, but Pope's lock of hair. Instead of the epic meals – the beefsteak in Homer, the loads of sausages in

Tassoni, the piled refectory fare in Boileau – there is in Pope the
lacquer and silver ceremonial of coffee. Ajax and Achilles had
their great shields magnificently displayed by Homer. Garth
had given Querpo a shield for the medical fracas.[15] In Pope
these shields have become Belinda's tremblingly expansive petticoat. Homer, Virgil, and Tassoni have their gods and goddesses;
Lucan, Tassoni, Boileau, and Garth have their personified gods
and goddesses – Fame, Fate, Time, Death, Piety, Law, Envy,
Sloth. But the machinery of Pope is mainly provided by the
sylphs, who unite the bodily fluidity of Milton's angels with the
minuteness of Shakespeare's fairies. Boileau had imitated the epic
battles by a skirmish of flung books; Garth's equivalent for books
had been gallipots, urinals, and brass weights, and he had made
Mirmillo boast of the patients he had dispatched in a single day.[16]
In Pope it is a game of cards drawn forth to combat on a velvet
plain and, later, a hullabaloo mainly of fans, silks, and milliners'
whalebone. Boileau had had his similes of bulls, wolf, and cranes;
Garth his of Leviathan and cranes. The mock-epic was incomplete without its simile, but Pope will not admit the beast. His
simile for the battle (at this point Boileau had brought out his
bull) is literary:

> So when bold *Homer* makes the Gods engage . . .

and the subsidary one for an incident in the battle is a gentle
adaptation from Ovid's Dido:

> Thus on *Meander*'s flow'ry Margin lies
> Th'expiring Swan, and as he sings he dies.

VII

Garth had spent some pains on providing beautiful description
in his poem. An account of evening will contain such a line as
'The Clouds aloft with golden Edgings glow'. Pope's theme
justifies such poetry more than Garth's did, and in following him
he was jealous of it. It is an element that has been grossly under-
valued by critics who at most can speak only of 'filigree'.[17] And
there have been other and graver oversights. It is seen that there

is diminution, but not that there is magnification, too.[18] In the same way that the poem mixes burlesque with mock-heroic, it applies these two contrasted scales. There is a game of cards instead of a battle; but, instead of coffee pouring into a cup, '*China*'s Earth receives the smoking Tyde',[19] a line gigantically increasing space and time. Instead of Hector there is Belinda, but her eyes radiate lightning. One is continually at a loss for definitions. And the critics also miss what an editor cannot – the way the poem beds itself in its city and in its time. The renaissance critics considered that the epic should be vast, containing the whole world. The whole world is represented in Pope's poem:

> This Casket *India*'s glowing Gems unlocks,
> And all *Arabia* breathes from yonder Box.

or 'The Fate of *Louis*, and the Fall of *Rome*'.

But the scene of the epics is empty desert beside the milieu of the *Rape of the Lock*, its close-packed London. And the epic is thing-less beside Pope's poem with its close-packed material objects. 'Coffee, tea, and Chocolate . . . are now become capital branches of this nation's commerce', wrote Defoe in 1713:[20] all three find a place in the *Rape of the Lock*. There are the white-gloved beaux, the tweezer-case, but also, flashed into the very bosom of Hampton Court, the coffee-house politicians with their half-closed eyes. The hour that Belinda sits down to ombre is the hour

> When hungry Judges soon the Sentence sign,
> And Wretches hang that Jury-men may Dine.

Nor are the intellectual interests of the time neglected. Pope's Catholic friends found phrases in the poem reminding them of the Primer,[21] Dennis discovers 'a bitter Bob for Predestinarians',[22] there is a hit at Presbyterians (v 121), contemporary educational theory is criticized by implication (1 29 ff) and the virtuosi and the casuists, both lay and ecclesiastical, are pinioned here as firmly as in the *Dunciad*: 'Dry'd Butterflies, and Tomes of Casuistry.' This sort of satire was expected of the mock-heroic. As it came to be practised in the seventeenth and eighteenth centuries, the mock-heroic mocked at epic but mocked more at contemporary society. But the social mockery of the *Rape of the Lock* is not simple, does not make a pat contribution to single-mindedness. Its world is vast and complicated. It draws no line of cleavage between its 'seriousness' and its mockery. Belinda is not closed up in a rigid coterie which Clarissa and the rest of the poem mock at. Pope, fierce and tender by turns, knows no more than Hazlitt, 'whether to laugh or weep' over the poem. He is aware of values that transcend his satire: '*Belinda* smil'd, and all the World was gay', and

> If to her share some Female Errors fall,
> Look on her Face, and you'll forget 'em all.

The criticism the poem provides is sometimes more a picture than a criticism. It is so elaborate, shifting, constellated, that the intellect is baffled and demoralised by the aesthetic sense and emotions. One is left looking at the face of the poem, as at Belinda's.

That Pope was aware of the complex response his poem elicits from its readers is shown by his letter to Mrs Marriot of 28 February 1713/14, which accompanies what is evidently the newly published *Rape of the Lock*, and contains the following:

What excuse then, can I offer for the poem that attends this letter, where 'tis a chance but you are diverted from some very good action or useful reflection for more hours than one. I know it is no sin to laugh, but I had rather your laughter should be at the vain ones of your own sex than at me, and therefore would rather have you read my poem than my letter. This whimsical piece of work, as I have now brought it up to my first design, is at once the most a satire, and the most inoffensive, of anything of mine. People who would rather it were let alone laugh at it, and seem heartily merry, at the same time that they are uneasy. 'Tis a sort of writing very like tickling. I am so vain as to fancy a pretty complete picture of the life of our modern ladies in this idle town from which you are so happily, so prudently, and so philosophically retired.[23]

VIII

Finally, Pope takes over from the serious epic another element which he does not mock at: the element of serious technical care. He spent on his eight hundred lines as much devotion as, say, Milton had spent on one (or more) of the Books of *Paradise Lost*. He even plays ombre with himself till he hits on the game which suits his purpose. With the economy for which he is the supreme poet, he makes the same vehicle carry both human and epic mockery. He makes the 'figures' carry the satire. The line 'Dost sometimes Counsel take – and sometimes *Tea*' is famous among grammarians as an instance of zeugma, but lying beyond its technical smartness is all the mixed power, hollowness, and public homeliness of royalty. There is more than literary surprise, than bathos, in 'And send the Godly in a Pett, to pray'; and the bathetic and alliteratively peppered disorder on Belinda's dressing table is fundamentally a moral disorder: 'Puffs, Powders, Patches, Bibles, Billet-doux.'

The integrity of Pope's art is well exhibited by the additions to the second edition. He considered that the manner in which he had contrived the sylphs to 'fit so well' with 'what was published before' constituted 'one of the greatest proofs of judgment of anything I ever did'. Addison, who had cited the first version of the poem as an instance of the appropriateness of pagan mythology for mock-heroic,[24] tried to dissuade him from altering a poem that was already 'a delicious little thing, and, as he expressed it, *merum sal*'. According to Warburton, Pope imputed Addison's advice to ungenerous motives, and his immediate revenge took the form of two stabs at *Rosamond* in which Addison had used machines facilely.

Pope saw to it that the additions included specimens of all the three kinds of machine noted by Le Bossu: the sylphs are 'theological' (they represent 'good' and 'bad'), 'physical' (they roll planets and attend to the weather), and 'allegorical' or 'moral' (the machines include Spleen). And if Ariel takes up a disproportionate space in cantos I and II – it will be recalled that Shock thought that Belinda had slept too long – it is mainly in his long

speeches that Pope contrives to set the poem most firmly in its
world of virgins, prudes, matrons, powders, essences, and jewels,
and to deliver some of his most telling satire. Nor must it be
overlooked – Pope[25] and later critics overlooked it[26] – that the
additions do not provide the only machinery in the poem. They
join a poem the machinery of which Addison had already com-
mended. In the first version of the poem the Baron had wor-
shipped 'Propitious Heav'n, and ev'ry Pow'r . . . But chiefly
Love'; had built an altar; had devised a prayer to which 'The
Pow'rs gave Ear', but only 'granted half'. Moreover, though it
was coffee, and not a god, which

> Sent up in Vapours to the *Baron*'s Brain
> New Stratagems, the radiant Locke to gain,[27]

the stroke which severed the lock is described as 'fatal', and
Fate is hymned, along with steel, in the concluding paragraph of
the canto. Belinda's hysterics are in vain since '*Fate* and *Jove* had
stopp'd the *Baron*'s Ears'. Jove hangs out the golden scales so
that the battle of fans and whalebone can reach an issue. And,
finally, Heaven, which at the outset granted only half the Baron's
prayer, consistently dooms him to lose the trophy:

> With such a Prize no Mortal must be blest,
> So Heav'n decrees! with Heav'n who can contest?

All this machinery is of the kind which Le Bossu had spoken of
most strongly: 'The *Gods* are the *Causes* of the Actions. They
make the *Plots*, and dispose the *Solution* of them too'; and in his
closing transformation Pope has also provided machinery of the
kind which Le Bossu had described as 'requir[ing] Divine Probability'. So that it is to all this august machinery that Pope added
the more exquisitely mechanised sylphs and the dour goddess
Spleen.[28] And it is for this reason that Dennis's charge that the
machinery does not affect the action is beside the point: he is
thinking only of the sylphs and is forgetting the active machines
which they supplement. For the same reason there is nothing to
be said for Dennis's verdict that in the *Rape of the Lock* the
machines are not opposed to each other. Pope's sylphs are

opposed to Fate[29] and are betrayed because Belinda, to the
improvement of the moral satire, transgresses the one condition
which gives them power, 'an inviolate Preservation of Chastity'.[30]
Moreover, Pope, unlike de Villars, makes some of his sylphs
'bad', and, though the bad are not actively confronted with the
good, they alternate within a split second:

> ... that sad moment, when the *Sylphs* withdrew,
> And *Ariel* weeping from *Belinda* flew,

in that moment, the gnome Umbriel 'Repairs to search the
gloomy Cave of *Spleen*'.

NOTES

1. Pope, with his eye on *Hudibras*, includes mockery of the romance
in the epic mockery of the *Rape*: see III 129 ff: 'So Ladies in Romance
...' and II 38.

2. 1699: translated anonymously as 'The Battel of the Pygmies and
Cranes', in *Poems on Several Occasions ... By Mr. Addison ... 1719*.

3. *Œuvres*, II 405: from the 'Au Lecteur' which appeared in the
first edition (1674).

4. *Essays* (1778 ed.) p. 396.

5. This rules out from mock-heroic John Philips's 'Splendid Shilling'
(1701). Philips borrows Milton's epic style for a modern low subject,
but does not mimic the structure of the epic.

6. Dryden, *Essays*, selected and edited W. P. Ker (Oxford, 1900)
I 211.

7. Homer is, for Pope, 'a historian antiquary ... as well as a poet
(Postscript to *Odyssey*, V 241).

8. Rymer, *Critical Essays of the Seventeenth Century*, ed. J. E.
Spingarn (Oxford, 1908) II 168.

9. Othello is mentioned (V 105 ff) and a song from *Camilla* quoted
(V 64); the other direct literary references are to epic. The poem provides, of course, continual literary echoes, parodies, and criticisms.

10. Pope's poem has its innuendos.

11. Ozell's translation of *Le Lutrin* (1708) owes something to
Garth in its interpolation of a six-line passage on spleen and the
fashionable world (p. 61); and, to take another instance, in its unwar-
ranted reference to Arabian tales and the way 'fair' readers are lulled

by them 'Supinely in soft Dreams' (p. 97) Ozell is helping to feminize the mock-heroic.

12. I have seldom drawn on this poem to illustrate the *Rape of the Lock*, since it is difficult to see which way the debt lies. The debt may well have been Pope's: he refers to news about the poem in August 1713, and is found asking Gay to let him 'take along with me [into the country] your poem of the *Fan*, to consider it at full leisure' at about the time when he was engaged on the additions to the *Rape of the Locke* – letters to Gay, 23 Aug. 1713 and 23 Oct. [1713].

13. Pope was no doubt familiar with Boileau's bagatelle, 'La Métamorphose de la Perruque de Chapelain en Comète' (1664); and see Pope's *Epilogue to the Satires*, II 231 and note.

14. Garth provides an altar built to Disease, the fire on which is lighted by prescriptions.

15.   His Arms were made, if we may credit Fame,
   By *Mulciber*, the Mayor of *Bromingham*.
   Of temper'd *Stibium* the bright Shield was cast,
   And yet the Work the Metal far surpass'd.
   A Foliage of dissembl'd *Senna* Leaves,
   Grav'd round the Brim, the wond'ring Sight deceives.
   Embost upon the Field, a Battel stood
   Of *Leeches* spouting Hemorrhoidal Blood . . . (p. 82)

16.   *Oxford* and all her passing Bells can tell,
   By this Right Arm, what mighty Numbers fell.
   Whilst others meanly ask'd whole Months to slay,
   I oft dispatch'd the Patient in a Day . . . (p. 54)

17. The best comment on the filigree of the poem is Beardsley's *The Rape of the Lock . . . Embroidered with Nine Drawings by Aubrey Beardsley . . . MDCCCXCVI*. The verso of the half-title reads 'Twenty-five copies of this Book have been printed on Japanese Vellum for Sale.' The drawings should be seen in this edition.

18. This seems to have been first pointed out by W. H. Auden – see *From Anne to Victoria*, ed. B. Dobrée (1937) p. 105.

19. Cf. 'wedg'd whole Ages in a *Bodkin*'s Eye' (II 128).

20. See D. George, *England in Transition* (1931) pp. 35 ff.

21. Cf. the charge (*Key*, supra, p. 44) that 'a Tendency to Popery . . . is secretly insinuated through the whole'.

22. In II 101–10 (*Remarks*, supra, p. 64).

23. *Correspondence*, ed. George Sherburn (Oxford, 1956) I 211.

24. *Spectator*, no. 523 (30 Oct. 1712): 'In Mock-Heroick Poems, the use of the Heathen Mythology is not only excusable but graceful, because it is the Design of such Compositions to divert, by adapting the fabulous Machines of the Ancients to low Subjects, and at the same time by ridiculing such kings of Machinery in Modern Writers.'

25. See dedicatory epistle.

26. Dennis is an exception, but he makes no use of his perception.

27. In the 1714 version it is even more explicitly part of the machinery: 'Fate urg'd the Sheers' (III 151).

28. He also took the opportunity to increase the role of the original machines.

29. See, especially, III 145 ff.

30. Dedicatory epistle.

Cleanth Brooks

THE CASE OF
MISS ARABELLA FERMOR (1943)

ALDOUS HUXLEY'S lovers, 'quietly sweating, palm to palm', may be conveniently taken to mark the nadir of Petrarchism. The mistress is no longer a goddess – not even by courtesy. She is a congeries of biological processes and her too-evident mortality is proclaimed at every pore. But if we seem to reach, with Huxley's lines, the end of something, it is well to see what it is that has come to an end. It is not the end of a naïve illusion.

The Elizabethans, even those who were immersed in the best tradition of Petrarchism, did not have to wait upon the advent of modern science to find out that women perspired. They were thoroughly aware that woman was a biological organism, but their recognition of this fact did not prevent them from asserting, on occasion, that she was a goddess, nevertheless. John Donne, for instance, frequently has it both ways: indeed, some of the difficulty which the modern reader has with his poems may reside in the fact that he sometimes has it both ways in the same poem. What is relevant to our purposes here is not the occurrence of a line like 'Such are the sweat drops of my mistress' breast' in one of the satiric 'elegies', but the occurrence of lines like

> Our hands were firmly cemented
> With a fast balm, which thence did spring

in a poem like *The Ecstasy*. The passage quoted, one may argue, glances at the very phenomenon which Huxley so amiably describes; but Donne has transmuted it into something else.

But if Donne could have it both ways, most of us, in this latter day, cannot. We are disciplined in the tradition of either-or, and lack the mental agility – to say nothing of the maturity of attitude – which would allow us to indulge in the finer distinctions and the more subtle reservations permitted by the tradition of both-and. Flesh *or* spirit, merely a doxy or purely a goddess (or alternately, one and then the other), is more easily managed in our poetry, and probably, for that matter, in our private lives. But the greater poems of our tradition are more ambitious in this matter: as a consequence, they come perhaps nearer the truth than we do with our ordinary hand-to-mouth insights. In saying this, however, one need by no means confine oneself to the poetry of Donne. If we are not too much blinded by our doctrine of either-or, we shall be able to see that there are many poems in the English tradition which demonstrate a thorough awareness of the problem and which manage, at their appropriate levels, the same kinds of synthesis of attitudes which we associate characteristically with Donne.

Take Pope's *Rape of the Lock*, for instance. Is Belinda a goddess, or is she merely a frivolous tease? Pope himself was, we may be sure, thoroughly aware of the problem. His friend Swift penetrated the secrets of the lady's dressing-room with what results we know. Belinda's dressing-table, of course, is bathed in a very different atmosphere; yet it may be significant that Pope is willing to allow us to observe his heroine at her dressing-table at all. The poet definitely means to give us scenes from the green room, and views from the wings, as well as a presentation 'in character' on the lighted stage.

Pope, of course, did not write *The Rape of the Lock* because he was obsessed with the problem of Belinda's divinity. He shows, indeed, that he was interested in a great many things: in various kinds of social satire, in a playful treatment of the epic manner, in deflating some of the more vapid clichés that filled the love poetry of the period, and in a dozen other things. But we are familiar with Pope's interest in the mock-epic as we are not familiar with his interest in the problem of woman as goddess; and moreover, the rather lurid conventional picture of Pope as the 'wicked wasp of Twickenham' – the particular variant of the either-or theory as applied to Pope – encourages us to take the poem as a dainty but rather obvious satire. There is some justification, therefore, for emphasizing aspects of the poem which have received little attention in the past and, perhaps, for neglecting other aspects of the poems which critics have already treated in luminous detail.

One further point should be made: if Pope in this account of the poem turns out to be something of a symbolist poet, and perhaps even something of what we call, in our clumsy phrase, a 'metaphysical poet' as well, we need not be alarmed. It matters very little whether or not we twist some of the categories which the literary historian jealously (and perhaps properly) guards. It matters a great deal that we understand Pope's poem in its full richness and complexity. It would be an amusing irony (and one not wholly undeserved) if we retorted upon Pope some of the brittleness and inelasticity which we feel that Pope was inclined to impose upon the more fluid and illogical poetry which preceded him. But the real victims of the maneuver, if it blinded us to his poem, would be ourselves.

Pope's own friends were sometimes guilty of oversimplifying and reducing his poem by trying to make it accord with a narrow and pedantic logic. For example, Bishop Warburton, Pope's friend and editor, finds an error in the famous passage in which Belinda and her maid are represented as priestesses invoking the goddess of beauty. Warburton feels forced to comment as follows: 'There is a small inaccuracy in these lines. He first makes his heroine the chief priestess, then the goddess herself.' The lines in question run as follows:

> First rob'd in white, the nymph intent adores
> With head uncover'd, the cosmetic pow'rs.
> A heav'nly image in the glass appears,
> To that she bends, to that her eyes she rears . . .

It is true that Pope goes on to imply that Belinda is the chief priestess (by calling her maid the 'inferior priestess'), and that, a few lines later, he has the maid 'deck [Belinda] the goddess with the glittering spoil'. But surely Warburton ought not to have missed the point: Belinda, in worshipping at the shrine of beauty, quite naturally worships herself. Whose else is the 'heav'nly

image' which appears in the mirror to which she raises her eyes?
The violation of logic involved is intended and is thoroughly
justified. Belinda *is* a goddess, but she puts on her divinity at her
dressing-table; and, such is the paradox of beauty-worship, she
can be both the sincere devotee and the divinity herself. We shall
certainly require more sensitive instruments than Bishop Warburton's logic if we are to become aware of some of the nicest
effects in the poem.

But to continue with the dressing-table scene:

> The fair each moment rises in her charms,
> Repairs her smiles, awakens every grace,
> And calls forth all the wonders of her face:
> Sees by degrees a purer blush arise,
> And keener lightnings quicken in her eyes.

It is the experience which the cosmetic advertisers take with a
dead level of seriousness, and obviously Pope is amused to have
it taken seriously. And yet, is there not more here than the
obvious humor? Belinda is, after all, an artist, and who should
be more sympathetic with the problems of the conscious artist
than Pope himself? In our own time, William Butler Yeats, a
less finicky poet than Pope, could address a 'young beauty' as
'dear fellow artist'.

In particular, consider the 'purer blush'. Why purer? One must
not laugh too easily at the purity of the blush which Belinda is
engaged in painting upon her face. After all, may we not regard
it as a blush 'recollected in tranquility', and therefore a more ideal
blush than the actual blush which the spontaneous overflow of
emotion – shame or hauteur on an actual occasion – might bring?
If we merely read 'purer' as ironic for its opposite, 'impurer' –
that is, unspontaneous and therefore unmaidenly – we shall miss
not only the more delightful aspects of the humor, but we shall
miss also Pope's concern for the real problem. Which is, after all,
the more maidenly blush? That will depend, obviously, upon
what one considers the essential nature of maidens to be; and
Belinda, we ought to be reminded, is not the less real nor the less
feminine because she fails to resemble Whittier's robust heroine
Maude Muller.

One is tempted to insist upon these ambiguities and complexities of attitude, not with any idea of overturning the orthodox reading of Pope's irony, but rather to make sure that we do not conceive it to be more brittle and thin than it actually is. This fact, at least, should be plain: regardless of what we may make of the 'purer blush', it is true that Belinda's dressing-table does glow with a special radiance and charm, and that Pope, though amused by the vanity which it represents, is at the same time thoroughly alive to a beauty which it actually possesses.

There is a further reason for feeling that we shall not err in taking the niceties of Pope's descriptions quite seriously. One notices that even the metaphors by which Pope characterizes Belinda are not casual bits of decoration, used for a moment, and then forgotten. They run throughout the poem as if they were motifs. For instance, at her dressing-table Belinda is not only a priestess of 'the sacred rites of pride', but she is also compared to a warrior arming for the fray. Later in the poem she is the warrior once more at the card-table in her conquest of the two 'adventurous knights'; and again, at the end of the poem, she emerges as the heroic conqueror in the epic encounter of the beaux and belles.

To take another example, Belinda, early in the poem, is compared to the sun. Pope suggests that the sun recognizes in Belinda a rival, and fears her:

> Sol through white curtains shot a tim'rous ray,
> And oped those eyes that must eclipse the day.

But the sun's fear of Belinda has not been introduced merely in order to give the poet an opportunity to mock at the polite cliché. The sun comparison appears again at the beginning of Canto II:

> Not with more glories, in th'ethereal plain,
> The sun first rises o'er the purpled main,
> Than issuing forth, the rival of his beams
> Launch'd on the bosom of the silver Thames.

Belinda is like the sun, not only because of her bright eyes, and not only because she dominates her special world ('But every eye was fix'd on her alone'). She is like the sun in another regard:

> Bright as the sun, her eyes the gazers strike,
> And, like the sun, they shine on all alike.

Is this general munificence on the part of Belinda a fault or a virtue? Is she shallow and flirtatious, giving her favors freely to all; or, does she distribute her largesse impartially like a great prince? Or, is she simply the well-bred belle who knows that she cannot play favorites if she wishes to be popular? The sun comparison is able to carry all these meanings, and therefore goes past any momentary jest. Granting that it may be over-ingenious to argue that Belinda in Canto IV (the Cave of Spleen) represents the sun in eclipse, still the sun comparison does appear once more in the poem, and quite explicitly. As the poem closes, Pope addresses Belinda thus:

> When those fair suns shall set, as set they must,
> And all those tresses shall be laid in dust;
> This lock, the Muse shall consecrate to fame
> And 'midst the stars inscribe Belinda's name.

Here, one notices, that the poet, if he is forced to concede that Belinda's eyes are only metaphorical suns after all, still promises that the ravished lock shall have a celestial eternity, adding, like the planet Venus, 'New glory to the shining sphere!' And here Pope, we may be sure, is not merely playful in his metaphor. Belinda's name has actually been inscribed in the only heaven in which a poet would care to inscribe it. If the sceptic still has any doubts about Pope's taking Belinda very seriously, there should be no difficulty in convincing him that Pope took his own work very seriously indeed.

We began by raising the question of Belinda's status as a goddess. It ought to be quite clear that Pope's attitude toward Belinda is not exhausted in laughing away her claims to divinity. The attitude is much more complicated than that. Belinda's charm is not viewed uncritically, but the charm is real: it can survive the poet's knowledge of how much art and artifice have gone into making up the charm.

To pursue the matter of attitude farther still, what, after all, is Pope's attitude toward the iridescent little myth of the sylphs which he has provided to symbolize the polite conventions which govern the conduct of maidens? We miss the whole point if we dismiss the sylphs as merely 'supernatural machinery'. In general, we may say that the myth represents a qualification of the poet's prevailingly naturalistic interpretation. More specifically, it represents his attempts to do justice to the intricacies of the feminine mind. For in spite of Pope's amusement at the irrationality of that mind, Pope acknowledges its beauty and its powers.

In making this acknowledgement, he is a good realist – a better realist, indeed, than he appears when he tries to parade the fashionable ideas of the Age of Reason as in his *Essay on Man*. He is good enough realist to know that although men in their 'learned pride' may say that it is Honor which protects the chastity of maids, actually it is nothing of the sort: the belles are not kept chaste by any mere abstraction. It is the sylphs, the sylphs with their interest in fashion notes and their knowledge of the feminine heart:

With varying vanities, from ev'ry part,
They shift the moving toy-shop of the heart;
Where wigs with wigs, with sword-knots sword-knots strive
Beaux banish beaux, and coaches coaches drive.

Yet the myth of the sylphs is no mere decoration to this essentially cynical generalization. The sylphs do represent the supernatural, though the supernatural reduced, of course, to its flimsiest proportions. The poet has been very careful here. Even Belinda is not made to take their existence too seriously. As for the poet, he very modestly excuses himself from rendering any judgment at all by ranging himself on the side of 'learned pride'.

Some secret truths, from learned pride conceal'd
To maids alone and children are reveal'd:
What, though no credit doubting wits may give?
The fair and innocent shall still believe.

In the old wives' tale of the child's fairy story may lurk an item
of truth, after all. Consider the passage carefully.

'Fair' and 'innocent' balance 'maids' and 'children'. Yet they
act further to color the whole passage. Is 'fair' used merely as a
synonym for 'maids' – e.g. as in 'the fair'? Or, is it that beauty is
easily flattered? The doctrine which Ariel urges Belinda to accept
is certainly flattering: 'Hear and believe! thy own importance
know / . . . unnumbered spirits round thee fly. . . .' Is 'innocent'
to be taken to mean 'guiltless', or does it mean 'naïve', perhaps
even 'credulous'? And how do 'fair' and 'innocent' influence
each other? Do the fair believe in the sylphs because they are still
children? (Ariel, one remembers, begins by saying: 'If e'er one
vision touch thy infant thought. . . .') Pope is here exploiting
that whole complex of associations which surround 'innocence'
and connect it on the one hand with more than worldly wisdom
and, on the other, with simple gullibility.

Pope, as we now know, was clearly unjust in suggesting that
Addison's advice against adding the machinery of the sylphs
was prompted by any desire to prevent the improvement of the
poem. Addison's caution was 'safe' and natural under the circumstances. But we can better understand Pope's pique if we
understand how important the machinery was to become in the
final version of the poem. For it is Pope's treatment of the sylphs
which allows him to develop, with the most delicate modulation,
his whole attitude toward Belinda and the special world which she
graces. It is precisely the poet's handling of the supernatural –
the level at which he is willing to entertain it – the amused qualifications which he demands of it – that makes it possible for him
to state his attitude with full complexity.

The sylphs are, as Ariel himself suggests, 'honor', though
honor rendered concrete and as it actually functions, not honor
as a dry abstraction. The sylphs' concern for good taste allows
little range for critical perspective or a sense of proportion.
To Ariel it will really be a dire disaster whether it is her honor
or her new brocade that Belinda stains. To stain her honor will
certainly constitute a breach of good taste – whatever else it
may be – and that for Ariel is enough. Indeed, it is enough for

the rather artificial world of manners with which Pope is concerned.

The myth of the sylphs is, thus, of the utmost utility to Pope: it allows him to show his awareness of the absurdities of a point of view which, nevertheless, is charming, delightful, and filled with a real poetry. Most important of all, the myth allows him to suggest that the charm, in part at least, springs from the very absurdity. The two elements can hardly be separated in Belinda; in her guardian, Ariel, they cannot be separated at all.

In this connection, it is well to raise specifically the question of Pope's attitude toward the 'rape' itself. We certainly underestimate the poem if we rest complacently in the view that Pope is merely laughing at a tempest in a teapot. There is such laughter, to be sure, and late in the poem, Pope expresses his own judgment of the situation, employing Clarissa as his mouthpiece. But the tempest, ridiculous though it is when seen in perspective, is a real enough tempest and related to very real issues. Indeed, Pope is able to reduce the incident to its true importance, precisely because he recognizes clearly its hidden significance. And nowhere is Pope more careful to take into account all the many sides of the situation than just here in the loss of the lock itself.

For one thing, Pope is entirely too clear-sighted to allow that the charming Belinda is merely the innocent victim of a rude assault. Why has she cherished the lock at all? In part at least, 'to the destruction of mankind', though mankind, of course, in keeping with the convention, wishes so to be destroyed. Pope suggests that the Baron may even be the victim rather than the aggressor – it is a moot question whether he has seized the lock or been ensnared by it. Pope does this very skilfully, but with great emphasis:

> Love in these labyrinths his slaves detains
> And mighty hearts are held in slender chains.
> With hairy springes we the birds betray,
> Slight lines of hair surprise the finny prey,
> Fair tresses man's imperial race ensnare,
> And beauty draws us with a single hair.

Indeed, at the end of the poem, the poet addresses his heroine, not as victim but as a 'murderer':

> For, after all the murders of your eyes,
> When after millions slain, yourself shall die. . . .

After all, does not Belinda want the Baron (and young men in general) to covet the lock? She certainly does not want to retain possession of the lock for ever. The poet naturally sympathizes with Belinda's pique at the way in which the Baron obtains the lock. He must, in the war of the sexes, coax her into letting him have it. Force is clearly unfair, though blandishment is fair. If she is an able warrior, she will consent to the young man's taking the lock, though the lock still attached to her head – and on the proper terms, honorable marriage. If she is a weak opponent, she will yield the lock, and herself, without any stipulation of terms, and will thus become a ruined maid indeed. Pope has absolutely no illusions about what the game is, and is certainly not to be shocked by any naturalistic interpretation of the elaborate and courtly conventions under which Belinda fulfills her natural function of finding a mate.

On the other hand, this is not at all to say that Pope is anxious to do away with the courtly conventions as a pious fraud. He is not the romantic anarchist who would abolish all conventions because they are artificial. The conventions not only have a regularizing function: they have their own charm. Like the rules of the card game in which Belinda triumphs, they may at points be arbitrary; but they make the game possible, and with it, the poetry and pageantry involved in it in which Pope very clearly delights.

The card game itself, of course, is another symbol of the war of the sexes. Belinda must defeat the men; she must avoid that debacle in which

> The Knave of Diamonds tries his wily arts,
> And wins (oh shameful chance!) the Queen of Hearts.

She must certainly avoid at every cost becoming a ruined maid. In the game as played, there is a moment in which she is 'Just in the jaws of ruin and Codille' and gets a thrill of dangerous excitement at being in so precarious a position.

If the reader objects that the last comment suggests a too obviously sexual interpretation of the card game, one must hasten to point out that a pervasive sexual symbolism informs, not only the description of the card game, but almost everything else in the poem, though here, again, our tradition of either-or may cause us to miss what Pope is doing. We are not forced to take the poem as either sly bawdy *or* as delightful fantasy. But if we are to see what Pope actually makes of his problem, we shall have to be alive to the sexual implications which are in the poem.

They are perfectly evident – even in the title itself, and the poem begins with an address to the Muse in which the sexual implications are underscored:

> Say what strange motive, goddess! could compel
> A well-bred lord to assault a gentle belle?
> Oh say what stranger cause, yet unexplored,
> Could make a gentle belle reject a lord?

True, we can take *assault* and *reject* in their more general meanings, not in their specific Latin senses, but the specific meanings are there just beneath the surface. Indeed, it is hard to believe, on the evidence of the poem as a whole, that Pope would have been in the least surprised by Sir James Frazer's later commentaries on the ubiquity of hair as a fertility symbol. In the same way, one finds it hard to believe, after some of the material in the 'Cave of Spleen' section ('And maids turn'd bottles call aloud for corks'), that Pope would have been too much startled to come upon the theories of Sigmund Freud.

The sexual implications become quite specific after the 'rape' has occurred. Thalestris, in inciting Belinda to take actior against the Baron, cries:

> Gods! shall the ravisher display your hair?
> While the fops envy and the ladies stare?

Even if we take *ravisher* in its most general sense, still the sexual symbolism lurks just behind Thalestris' words. Else why should honor be involved as it is? Why should the Baron desire the lock, and why should Belinda object so violently, not as to an act of simple rudeness, but to losing 'honor' and becoming a 'degraded toast'? The sexual element is involved at least to the extent that Belinda feels that she cannot afford to suffer the Baron, without protest, to take such a 'liberty'.

But a deeper sexual importance is symbolized by the whole incident. Belinda's anguished exclamation –

> Oh hadst thou, cruel! been content to seize
> Hairs less in sight, or any hairs but these!

carries on, unconsciously, the sexual suggestion. The lines indicate, primarily, of course, Belinda's exasperation at the ruining of her coiffure. The principle ironic effect, therefore, is one of bathos: her angry concern for the prominence of the lock deflates a little her protests about honor. (Something of the bathos carries over to the sexual parallel: it is hinted, perhaps, that for the belle the real rape might lose some of its terrors if it could be concealed.) But though Belinda's vehemence gives rise to these ironies, the exclamation itself is dramatically appropriate; and Belinda would doubtless have blushed to have her emphasis on 'any' interpreted literally and rudely. In her anger, she is obviously unconscious of the *faux pas*. But the fops whose admiring and envious comments of the exposed trophy Thalestris can predict – 'Already hear the horrid things they say' – would be thoroughly alive to the unconscious *double entendre*. Pope's friend, Matthew Prior, wrote a naughty poem in which the same *double entendre* occurs. Pope himself, we may be sure, was perfectly aware of it.

In commenting on Pope's attitude toward the rape, we have suggested by implication his attitude toward chastity. Chastity is one of Belinda's most becoming garments. It gives her her retinue of airy guardians. As a proper maiden, she will keep from staining it just as she will keep from staining her new brocade. Its very fragility is part of its charm, and Pope becomes something of a symbolist poet in suggesting this. Three times in the poem he refers to the breaking of a frail china jar, once in con-

nection with the loss of chastity, twice in connection with the
loss of 'honor' suffered by Belinda in the 'rape' of the lock:

> Whether the nymph shall break Diana's law,
> Or some frail china jar receive a flaw . . .

> Or when rich China vessels, fall'n from high,
> In glitt'ring dust and painted fragments lie!

> Thrice from my trembling hands the patch-box fell;
> The tott'ring china shook without a wind . . .

Pope does not say, but he suggests, that chastity is, like the fine
porcelain, something brittle, precious, useless, and easily broken.
In the same way, he has hinted that honor (for which the sylphs,
in part, stand) is something pretty, airy, fluid, and not really
believed in. The devoted sylph who interposes his 'body' between
the lock and the closing shears is clipped in two, but honor
suffers little damage:

> Fate urged the shears, and cut the sylph in twain,
> (But airy substance soon unites again).

It would be easy here to turn Pope into a cynic; but to try
to do this is to miss the point. Pope does not hold chastity to be
of no account. He definitely expects Belinda to be chaste; but, as
a good humanist, he evidently regards virginity as essentially a
negative virtue, and its possession, a temporary state. He is very
far from associating it with any magic virtue as Milton had in his
Comus. The only magic which he will allow it is a kind of charm –
a *je-ne-sais-quoi* such as the sylphs possess.

Actually, we probably distort Pope's views by putting the
question in terms which require an explicit judgment at all. Pope
accepts in the poem the necessity for the belle to be chaste just
as he accepts the necessity for her to be gracious and attractive.
But in accepting this, he is thoroughly alive to the cant frequently
talked about woman's honor, and most of all, he is ironically,
though quietly, resolute in putting first things first. This, I take
it, is the whole point of Clarissa's speech. When Clarissa says:

> Since painted, or not painted, all shall fade,
> And she who scorns a man must die a maid,

we need not assume with Leslie Stephen that Pope is expressing a smug masculine superiority, with the implication that, for a woman, spinsterhood is the worst of all possible ills. (There is actually no reason for supposing that Pope thought it so.) The real point is that for Belinda perpetual spinsterhood *is* the worst of all possible ills. In her own terms, it would be a disaster to retain her locks for ever – locks turned to gray, though still curled with a pathetic hopefulness, unclaimed and unpossessed by any man. Belinda does not want *that*; and it is thus a violation of good sense to lose sight of the fact that the cherished lock is finally only a means to an end – one weapon to be used by the warrior in the battle, and not the strongest weapon.

Clarissa is, of course, promptly called a prude, and the battle begins at once in perfect disregard of the 'good sense' that she has spoken. Pope is too fine an artist to have it happen otherwise. Belinda *has* been sorely vexed – and she, moreover, remains charming even as an Amazon. After all, what the poet has said earlier is sincerely meant:

> If to her share some female errors fall,
> Look on her face, and you'll forget them all.

Though Pope obviously agrees with Clarissa, he is neither surprised nor particularly displeased with his heroine for flying in the face of Clarissa's advice.

The ensuing battle of the sexes parodies at some points the combat in the great epic which Milton fashioned on the rape of the apple. But the absurdity of a battle in which the contestants cannot be killed is a flaw in Milton's great poem, whereas Pope turns it to beautiful account in his. In *Paradise Lost* the great archangels single each other out for combat in the best Homeric style. But when Michael's sword cleaves the side of Lucifer, the most that Milton can do with the incident is to observe that Lucifer feels pain, for his premises force him to hurry on to admit that

> . . . th'Ethereal substance clos'd
> Not long divisible . . .

Lucifer is soon back in the fight, completely hale and formidable as ever. We have already seen how delightfully Pope converts this cabbage into a rose in the incident in which the sylph, in a desperate defence of the lock, is clipped in two by the shears. The absurdity of a war fought by invulnerable opponents gives an air of unreality to the whole of Milton's episode. There is a bickering over rules. Satan and his followers cheat by inventing gunpowder. The hosts under Michael retort by throwing the celestial hills at the enemy; and the Almighty, to put a stop to the shameful rumpus, has the Son throw the trouble-makers out. But if the fight were really serious, a fight to the death, why does the heavenly host not throw the hills in the first place? Or, why does not the Almighty cast out the rebels without waiting for the three days of inconclusive fighting to elapse? The prevailing atmosphere of a game – a game played by good little boys and by unmannerly little ruffians, a game presided over by the stern schoolmaster, haunts the whole episode. The advantage is wholly with Pope here. By frankly recognizing that the contest between his beaux and belles is a game, he fulfills his basic intention.

The suspicion that Pope in this episode is glancing at Milton is corroborated somewhat by Pope's general use of his celestial machinery. The supernatural guardians in *The Rape of the Lock* are made much of, but their effectiveness is hardly commensurate with their zeal. The affinities of the poem on this point are again with *Paradise Lost*, not with the *Iliad*. In Milton's poem the angels are carefully stationed to guard Adam and Eve in their earthly home, but their protection proves, in the event, to be singularly ineffectual. They cannot prevent Satan from finding his way to the earth; and though they soar over the Garden, their 'radiant Files, / Daz'ling the Moon', they never strike a blow. Even when they discover Satan, and prepare to engage him in combat, God, at the last moment, prevents the fight. Indeed, for all their numbers and for all their dazzling splendor, they succeed in determining events not at all. They can merely (for instance, Raphael) give the human pair advice and warning. Milton, though he loved to call their resonant names and evidently tried to provide them with a realistic function, was apparently so fearful lest he divert attention from Adam's own freely made decision that he succeeded in giving them nothing to do.

If this limitation constitutes another ironical defect, perhaps, in Milton's great epic, it fits Pope's purposes beautifully. For, as we have seen, Pope's supernatural machinery is as airy as gossamer, and the fact that Ariel can do no more than Raphael, advise and warn – for all his display of zeal – again fulfills Pope's basic intention. The issues in Pope's poem are matters of taste, matters of 'good sense', and the sylphs do not violate the human limitations of this world which Pope has elected to describe and in terms of which judgments are to be made. Matters of morality – still less, the ultimate sanctions of morality – are never raised.

To return to the battle between the beaux and belles: here Pope beautifully unifies the various motifs of the poem. The real nature of the conventions of polite society, the heroic pretensions of that society as mirrored in the epic, the flattering genial ragging. Indeed, the clichés of the ardent lover become the focal point of concentration. For the clichés, if they make the contention absurd and pompous, do indicate, by coming alive on another level, the true, if unconscious, nature of the struggle.

> No common weapons in their hands are found,
> Like Gods they fight, nor dread a mortal wound.

'Like Gods they fight' should mean in the epic framework 'with superhuman energy and valor'. And 'nor dread a mortal wound' logically completes 'Like Gods they fight' – until a yet sterner logic asserts itself and deflates the epic pomp. A fight in which the opponents cannot be wounded is only a sham fight. Yet, this second meaning is very rich after all, and draws 'Like Gods they fight' into its own orbit of meanings: there may be extra zest in the fighting because it *is* an elaborate game. One can make godlike gestures because one has the invulnerability of a god. The contest is godlike, after all, because it is raised above the dust and turmoil of real issues. Like an elaborate dance, it symbolizes real issues but can find room for a grace and poetry which in a more earnest struggle are lost.

I have said earlier that Pope, by recognizing the real issues involved, is able to render his mock-epic battle meaningful. For the beaux of Hampton Court, though in truth they do not need to dread a mortal wound, can, and are, prepared to die. 'To die' had at this period, as one of its submeanings, to experience the consummation of the sexual act. (Donne, Dryden, and even Shakespeare use the term with a glance at this meaning; sceptics may consult the second song in Dryden's *Marriage à La Mode*.) Pope's invulnerable beaux rush bravely forward to achieve such a death; for the war of the sexes, when fought seriously and to the death, ends in such an act.

The elegant battleground resounds with the cries of those who 'die in metaphor . . . and song'. In some cases, little more is implied than a teasing of the popular clichés about bearing a 'living death' or being burnt alive in Cupid's flames. But few will question the sexual implications of 'die' in the passage in which Belinda overcomes the Baron:

> Nor fear'd the chief th'unequal fight to try,
> Who sought no more than on his foe to die . . .
> 'Boast not my fall, (he cried) insulting foe!
> Thou by some other shalt be laid as low . . .'

The point is not that Pope is here leering at bawdy meanings. In the full context of the poem, they are not bawdy at all – or, perhaps we put the matter more accurately if we say that Pope's *total* attitude, as reflected in the poem, is able to absorb and digest into itself the incidental bawdy of which Pope's friends, and obviously Pope himself, were conscious. The crucial point is that Pope's interpretation of Belinda's divinity does not need to flinch from bawdy implications. The further meanings suggested by the naughty *double entendres* are not merely snickering jibes which contradict the surface meaning: rather those further meanings constitute the qualifying background against which Belinda's divinity is asserted. Pope's testimony to Belinda's charm is not glib; it is not thin and one-sided. It is qualified, though not destroyed by a recognition of all the factors involved – even of those factors which seem superficially to negate it.

The touch is light, to be sure, but the poem is not flimsy, not mere froth. The tone is ironical, but the irony is not that of a narrow and acerb satire; rather it is an irony which accords with a wise recognition of the total situation. The 'form' of the poem is, therefore, much more than the precise regard for a set of rules and conventions mechanically apprehended. It is, finally, the delicate balance and reconciliation of a host of partial interpretations and attitudes.

It was observed earlier that Pope is able to reduce the 'rape' to its true insignificance because he recognizes, as his characters do not, its real significance. Pope knows that the rape has in it more of compliment than of insult, though he naturally hardly expects Belinda to interpret it thus. He does not question her indignation, but he does suggest that it is, perhaps, a more complex response than Belinda realizes. Pope knows, too, how artificial the social conventions really are and he is thoroughly cognizant of the economic and biological necessities which underlie them – which the conventions sometimes seem to mask and sometimes to adorn. He is therefore not forced to choose between regarding them as either a hypocritical disguise or as a poetic and graceful adornment. Knowing their true nature, he can view this outrage of the conventions with a wise and amused tolerance, and can set it in its proper perspective.

Here the functional aspect of Pope's choice of the epic framework becomes plain. The detachment, the amused patronage, the note of aloof and impartial judgment – all demand that the incident be viewed with a large measure of aesthetic distance. Whatever incidental fun Pope may have had with the epic conventions, his choice of the mock-epic fits beautifully his general problem of scaling down the rape to its proper insignificance. The scene is reduced, and the characters become small and manageable figures whose actions can always be plotted against a larger background.

How large that background is has not always been noticed. Belinda's world is plainly a charming, artificial world; but Pope is not afraid to let in a glimpse of the real world which lies all about it:

> Meanwhile, declining from the noon of day,
> The sun obliquely shoots his burning ray;
> The hungry judges soon the sentence sign,
> And wretches hang that jurymen may dine;
> The merchant from th' exchange returns in peace,
> And the long labours of the toilet cease.
> Belinda now. . . .

It is a world in which business goes on and criminals are hanged for all that Belinda is preparing to sit down to ombre. This momentary glimpse of the world of serious affairs, of the world of business and law, of the world of casualness and cruelty, is not introduced merely to shrivel the high concerns of polite society into ironical insignificance, though its effect, of course, is to mock at the seriousness with which the world of fashion takes its affairs. Nor is the ironical clash which is introduced by the passage uncalculated and unintentional: it is not that Pope himself is unconsciously callous – without sympathy for the 'wretches'. The truth is that Pope's own perspective is so scaled, his totality of view so honest, that he can afford to embellish his tempest in a teapot as lovingly as he likes without for a moment losing the sense of its final triviality. A lesser poet would either have feared to introduce an echo of the 'real' world lest the effect prove to be too discordant, or would have insisted on the discord and moralized the contrast between the gay and the serious too heavily and bitterly. Pope's tact is perfect. The passage is an instance of the complexity of tone which the poem possesses.

Maynard Mack

MOCK-HEROIC IN
THE RAPE OF THE LOCK (1950)

WITH *The Rape of the Lock* we come to a more comprehensive instance than *Mac Flecknoe* of what was perhaps the Augustan writer's favorite literary form – the mock-epic or mock-heroic. Heroic poems are poems like the *Odyssey*, the *Aeneid*, and *Paradise Lost*, dealing with man in his exalted aspects. Their action is weighty, their personages are dignified, and their style is elevated. Mock-heroic writings imitate this style, and by applying it to situations that are not at all exalted, secure a ludicrous effect. One purpose of this, we must never forget, is wit and pleasure. The other is the criticism that comes from comparing what man has been or can be with what he usually is.

In the *Rape of the Lock* Pope applies his high style, and along with it a complete set of epic conventions, to the world of contemporary fashion. The poem originated from an incident that actually occurred in Pope's circle of acquaintances, when Robert, Lord Petre (the Baron), cut a lock of hair from the pretty head of Arabella Fermor (Belinda), and Pope was asked by a mutual friend of the Petre and Fermor families to toss off a jesting poem that would heal the resulting rancor. Pope did so; but the poem, as his imagination worked over it, expanded from a jest into a witty and tender analysis of the perennial war of the sexes (compare the theme of James Thurber), executed against a shimmering background of upper-class decorums.

The parodies of epic convention in the poem are too numerous to be itemized, but among them may be singled out these: the dream message from the gods and the arming of the champion (I 23 ff, 121 ff); the sacrifice to the gods and the 'charge' to the troops (II 35 ff, 73 ff); the single combat at Ombre, and the epic feast (III 25 ff, 105 ff); the journey to the underworld (IV 11 ff); the general combat, divine intervention, and the apotheosis of the lock (v 35 ff, 71 ff, 113 ff). The reader familiar with *Paradise Lost* will notice a particularly large number of mock-parallels with that poem – for example, between the situation of the fallen angels at the opening of Milton's first book and the punishments promised by Pope's Ariel to careless sylphs (II 125 ff). As for the sylphs themselves, they are a splendid re-creation in social terms of the divine powers who watch over the fortunes of epic heroes. And they are also Pope's way of rendering – in their luminosity, fragility, and grace – the womanliness of woman.

The 'action' of the *Rape of the Lock* has many layers of complexity. The surface level is simply a narrative of Belinda's day: how she awakes, dresses for conquest, is conveyed down the Thames to Hampton Court, bests the Baron at Ombre, exults too proudly and therefore suffers an Aristotelean reversal of fortune in the loss of her lock, screams, collapses in a tantrum, receives good advice from Clarissa, but refuses to take it, and finally participates in the general huffing and puffing of polite indignation with which the poem ends. The progress of Belinda's day is denoted by successive references to the sun, the last of them (v 147) suggesting an implicit relation between the pattern of her day and the pattern of human life.

A second level in the action takes up the war between the sexes. Here we recognize that Pope's title has a possible literal as well as figurative significance, and that the poem is concerned with the elaborate forms that surround the courtship of man and woman. Belinda arms her beauty for an encounter the object of which is not to defeat the enemy but to yield to him – on the proper terms. By using force, the Baron violates the rules of the game. But on the other hand, as Clarissa wisely points out, Belinda should not profess to be ignorant of or outraged by the game's objective: 'she who scorns a man, must die a maid'.

On a third level the movement of the poem is psychological. We first see Belinda fancy-free, i.e. surrounded with the influence of the sylphs (her own maidenly coquetries), whose protective power depends on her remaining fancy-free. At the critical moment, however, the sylphs are helpless to save the lock because Belinda's affections have become engaged: an earthly lover lurks at her heart, and as a consequence the lock of maidenliness is forfeit. This is the purpose for which the rituals of courtship exist, and it is therefore prudish in Belinda to affect such horror at the event. To represent this, Ariel the sylph is now replaced by Umbriel the gnome – for the gnomes are reincarnations of women who were prudes. Hence it is Umbriel who penetrates down into that dusky cavern of neuroses, the Cave of Spleen, returns thence with rages which are largely affectation, and presides 'on a sconce's height' over the fracas of the last canto, which affectation has precipitated. The nature of the affectation is made clear in Thalestis's speech (IV 95 ff), where we see that the pose of outraged innocence she urges Belinda to adopt rests on a confusion of values. 'Honour', in Thalestris's vocabulary, does not mean the reality of chastity, but the reputation; and in the interest of the reputation, she is prepared, if necessary, to sacrifice the reality itself: 'Honour forbid! at whose unrivalled shrine Ease, pleasure, *virtue, all,* our sex resign.' Belinda's final couplet in this canto shows that she too has started putting appearance first.

The final level of meaning takes us to the general social criticism which forms the background of the poem. Here confusion of values is again the theme, but on a broader scale. Pope presents the absurdities of the fashionable world with affection, and with an eye to the delicate beauties that its best graces unfold. But he never allows us to forget that it is also a world whose ethical judgments are in sad disarray. Hearts and necklaces, lapdogs and lovers, statesmanship and tea, queens and Indian screens, the hunger of jurymen and justice, Bibles and billets-doux: the verse of the poem entangles these trifles and values together in order to reflect a similar entanglement in this society's mind. And it is just here, in the presentation of a moral muddle, that the mock-heroic structure proves itself invaluable. By juxtaposing the contemporary with the heroic, the poet can emphasize both the epic proportions to which this society has magnified its trifles (like the estrangement of families over a lock of hair) and also their real triviality. Furthermore, by the contrast between the social ephemera that his verse licks up as it flows along – watches, sedan chairs, coaches, cosmetics, curling irons, men, monkeys, lap-dogs, parrots, snuff boxes, bodkins – and the quite different world of heroic activity invoked through the epic parodies and the style, he can remind us of the inexorable conditions of life, death, and self-giving that not even the most glittering civilization can afford to ignore.

Hugo M. Reichard

THE LOVE AFFAIR IN POPE'S
THE RAPE OF THE LOCK (1954)

THE love affair which has a title part in the *Rape of the Lock* was perhaps once so obvious as to need no comment; at least Dr Johnson thought 'the subject of the poem . . . an event below the common incidents of common life'.[1] By the twentieth century the love story seemed so obscure as to defy analysis; at least Geoffrey Tillotson thought that the rejection of the hero by the heroine was unaccountable.[2] A decade ago Cleanth Brooks refurbished the action as a neo-classic campaign in the unending 'war of the sexes' over rites of possession.[3] Some such pattern of pre-marital courtship is doubtless a norm assumed for the comedy of the poem, as it is – William K. Wimsatt reminds us – for Molière's *Misanthrope*, Congreve's *Way of the World*, and Meredith's *Egoist*.[4] While suggestively approaching the plan of the action, however, Brooks has rather too closely assimilated Pope's particular campaign to the general war. If the comedy of the poem posits a norm, it also sets forth a divergence. One is free to speculate that in a hypothetical sequel to Pope's poem the Baron and Belinda might have gone on (like other gallivanting young people, indeed like Arabella Fermor and Lord Petre) to get married – he to another woman, she to another man.[5] But as it stands the poem is not directly concerned with what Brooks calls 'the elaborate and courtly conventions under which Belinda fulfills her natural function of finding a mate' (p. 144). Both Belinda and the Baron are at the age of exuberance where the armor of courtship fits rather loosely, like the helmet Swift stuck on Dryden. Feigning 'death', sophisticating love, and shunning marriage, they wage a mock war in a mock-heroic poem. Their maneuvers, I wish to show, make the plot of the poem a contest of wiles between commanding personalities – an uninhibited philanderer and an invincible flirt.

The showing rests in the first place on Pope's own words, in the *Rape of the Lock* and in his other poems about belles and beaux. Corroboration, which is abundantly available because of the great interest which art and literature of the eighteenth century took in a coquette's or rake's progress,[6] is limited here to some periodical essays. As it happens, the relevance of Addison and Steele bears out George Sherburn's opinion·that the 'tone of the poem was certainly learned from those sober discourses on the foibles of women that adorned the *Tatler* and *Spectator*'.[7] But analogues in the essays to the characters, sentiments, and fable of the little epic will be used here, not to argue influence, but to guide explication. The analogues, I need hardly add, leave the poem neither dated nor dimmed. Though periodical essays – like newspapers now – exhibit members of Belinda's and the Baron's species, they certainly do not contain Belinda and the Baron themselves, much less Pope's total poem, which has a world of things to itself. In allowing the essays to hold a candle to the poem, I mean only to cast some light on the love story.

The axis of the story is the character of Belinda. Brooks thinks apparently that the girl is – or ought to be – out to catch a husband.[8] Doubtless the girl would be well advised to become a wife before she passes her heyday as a reigning beauty. But Belinda is not noticeably forehanded. The girls in the poem who plan for marriage are not her sort: they are protégées of the gnomes, with whom she has no dealings until Umbriel appears in the fourth of the five cantos; even after Umbriel replaces Ariel, there is not the slightest sign that she is meditating matrimony. After as well as before Umbriel's advent the poem pauses over the latent irony of Belinda's self-sufficiency as a reigning beauty.[9] Perhaps extending the earlier suggestion that the Baron's scissors portend time's wear-and-tear (III 171–8), Pope prophetically compares the distress of the shorn girl to the chagrin of old maids – 'scornful virgins who their charms survive' and 'ancient ladies when refused a kiss' (IV 4–10). Likewise Clarissa pointedly reminds Belinda that 'since locks will turn to grey . . . she who

scorns a man, must die a maid' (v 26–8). Both the comparison
and the reminder would not be half so telling if Belinda did not
persistently disdain wedlock. Her quest is plainly, not for a man
in her life, but for men at her feet. Willing to be wanted, she
devotes herself 'to the destruction of mankind' (II 19); averse to
captivity, she 'rejects mankind' (I 68). She likes 'with youthful
lords to roam' (IV 159) and yet chooses to 'reject a lord' as lover
or husband (I 10). Besides declining the Baron's improper advances, 'oft she rejects' other offers (II 12).

On the evidence of the text, by the standards of Sir James
Murray, Addison, Steele, and Ariel, Pope's heroine is not a
bride-to-be, but a coquette *par excellence*. Oxford, ever providing
a liberal education, says that a coquette is 'a woman (more or
less young) who uses arts to gain the admiration and affection of
men, merely for the gratification of vanity or from a desire of
conquest, and without any intention of responding to the feelings
aroused; a woman who habitually trifles with the affections of
men'. For Steele a coquette is a 'happy self-loving dame, that
takes all the admiration she can meet with, and returns none of it
in love to her admirers'. Her forte, he says, 'is to win hearts and
throw 'em away, regarding nothing but the triumph' (*Spectator*,
no. 515). In view of Brooks's enthusiasm for the 'divinity' of
Belinda, Addison's extended definition of a coquette is especially
tonic. Bearing the Virgilian epigraph 'O Dea certe', *Spectator*,
no. 73, deals with 'the vain part of the sex, whom . . . I shall dis-
tinguish by the name of idols'. Inevitably it calls to mind
Belinda's patience before her mirror, her fondness for barges and
courts, her delight in fulsome love letters, the bounds she puts
on her blandishments, and the assault she incurs from one of her
unsatisfied admirers. Here, in part, is Addison's satiric apotheosis
of the coquette:

An Idol is wholly taken up in the Adorning of her Person. You
see in every Posture of her Body, Air of her Face, and Motion
of her Head, that it is her Business and Employment to gain
Adorers. For this Reason your Idols appear in all public Places
and Assemblies, in order to seduce Men to their Worship. The
Playhouse is very frequently filled with Idols; several of them are

carried in Procession every Evening about the Ring, and several of them set up their Worship even in Churches. They are to be accosted in the Language proper to the Deity. Life and Death are in their Power: Joys of Heaven and Pains of Hell are at their disposal . . . Raptures, Transports, and Extasies are the Rewards which they confer; Sighs and Tears, Prayers and broken Hearts are the Offerings which are paid to them. Their Smiles make Men happy; their Frowns drive them to despair. . . .

It has indeed been known, that some of them have been used by their incensed Worshippers like the Chinese Idols, who are Whipped and Scourged when they refuse to comply with the Prayers that are offered to them. . . .

From this severe indication that coquettes are 'the most charming, but the most unworthy, sort of women' (*Tatler*, no. 107), we turn to the dulcet testimony of Ariel and Pope.

Ariel is an expert witness. He himself, like other sylphs, is a deceased and metamorphosed coquette:

> For when the Fair in all their Pride expire,
> To their first Elements their Souls retire . . .
> The graver Prude sinks downward to a *Gnome*,
> In search of Mischief still on Earth to roam.
> The light Coquettes in *Sylphs* aloft repair
> And sport and flutter in the Fields of Air.[10]

He is affiliated with live coquettes by way of duty, for sylphs chaperon girls – Belinda for one – who are 'fair and chaste', guide them through their flirtations, and keep them pure and fancy-free (i 67–78, 91–104). Though not all coquettes are escorted by sylphs (i 87–8), all sylphs seem to confine their services to coquettes. Presiding over much more than lotions and brocade, they see to it that a girl in their care is distracted from the seductive treats, clothes, and advances of one man to those of another; in thus embodying the 'levity', or inconstancy, of such a girl, the sylphs hold a coquette in character – that is, interested in one man after another.[11]

Belinda's behavior matches her retinue. Not every gesture, it is true, is plain coquetry. When the Baron comes up behind the

girl with his scissors, for example, 'Thrice she look'd back, and
thrice the foe drew near.' The glances may be allurement, or they
may be nothing more than innocent responses to the sylphs'
puffs and twitches of warning. There is no such ambiguity in the
girl's performance on the Thames barge. She executes a tour de
force of flirtation:

> Fair Nymphs, and well-drest Youths around her shone,
> But ev'ry Eye was fix'd on her alone . . .
> Favours to none, to all she Smiles extends,
> Oft she rejects, but never once offends.
> Bright as the Sun, her Eyes the Gazers strike,
> And, like the Sun, they shine on all alike.   (II 5–14)

In charming men by the boatload, Belinda deftly maintains the
style, in eighteenth-century terms, of a coquette as distinguished
from a jilt. For she stays chaste while offering temptation, and
sweetly genial even when saying no.[12]

Belinda's motives, like her spirits and actions, stamp her as a
coquette. If her conduct is in the long run stultifying, it is in the
short run purposeful: living in the present, she prefers her heady
triumphs as a maiden to the dull glories of a virtuous wife. Her
motives are those which observers of the species have singled out
– 'vanity', 'desire of conquest', 'self-love'. She herself protests
after her debacle that she does not know 'what mov'd my mind
with youthful lords to roam' (IV 159). Pope, however, does not
mean to leave his readers baffled too. The reason for the roaming
is rhymed plainly and reminiscently in the second of the *Moral
Essays*, a later and harsher poem that deals with coquettes and
their 'love of sway': 'For foreign glory, foreign joy, they roam; /
No thought of peace or happiness at home' (223–4). The reason
is made abundantly clear in the *Rape of the Lock* itself. With a
characteristic inconsistency, the girl who wonders what moved
her mind also exclaims wistfully, 'Oh had I rather un-admir'd
remain'd / In some lone isle' (IV 153–4). The exclamation seems
the oblique equivalent of what one coquette avows in *Spectator*,
no. 515: 'To tell you the plain truth, I know no pleasure but in
being admired.' Belinda has sought all the glories that, in

Clarissa's vivid review, can come to a young beauty who takes pains with her charms (v 9–16). With tresses curled to seize and enslave the hearts of men (II 19–28), Belinda plays her cards against dashing males for the fame that comes from maidenly conquests:

> *Belinda* now, whom Thirst of Fame invites,
> Burns to encounter two adventrous Knights,
> At *Ombre* singly to decide their Doom;
> And swells her Breast with Conquests yet to come.
>
> (III 25–8)

With a combination of emphasis and finesse Pope renders Belinda's ruling passion unmistakable pride, in the dual sense of self-conceit and self-assertion.[13] For this purpose as for many others he uses the sylphs. They are as solicitous as the girl herself not merely for her dress and coiffure, but also for her inner satisfaction. 'Fairest of mortals,' Ariel addresses Belinda in her dream; 'Hear and believe! thy own importance know' (I 27–46). Ariel's sound cajolery must seem an echo to Belinda's own sense of values. But his catechism on honor is his most impressive, because least obvious, reflection of Belinda's vanity. It begins and ends:

> What guards the Purity of melting Maids . . .?
> 'Tis but their *Sylph*, the wise Celestials know,
> Tho' *Honour* is the Word with Men below.
>
> (171–8)

The 'sylph' that actually keeps a girl chaste represents something different from the 'honour' that is supposed to preserve her. The pretence is, as we say, a high sense of honor – according to Johnson 'nobleness of mind', according to a recent dictionary 'a fine sense of, and strict conformity to, what is considered morally right or due'. For Brooks the 'sylph' in Ariel's dictum signifies 'concern for good taste'. The gloss takes us in the right direction – towards a vulgarization of honor – but not, I think, far enough.

We can go the full distance by noting how Pope and others

elsewhere play on shades of meaning in the spectrum of *honour*.
Consider Thalestris' outburst:

> *Honour* forbid! at whose unrival'd Shrine
> Ease, Pleasure, Virtue, All, our Sex resign.
>
> (IV 105–6)

At first glance the shade of *honour* meant here seems to be 'chastity, purity, as a virtue of the highest consideration', but on
inspection the force of the word fades into 'reputation for this
virtue, good name' (*OED*). Under honorific cant, the couplet
suggests, ladies of fashion mask a shabby obsession with appearances and prestige. For such illumination Pope has familiar
precedents. Speaking of honor as an idol in the *Dispensary*, for
example, Garth punned significantly on the word *name* (de-
noting both illusion and reputation):

> Bigotted to this Idol, we disclaim
> Rest, Health, and Ease, for nothing but a Name.[14]

Similarly, Congreve gave Mirabell in *The Way of the World* an
insight into the cult of public relations: 'Why do we daily commit disagreeable and dangerous Actions? To save that Idol
Reputation' (II iii). In all these passages the honor men and
women live by is seen to be the variety defined in one of Johnson's illustrative quotations: 'If by *honour* is meant any thing
distinct from conscience, 'tis no more than a regard to the censure
and esteem of the world.' Such honor, moreover, is precisely
the kind of pride which Lovejoy discriminates as 'the desire for,
and pleasure in, the esteem, admiration or applause of others,
especially the craving for "distinction" '. This triple identifica-
tion of honor, desire for prestige (name or fame), and pride is
expressly made by Pope himself. In his epistle *To a Young Lady*,
with the Works of Voiture (1712) he thus analyzes chastity:

> Your pleasure is a vice, but not your *pride*;
> By nature yielding, stubborn but for *fame*;
> Made slaves by *honour*, and made fools by shame.[15]
>
> (34–6)

When Ariel tells Belinda, ' 'Tis but their Sylph, the wise Celestials know, / Tho' Honour is the Word with Men below', he is really saying that pride rather than nobility keeps a girl like her pure. He is saying (with a difference) what *Guardian*, no. 152, said – that among females of the species lust is checked by two restraints, the one given the 'name of modesty', and the other 'called by men honour, and by the gods, pride'. The sylph behind Belinda's purity is symbolically her *alter ego*.

She displays her self most vividly in what is perhaps the purplest of the poem's purple passages – the ritual at her dressing table (1 121–48). The scene, set in religious metaphor, contains a famous crux. Taking the vanity table as an 'altar', what are we to make of Belinda's double role? For she is in person the chief 'priestess' and in the mirror the 'goddess'. Brooks solves the mystery with a paradox – 'such is the paradox of beauty-worship, she can be both the sincere devotee and the divinity herself'. Though he elsewhere affirms Pope's resolution in putting first things first, he here regards Pope as only incidentally 'amused by the vanity' of Belinda's performance. Hazlitt, it seems to me, comes closer to the first principles of Belinda's soul and Pope's text: 'A toilette is described with the solemnity of an altar raised to the Goddess of vanity.'[16] In keeping with her honor, Belinda's religion is primarily not beauty-worship, but self-worship. She is her own 'goddess' – precisely the 'woman whom one "worships" or devotedly admires' (*OED*).

Steele, Addison, and Milton can help one approach this altar in the right spirit for communion with Belinda and Pope. *Spectator*, no. 79, unveils a boudoir similar to Belinda's, so similar that it even calls to mind the marvellous 'Puffs, powders, patches, Bibles, billet-doux'. The boudoir which Steele describes belongs to the 'beauteous Philauthia', who is an 'idol' of the variety previously noticed. Philauthia

has a very pretty furnished Closet, to which she retires at her appointed Hours; This is her Dressing-room, as well as Chappel; she has constantly before her a large Looking-glass, and upon the Table, according to a very witty Author,

Together lye her Prayer-Book and Paint
At once t'improve the Sinner and the Saint.[17]

It must be a good Scene, if one could be present at it, to see this
Idol by turns lift up her Eyes to Heav'n, and steal Glances at her
own dear Person. It cannot but be a pleasing Conflict between
Vanity and Humiliation.

Both the essay and the poem, one perceives, arrange the scene to
contrast heaven and self, piety and vanity: in the essay the
dressing-room is a chapel, and in the poem the dressing-table is
an altar. But there are notable differences between the vaguely
beauteous Philauthia in her sketchy chapel and the fully imagined
Belinda at her laden altar: while Philauthia is sufficiently orthodox to turn at times from her image to her God and even possibly to experience a conflict between vanity and humiliation,
Belinda is so idolatrous as to fix her eyes solely on her own
image. Evidently Pope has established the conflict of his scene,
not in the consciousness of the coquette, but in the insight of the
reader. The single-minded Belinda feels no strain; untroubled
by humiliation or piety, she is all vanity.

Brooks, who comments aptly on Miltonic parallels found in
the poem, seems to have missed a telltale echo in Belinda's
boudoir. Once again the *Spectator* is instructive. Talking of the
familiar passage in *Paradise Lost* (IV 449–91) where newborn
Eve is bemused by a face in the water, Addison draws the moral:
'the poet lets us know, that the first woman immediately after
her creation, ran to a looking-glass, and became so enamoured
of her own face, that she had never removed, to view any of the
other works of nature, had not she been led off to a man' (no.
325). In describing his pious maid and her goddess, Pope makes
use of Milton's, if not Addison's, exhibit of the narcissism of
women. Before a mirror in London rather than a pool in Eden,
Pope's Belinda is discovered in the posture of Milton's Eve. As
the first beauty of antiquity 'bent down to look' into her lake,
'a shape within the wat'ry gleam appear'd' – a 'wat'ry image'
(*PL* IV 460–1, 480). In just the same fashion and much the same
words 'a heav'nly image in the glass appears' to Belinda, and 'to

that she bends' (*RL* i 125–6). Like Eve and Narcissus, Belinda is vain and is enamored of her own image. But she manages her love affair in her own way. She does not languish over the image like Narcissus; nor is she so easily distracted from it by a man, as is Eve. Raising her egotism into a militant religion, Belinda does much more than worship a deity which is herself: she 'decks the goddess' to evoke the worship of mankind. These are in earnest 'the sacred rites of pride'.[18]

Belinda's antagonist, the Baron, is as removed as she herself from the conventional warfare in which the female studiously maneuvers the male into matrimony. After Belinda over-powers the man who has embarrassed her, she does not demand and he does not offer a ring. The pair have some resemblance to a stage couple fairly common in Pope's day – in Addison's words, 'a fine man who is . . . a whoremaster' and 'a fine woman that is . . . a jilt' (*Spectator*, no. 446). Although Belinda, as we have seen, is not quite that kind of woman, the Baron is just that kind of man, the kind of 'well-bred lord t'assault a gentle belle' (i 8) rather than join the siege of an army or a city. This 'ad-ventrous Baron', a 'bold lord, with manly strength indu'd', is of a perennial rather than medieval order of 'adventrous knights' (ii 29, iii 26, v 79). The order is baldly classified in the *Guardian*: speaking explicitly of 'men of rank and figure', no. 123 investi-gates the 'sort of knights-errant in the world, who, quite con-trary to those in romance, are perpetually seeking adventures to bring virgins into distress, and to ruin innocence'.

Since Belinda's pretty lock is an amatory symbol, the pursuit of it involves the Baron in 'a lover's toil' (ii 29–34). His aims are to kiss and tell – 'on his foe to die' (v 78) and to boast of the exploit:

> While Nymphs take Treats, or Assignations give,
> So long my Honour, Name, and Praise shall live!
>
> (iii 169–70)

His souvenirs prove this rake's prowess: 'three garters, half a pair of gloves; / And all the trophies of his former loves'.[19] The collection seems authentic: *Tatler*, no. 113, for example, lists

among the effects of a deceased roué 'five billet-doux . . ., a silk
garter, a lock of hair, and three broken fans'.[20] The Baron burns
the collection to propitiate the gods because the matchless
Belinda's lock of hair will make the grandest of trophies. Against
her he plans the same kind of campaign he has evidently waged
in the past, upon the other women he has loved and left:

> Resolv'd to win, he meditates the way,
> By Force to ravish, or by Fraud betray.

The Baron's preference for 'fraud or force' (II 31–4) is a
marauder's choice from the 'three ways to overcome another,
by violence, by persuasion, or by craft', as canvassed in Pope's
Iliad (XIV 216 n). Though it may make him all the more eligible
to women,[21] the Baron's adventurism has no place for persuasion
– and matrimony.

In the game of ombre the Baron and Belinda first encounter
each other by name. The episode is, to be sure, like the later
mêlée with fans and frowns and snuff, a parlour version of an
epic battle. Yet it is also an amatory passage. After losing the
first four tricks, the Baron starts winning. With two 'diamonds',
his best suit, he advances apparently on 'an easy conquest'. With
a third diamond he 'wins (oh shameful chance) the Queen of
Hearts' and is now within an ace of taking the last of her cards,
indeed the last of her hearts. Here, 'just in the jaws of ruin, and
codille', Belinda blanches and quivers (III 75–92). The play
must be interpreted not only according to Hoyle and Homer, but
also according to Ariel, who has strict rules on hearts. Though he
tolerates a heart which is a 'moving toyshop' of a succession of
beaux (I 91–104), he would not like to have Belinda 'lose her
heart' to any one beau (II 101–10); and when he presently
detects 'an earthly lover lurking at her heart', he abandons the
girl (III 139–46). Accordingly, when the Baron's diamonds are
brought out, a free heart is in danger. So is something else of
moment to the girl and the sylph. Ariel, guardian of purity, is
sufficiently anxious about Belinda's purity to call attention to it
thrice in his briefing of the troops (II 105, 107, 118–22), and to
assign for protection of the petticoat, not the usual solitary

sentinel, but a patrol of 'fifty chosen sylphs, of special note' (II 117). Ariel prepares both readers and troops to respond at Hampton Court to challenges to Belinda's virtue and reputation, climactically of course in the work of the scissors, but earlier also in the momentary success of the diamonds. When the Queen of Hearts is taken it is a 'virgin's cheek' that turns pale.[22] The 'shameful' catastrophe before which the maiden shudders is the upshot of an 'easy conquest' – the disparate calamities of 'ruin, and codille'. If at one level the disparity tickles the catastrophe with bathos, at another level it insinuates that the beaten player would also be a fallen woman.[23] Because Belinda holds a king that can take the Baron's ace of hearts, she averts the catastrophe and emerges without attachments or tarnish, with new honours as a heart-breaker (III 99–104). Her exultation, uncommonly plain, even obstreperous, is ironically premature.

In a matter of moments Belinda now passes from this repulse of the Baron to defeat by him. On the way she falls in love. The lover in her heart – probably the Baron[24] – does not directly affect her status or her further adventures. What the Baron does not know – Belinda's secret heart, Ariel's invisible flight – cannot help him plan 'new stratagems' (III 117–24). What Belinda has lost – the detachment of her heart, the bodyguard of winged ineffectuals – does not disarm her: only a woman with eyes in the back of her head could defend herself from a prank like the Baron's. Nor does her passion alter her status as a coquette. In 'the close recesses of the virgin's thought' she keeps her new ideas to herself; thanks to 'all her art' only Ariel detects them. Soon, of course, the Baron's ideas, which are something else again, will jeopardize her career, as he trumps up evidence of love and indiscretion. Though the impulse and the hoax coincide, Belinda distinguishes herself by succumbing to neither. For the rest of the story she fights desperately to retain her status as a free lass. Unlike either Millamant or Laetitia Dale, Belinda betrays no sign of languishing into a wife; on the contrary she flouts Clarissa's adjuration to resignation, housewifery, and marriage. In labouring to retrieve the lock, she seeks to spike the Baron's claims. And when Pope brings the story to a close, he refrains from recording 'all the murders' of her eye in the past tense (v 141–50).[25]

Nevertheless, after falling in love, Belinda is not all that she used to be. Ariel, abandoning her because she no longer meets his high standards of purity, levity, and honor, leaves her diminished. In her heart of hearts she is no longer utterly her own woman, flawlessly self-centered, pure, and fancy-free. Even Belinda, who enjoys stirring and balking desire in others, can fall in love. Her lapse is all the dizzier because the beau who figures in it is the Baron or his like – a well-dressed fop.[26] But Ariel's moment of discovery and departure is not simple irony. 'You hardly know', Hazlitt says, 'whether to laugh or weep.' Like the withdrawal of Adam and Eve's guardian angels 'mute and sad for man', still more like the exit of the god whom Antony loved, the retirement of Ariel 'with a sigh' brings an aching sense of waste and doom. With the sylphs, who have glorified her, disappears some of Belinda's loveliness; more of it will go as she drops from 'graceful ease and sweetness' to hysterical screaming, scolding, and crying. With the Baron poised to snip off the lock, Ariel's fated departure is an omen of still larger losses to come.

Beside the injuries of Helen or Lucrece, the rape at Hampton Court is a preposterous scratch. Yet it nonetheless leaves the virgin 'to num'rous ills betray'd' (IV 152). When long hair is *de rigeur*, F. Scott Fitzgerald reminds us in 'Bernice Bobs Her Hair', cropped hair can be a panic disfigurement. More soberly, the theft of Belinda's lock is degrading. Since the action is 'a frolic of gallantry, rather too familiar',[27] Sir Plume rightly deems it 'past a jest' (IV 129), and Brooks rightly judges that Belinda 'cannot afford to suffer the Baron, without protest, to take such a "liberty"'. Since the damage is to be compounded by misrepresentation, Brooks wrongly judges that 'the rape has in it more of compliment than of insult'. The lock is a 'prize' worth winning, keeping, and displaying only at Belinda's expense. More than all the other 'trophies of his former loves' the lock will augment this philanderer's renown.[28] Though the new honours are shams, the Baron is not one to boggle at fraud. His species is seen in the periodical essays[29] and, notably, in Pope's *Temple of Fame* (1715), where several feckless 'men of pleasure, dress, and gallantry' apply for unearned glory:

> The Joy let others have, and we the Name,
> And what we want in Pleasure, grant in Fame.
>   The Queen assents, the Trumpet rends the Skies,
> And at each Blast a Lady's Honour dies.   (390–3)

It is the Baron's luck that Hampton Court is as receptive to calumny as is the Temple of Fame; in his set too 'at ev'ry word a reputation dies' (III 16), and Umbriel can plant heads 'with airy horns' and cause 'suspicion when no soul was rude' (IV 71–3). As the Baron has his counterparts in Pope's modernization of Chaucer, Belinda has hers in Pope's allusions to Virgil and Shakespeare. When she and Thalestris appeal to the Baron, 'Not half so fixt the Trojan cou'd remain, / While Anna begg'd and Dido rag'd in vain' (V 5–6). One remembers Dido's complaint to Aeneas: 'For you alone, I suffer in my fame, / Bereft of honour, and exposed to shame' (Dryden's *Aeneid*, IV 465–6). Similarly, Belinda's furor over her loss parallels Othello's agitation over Desdemona's: 'Not fierce Othello in so loud a strain / Roar'd for the handkerchief that caus'd his pain' (V 105–6).[30] Because the lock, like the handkerchief, gives leverage to scandal, Thalestris prophesies:

> Gods! shall the Ravisher display your Hair,
> While the Fops envy, and the Ladies stare!
> *Honour* forbid! at whose unrival'd Shrine
> Ease, Pleasure, Virtue, All, our Sex resign.
> Methinks already I your Tears survey,
> Already hear the horrid things they say,
> Already see you a degraded Toast,
> And all your Honour in a Whisper lost!   (IV 103–10)

By Belinda's own calculations such publicity is worse than intimacy (IV 175–6).

Since the severed lock can compromise her, Belinda tries to recover it, in the fourth canto by words, in the fifth by violence. The order of battle, Belinda's sex against the Baron's, can easily

be misconstrued. The 'real issues' of the fifth canto for Brooks
are that 'the beaux of Hampton Court . . . can, and are prepared
to, die' in the sexual act. In his view of the combat 'Pope's
invulnerable beaux rush bravely forward to achieve such a
death; for the war of the sexes, when fought seriously and to the
death, ends in such an act'. Though an orgy might be harmonized
paradoxically with the conventions of pre-marital courtship, it
cannot be reconciled with the text of the poem. Death, to begin
with, is involved in twenty of the seventy-six lines of the battle
royal (v 37–112). But sixteen of the twenty lines are not at all
sexual – one couplet asserting gayly that the combatants have no
fear of mortal wounds (v 43–4), seven couplets proving the
deadliness of Thalestris' eyes and Chloe's frown (v 57–70).[31]
Naughty deaths do not begin to dominate the war: only two
couplets, one clearly (v 77–8) and the other conjecturally (v
97–8), lend any colour at all to the notion that the Baron's troops,
more literally than those of Fortinbras, go to their graves like
beds. Since these four lines deal solely with the feelings of the
Baron himself, they tell us nothing whatsoever about the other
beaux who have been drawn into the quarrel.

If we must not make too much of the fatalities of the war, we
must also avoid mistaking the defense for the offense. For three
of the four men noticed by name there are no grounds for saying
that Pope's beaux rush bravely forward. Only one beau is at all
aggressive – Sir Plume, who is 'bold' and eccentric enough to
draw Clarissa down. Yet even this 'unthinking' fellow, who
previously erred by scolding the Baron when other beaux were
united in silent envy of the man (IV 103–4, 121–32), awakes to
the unreality of the warfare: after wrestling stolidly with Clarissa,
he lets himself be slain by the frown of Chloe (v 67–70). Sir
Plume's comrades in arms are perfectly futile at once. Without
stirring a limb, Dapperwit and Fopling tumble at once when
Thalestris, with her eyes, inflicts the first recorded casualties of
the war (v 57–66). The Baron, for all his libido, strikes nothing
but an attitude until he is floored by Belinda (v 75–98). It is the
belles, not the beaux, who enjoy the initiative in Belinda's war.
And when the girls rush bravely forward, they are flirting, not

with death or dishonor, but with the men. As the enemy gentlemen bow gallantly, the girls limit themselves to light-hearted artillery. This fraternizing suits not only mock heroics and the manners of a drawing-room, but also the envy felt by fops for another beau's conquest and the joy felt by belles for another beauty's shame (IV 103–10).[32]

We can visualize the war of the fifth canto without reversing the tide of battle, adding new pleasures to its death, or omitting its chief belligerent. Though enlivened by the soldiering of lesser warriors, the war turns on Belinda's exploits (v 75–112 – half of the battle report) in quest of the lock. Singlehanded, Belinda wins the war. For in Jove's scales the singular 'lady's hair' outweighs the multiple 'men's wits' (v 71–4) – meaning in general the brains which guide beaux and fit in 'tweezer-cases' (v 115–16), meaning particularly the intelligence shown by the Baron and his fellows. Since such peccant parts are taken into account by Jove, the judgment in Belinda's favor seems not only courteous but almost equitable. In the individual combat which fulfills the judgment Belinda, for all her rage, selects weapons which are at once ladylike, uncommon, and potent (v 75–96). The double point of her 'bodkin' – a lovely hair ornament flourished as a dagger – is utterly disarming. Even more breathtaking is her 'charge of snuff'. As a nerve gas this 'dust' is an absolute weapon. While only momentarily suffocating the adventurer who vowed to keep the lock as long as he could breathe (IV 137), its 'atoms' completely explode his pretensions to manhood. Felled before witnesses, by a woman, with a snap of her fingers, in a puff of tobacco powder, amid a fit of tears and sneezes, the Baron is routed because he is quite humiliated: 'this bold lord, with manly strength indu'd, / She with one finger and a thumb subdu'd'. 'The lock, obtain'd with guilt', has been 'kept with pain' (v 109). Standing over the poor beau who exposed her honor to unfair whispers, Belinda threatens to skewer him to everlasting shame with a hairpin.

She is, of course, denied a complete revenge by the Baron and by Fate. Catching his breath and, after a whine and a curse, gathering all his wits about him, the Baron plays Belinda's vanity

against her fury. With face-saving equivoque of his burning
love (v 97–102), he succeeds in checking his assailant and
humoring the spectators. Now, to restore the prewar equilib-
rium completely, all the value of the prize vanishes by heavenly
decree from both Belinda and the Baron (v 103–12). After they
have fought this affair of honor with cards, scissors, and snuff,
their 'ambitious aims' are thwarted and the contest is drawn. For
the disappearance of the lock leaves the Baron without a trophy
of conquest and Belinda without a trophy of reprisal. Presumably
there is no better way of settling the point of precedency between a coquette and a beau. To be sure, the star which is born
from the lost lock shines to Belinda's advantage (v 113–50). But
it is hers only by special providence of Pope. Because he has
graced her career with sense, good humor, and a poet,

> This Lock, the Muse shall consecrate to Fame,
> And mid'st the Stars inscribe Belinda's Name.

The consecration, the last rites paid her pride, invests her with a
finer and surer glory than any she could achieve by her own arts
as a coquette.

NOTES

1. See supra, p. 68.
2. *The Rape of the Lock and Other Poems*, Twickenham Edition of
the poems of Pope, II, ed. G. Tillotson (1940) p. 92.
3. See supra, p. 144.
4. *Alexander Pope: Selected Poetry & Prose* (New York, 1951) p.
xxxvii.
5. The *Lock* is a surprisingly clear illustration that though Pope is
an occasional poet, his poems usually transcend their occasions. Its
amour is quite unaffected by the marriage and death of the Baron's
prototype, even though the first version of the poem (1712) was
published some two or three months after Lord Petre's marriage to
Catherine Warmsley, and the second version (1714) followed Lord
Petre's death by almost twelve months (Tillotson, pp. 93, 96, 99, 353).
We know only one way in which the amour of the poem is modelled
on the relationship of Lord Petre and Miss Fermor, for we know only
one solitary event in their relationship – the shearing of the lock. We

know also that – but not *why* – Miss Fermor was piqued at the published poem (Tillotson, pp. 89–93). She might well be piqued if she saw Belinda as I see her.

6. The very term *coquette* seems, in the *OED*, to have first found much use only after the Restoration. The *Spectator* hints that it was a smart word in the early century: it reports that an amorous but unworldly young Oxonian who was vexed by a pert young lady in London 'railed at *coquettes* as soon as he had got the word' (no. 605). My citations from the essays are to these editions: *The Tatler*, ed. George A. Aitken, 4 vols (1898–9); *The Spectator*, ed. G. Gregory Smith, 4 vols (Everyman's Library: 1945) *The Guardian*, in *The British Essayists*, ed. Alex. Chalmers (Boston, 1846) XIII–XX.

7. *The Best of Pope* (New York, 1945) p. 398.

8. Supra, pp. 143 ff. In a paraphrase of Brooks's doctrine, Maynard Mack – supra, p. 155 – says that 'Belinda arms her beauty for an encounter the object of which is not to defeat the enemy but to yield to him – on the proper terms'.

9. Like Pope, the *Spectator* appreciated both the brief joys and prolonged punishments of incorrigible coquettes. On the one hand nos. 73, 89, 187, 254, 272, 342, and 605 chuckled over the woes of superannuated coquettes. On the other hand no. 486 noted that 'the fair sex reigns with greater tyranny over lovers than husbands'. And no. 605 saw without surprise that young beauties prefer admirers to husbands: 'Women, who have been married some time, not having it in their heads to draw after them a numerous train of followers, find their satisfaction in the possession of one man's heart. I know very well, that ladies in their bloom desire to be excused in this particular.'

10. The distinction made in this passage (1 57–66) between the *light* coquette and the *grave* prude is in effect glossed by *Tatler*, no. 126: 'The prude and coquette (as different as they appear in their behaviour) are in reality the same kind of women: the motive of action in both is the affectation of pleasing men. They are sisters of the same blood and constitution, only one chooses a *grave*, the other a *light*, dress. The prude appears more virtuous, the coquette more vicious, than she really is. The distant behaviour of the prude tends to the same purpose as the advances of the coquette; and you have as little reason to fall into despair from the severity of the one, as to conceive hope from the familiarity of the latter.' The italics are mine.

11. Pope so arranges the device of having former coquettes superintend active coquettes as to soften his exposure of Belinda and indeed blend it with adornment. The device in other hands could be a fairly blunt means of enlarging on the workaday evils of coquettes. Thus *Spectator*, no. 272, charges an ex-coquette with mischievously balking the honorable intentions of a fine young man toward a pretty young

girl. This 'creature', the essay explains, 'during the time of her bloom and beauty was so great a tyrant to her lovers, so overvalued herself and underrated all her pretenders, that they have deserted her to a man; and she knows no comfort but that common one to all in her condition, the pleasure of interrupting the amours of others. . . . Dear Sir, do not omit this true relation, nor think it too particular; for there are crowds of forlorn coquettes who intermingle themselves with other ladies, and contract familiarities out of malice, and with no other design but to blast the hopes of lovers, the expectation of parents, and the benevolence of kindred.' The relationship between Steele's ex-coquettes and Pope's deceased coquettes becomes all the more curious because the misguided belle of the essay is named Belinda.

12. *Spectator*, no. 187, makes one of the distinctions: 'The coquette is indeed one degree towards the jilt; but the heart of the former is bent upon admiring herself, and giving false hopes to her lovers; but the latter is not contented to be extremely amiable, but she must add to that advantage a certain delight in being a torment to others.' *Tatler*, no. 107, makes the other distinction: 'A coquette is a chaste jilt, and differs only from a common one, as a soldier, who is perfect in exercise, does from one that is actually in service.' But the distinctions were not universally recognized. For John Dennis interchangeably called Belinda a 'jilt' and a 'coquette' – *The Critical Works of John Dennis*, ed. E. N. Hooker (Baltimore, 1943) II 335, 341.

13. Arthur O. Lovejoy, ' "Pride" in Eighteenth-Century Thought', in *Essays in the History of Ideas* (Baltimore, 1948) p. 62.

14. Garth is quoted by Tillotson (p. 189) in the edifying note on IV 106.

15. The idea is also expressed, more cryptically, in the *Essay on Man*: 'Nor Virtue, male or female, can we name, / But what will grow on Pride, or grow on Shame' (II 193–4).

16. Supra, p. 93.

17. The author of the couplet seems unknown. Are the lines simply a garbled variant of Halifax's couplet, to which Tillotson (following Wakefield) compares *RL* I 138: 'Prayer-book, patch-boxes, sermon-notes and paint, / At once t'improve the sinner and the saint'? Prior's *Hans Carvel* puts the idea in another vein: 'An untouch'd Bible grac'd her toilet: / No fear that thumb of hers should spoil it' (59–60).

18. Is it inconsistent of Pope, after dwelling on 'the sacred rites of pride', to present Belinda on the barge with 'graceful ease, and sweetness void of pride' (II 15–18)? It was the *Spectator*'s opinion that consummate coquettes are masters of that 'eloquence of beauty, an easy mien . . . one which can be on occasion easily affected' (no. 515). The *Spectator* perceived, too, that coquettes could affect sweet humility: 'Albacinda has the skill as well as power of pleasing. Her form is

majestic, but her aspect humble. All good men should beware of the destroyer. She will speak to you like your sister, till she has you sure; but is the most vexatious of tyrants when you are so' (no. 144). Pope is, not acquitting, but rather once again accusing Belinda of pride when he says that her sweet and easy humility 'might hide her faults, if belles had faults to hide'. In his book belles certainly had.

19. In the 1712 two-canto version of the poem the 'trophies' are somewhat more fully catalogued: the offerings include a corset 'busk' and a 'fan' as well as a garter and a glove (I 55–8).

20. For similar collections, see *Spectator*, nos. 30, 245; *Guardian*, no. 151.

21. The periodical essays report regularly that women are especially attracted to dangerous rakes. See *Spectator*, nos. 156, 602; *Guardian*, no. 45.

22. Belinda is here (III 89) designated a virgin for the first time in the poem. She is so designated on three other occasions (III 139–40, IV 9–10, V 82). In all but the last of these cases and in two other uses of the word (I 97, IV 4) the designation is significantly pointed.

23. For periodical accounts of the dishonor risked by gambling ladies see *Guardian*, nos. 120 and 174.

24. An unknown of rank higher than the Baron's would neatly correlate Belinda's conduct from ombre to coffee (III 99–146) with Ariel's remarks on the gnomes' wards (I 79–86). But the odds are against an unknown. Though her heart of hearts is denied him in public at ombre, it might secretly be the Baron's later. When she protests his theft of her hair, she is not necessarily rejecting him from the heart; she is primarily defending on principle her prestige as a virgin and a coquette. After all she is not so fond of an unknown or indifferent to the Baron as to view all familiarities from the latter as odious (IV 175–6). Though she presents 'one finger and a thumb' of her hand only for the unaffectionate purpose of snuffing out his manhood, she would not be unique if she combined the violence of angry pride with the reticence of love. When he speaks up from the floor, he seems sure that the man to lay her as low will be 'some other' (V 97–8), but he has no way of guessing that she has already fallen in love, with him or anybody else. Standing far out from Belinda's otherwise faceless following, the Baron alone seems available for 'lurking at her heart'.

25. In being covertly in love with one man without ceasing to flirt with many others, Belinda is hardly a pioneer woman in literature. For a convenient counterpart see the coquette (of *Spectator*, no. 281) described in my next footnote.

26. All along Belinda seems to rate a beau – in Johnson's definition, 'a man of dress' – as a man of worth. (In this estimate she resembles

many girls in the periodical essays – e.g. *Tatler*, no. 151; *Spectator*, nos. 15, 281, 311, 506; *Guardian*, nos. 34, 149.) She glows when she moves among or even dreams of fashion plates (I 23–4; II 5–14). Up to a point, like Ariel's other wards, she finds safety in numbers of modish wigs, sword-knots, and coaches; and 'beaus banish beaus' from her heart. (I 99–102). In finally falling in love she shows her taste in men of distinction and Pope's taste in ironies. (For Pope's taste, see I 90 and *Moral Essay*, II 247, 93–4, 265.) There is in *Spectator*, no. 281, a heart very similar to Belinda's, entered with an irony very similar to Pope's. In a previous essay (no. 275) Addison made a satiric report (much like Pope's at V 71–4, 115–16) of the imaginary 'dissection of a beau's head'. No. 281, a sequel, is the report of the imaginary 'dissection of a coquette's heart'. (Coming from the *Rape*, one sees that the subject here is a cadaver and that the speaker is explicit.) When first explored, the heart of the consummate coquette proved light, hollow, and impressively manproof, even though 'the lady of this heart, when living, received the addresses of several who made love to her, and did not only give each of them encouragement, but made every one she conversed with believe that she regarded him with an eye of kindness'. But at last, concealed in the centre of the heart, was discovered 'a little figure . . . dressed in a very fantastic manner'. And 'the little idol that was thus lodged in the very middle of the heart was the deceased beau' of the earlier dissection.

27. Johnson, supra, p. 66.
28. II 30, 44; III 165–70; IV 113–16, 139–40; V 108–11.
29. *Tatler*, no. 88; *Guardian*, no. 92.
30. For Othello's interpretation of Cassio's having the handkerchief, see *Othello*, V ii 213–15.
31. These lines are properly subsumed under Brook's concession that 'in some cases little more is implied than a teasing of the popular clichés' about dying for love. Tillotson's notes to V 57–70 are very helpful. Two additional exhibits may be added – *Tatler*, no. 110, and *Spectator*, no. 377. The latter essay is an especially valuable analogue of Pope's ridicule of the clichés. To rid the language of 'metaphorical deaths', Addison asks the 'dying' lover to note 'that all his heavy complaints of wounds and deaths rise from some little affections of coquetry, which are improved into charms by his own fond imagination'. In a jocose 'Bill of Mortality' Addison illustrates how lovers may perish fancifully: 'wounded by Belinda's scarlet stocking . . . smitten at the opera by the glance of an eye . . . killed by the tap of a fan on his left shoulder by Coquetilla . . . hurt by the brush of a whalebone petticoat . . . shot through the sticks of a fan . . . struck thro' the heart by a diamond necklace . . . slain by a blush from the Queen's Box . . . cut off in the twenty-first year of his age by a white-wash . . . slain by an

arrow that flew out of a dimple in Belinda's left cheek . . . hurt from a pair of blue eyes . . . dispatch'd by a smile . . . murder'd by Melissa in her hair . . . drowned in a flood of tears'.

32. See also 'The Fourth Satire of Dr. John Donne, Versifyed', lines 258–9, unexpectedly evolved from Donne's own lines 217–18.

Reuben A. Brower

'AM'ROUS CAUSES' (1959)

> What dire Offence from am'rous Causes springs,
> What mighty Contests rise from trivial Things . . .

WE can imagine the amusements with which Pope and his fellow Scriblerians might overhear a discourse on the *Rape of the Lock* and heroic tradition. The *Key to the Lock* and the *Art of Sinking in Poetry* show what they might do with the theme – sufficient warning to any critic 'who delights to trace the mind from the rudeness of its first conceptions to the elegance of its last'. However much we may learn from such a study about the growth of the poem and the richness of its texture, we cannot, as Valéry reminds us, confuse the process of composition with poetic effect. For the critic, as for the common reader, the *Rape of the Lock* must be the final 'elegance', the 'easy art', the wit and good nature that Pope praised in Voiture:

> In these gay Thoughts the Loves and Graces shine,
> And all the Writer lives in ev'ry Line;
> His easie Art may happy Nature seem,
> Trifles themselves are Elegant in him.

The 'Epistle to Miss Blount, With the Works of Voiture', from which these lines come, and which is so close in tone and subject to the *Rape of the Lock*, was completed only a year or so before Pope wrote the first version of his 'Heroi-Comical Poem'.

Pope's poetry of wit in the *Rape of the Lock* is probably most perfect in the passage on the ceremony of afternoon coffee and the cutting of the lock:

> For lo! the Board with Cups and Spoons is crown'd,
> The Berries crackle, and the Mill turns round.
> On shining Altars of *Japan* they raise

The silver Lamp; the fiery Spirits blaze.
From silver Spouts the grateful Liquors glide,
While *China*'s Earth receives the smoking Tyde.
At once they gratify their Scent and Taste,
And frequent Cups prolong the rich Repast.
Strait hover round the Fair her Airy Band;
Some, as she sip'd, the fuming Liquor fann'd,
Some o'er her Lap their careful Plumes display'd,
Trembling, and conscious of the rich Brocade.
Coffee, (which makes the Politician wise,
And see thro' all things with his half-shut Eyes)
Sent up in Vapours to the *Baron*'s Brain
New Stratagems, the radiant Lock to gain.
Ah cease rash Youth! desist ere 'tis too late,
Fear the just Gods, and think of *Scylla's* Fate!
Chang'd to a Bird, and sent to flit in Air,
She dearly pays for *Nisus*' injur'd Hair!
But when to Mischief Mortals bend their Will,
How soon they find fit Instruments of Ill!
Just then, *Clarissa* drew with tempting Grace
A two-edg'd Weapon from her shining Case;
So Ladies in Romance assist their Knight,
Present the Spear, and arm him for the Fight.
He takes the Gift with rev'rence, and extends
The little Engine on his Fingers' Ends,
This just behind *Belinda*'s Neck he spread,
As o'er the fragrant Steams she bends her Head:
Swift to the Lock a thousand Sprights repair,
A thousand Wings, by turns, blow back the Hair,
And thrice they twitch'd the Diamond in her Ear,
Thrice she look'd back, and thrice the Foe drew near.
Just in that instant, anxious *Ariel* sought
The close Recesses of the Virgin's Thought;
As on the Nosegay in her Breast reclin'd,
He watch'd th' Ideas rising in her Mind,
Sudden he view'd, in spite of all her Art,
An Earthly Lover lurking at her Heart.
Amaz'd, confus'd, he found his Pow'r expir'd,
Resign'd to Fate, and with a Sigh retir'd.
The Peer now spreads the glitt'ring *Forfex* wide,

T'inclose the Lock; now joins it, to divide.
Ev'n then, before the fatal Engine clos'd,
A wretched *Sylph* too fondly interpos'd;
Fate urg'd the Sheers, and cut the *Sylph* in twain,
(But Airy Substance soon unites again)
The meeting Points the sacred Hair dissever
From the fair Head, for ever and for ever!   (III 105–54)

It is easy enough to pick out the phrases that catch the essence of the poem: 'shining Altars', 'glitt'ring *Forfex*', 'fatal Engine', 'Airy Band'. All are characteristic of the whole, and yet perfect for the occasion. What do we mean by the 'poetry of wit' as illustrated by these expressions? 'Glitt'ring *Forfex*', for example, sounds like an epic formula, the usual combination of epithet and noun with a flavour of mystery about its exact meaning. The use of a solemn Latin term for a familiar object, the word in which the point (!) focuses, is in Dryden's finest satirical-heroic style, but 'glitt'ring', a favourite adjective in the *Rape of the Lock* and other early poems, is pure Pope. It is the adjective that makes us feel the minuteness of the actual 'Forfex' and that diverts our attention to an irrelevant beauty. The Baron's heroic act seems very slight by the Homeric standard, yet exquisitely beautiful and touched somehow with the fire of that splendid world. The essence of Pope's wit in the *Rape of the Lock* lies in this beautiful diminution, where 'beautiful' implies the appeal of the surface and the appeal of a better world of noble manners and actions. Cutting the lock is absurd, but also much more than absurd.

Of the phrases we have chosen, 'fatal Engine' probably comes closest to the allusive irony of Dryden, with its echoes of Virgil and Milton. Dryden's *Aeneis* serves here for Virgil, the phrase being his translation of *fatalis machina*. For a moment Pope sustains the grander tone of *Absalom and Achitophel*, 'Ev'n then, before the fatal Engine clos'd . . .', but with the next line, 'A wretched *Sylph* too fondly interpos'd . . .', he restores the scale of the scene, and 'the fatal Engine' is reduced to 'The little Engine on his Fingers' Ends . . .' Both phrases give us in passing a sense of the precious slightness of objects and actions. Presently,

as in his *Iliad*, Pope reinforces the heroic by borrowing from
Milton:

> Fate urg'd the Sheers, and cut the *Sylph* in twain,
> (But Airy Substance soon unites again) . . .

Milton's '. . . but th' Ethereal substance clos'd' is adjusted to fit
Pope's more delicate myth and tone, where Dryden would easily
have taken 'ethereal'[1] in his stride. 'Airy', reminding us of
Pope's closeness to Donne, amuses by the contrast with Milton
and evokes the misty charm of Ariel and his 'lucid Squadrons'.
In 'shining Altars' there is the same witty diminution and sensuous appeal as in 'glitt'ring *Forfex*', but here the visual detail
fits into a scene of the heroic pictorial type familiar in Pope's
Iliad, a description that gives an initial impression of being in
Dryden's grandest epic manner. Opening with Virgilian rhetorical pomp ('For lo!'), it rises to a Latin gravity in 'frequent Cups
prolong the rich Repast'.

But with 'hover round the Fair', we hear the familiar accent of
'society', and with

> *Coffee*, (which makes the Politician wise,
> And see thro' all things with his half-shut Eyes)

we are in the coffeehouse where a worldly observer is speaking to
us in an aside. 'Sent up in Vapours' is fashionable psychology
served up as a joke. In the *Rape of the Lock* the epic grandeur is
always being lightly qualified by this voice that takes us into the
poet's confidence. Compared to the delicate game of innuendo
that Pope plays with such consummate skill, the usual mock-epic
tricks of inflation seem almost crude. Even at the climax of the
action, the most heroic moment in the poem, Pope manages to
insinuate this confidential tone by the lightest of touches:

> But when to Mischief Mortals bend their Will,
> How soon they find fit Instruments of Ill!

The couplet, as the notes remind us, is indebted to *Henry VI* and
to *Absalom and Achitophel*. But,

> Just then, *Clarissa* drew with tempting Grace
> A two-edg'd Weapon from her shining Case . . .

'Just then' (the transition in a children's story), and a little later, 'just behind' (the feminine accent of 'just *there*, my dear'), incline the tone towards cosy intimacy. Dryden's manner is by comparison elephantine.

Yet Pope's '*Spectator*' tone, as Sherburn calls it, makes possible a personal moral seriousness rare in Dryden (to speak in these terms may be worse than elephantine). In the present passage the tone allows Pope to move out from 'coffee' to a sharp criticism of statesmanship. Although in recent years too much has been said too solemnly about Pope's serious concerns in the *Rape of the Lock*, it would be light-minded to disregard them. In the better 'case' implied by Pope's satire, marriage is not entered into lightly or unadvisedly, the ceremony of innocence is not drowned, and beauty in nature and in art are truly wonderful. But the chief moral, like all poetic 'morals', is inseparable from the poetry, from Pope's peculiar wit and tone:

> What then remains, but well our Pow'r to use,
> And keep good Humour still whate'er we lose?
> And trust me, Dear! good Humour can prevail,
> When Airs, and Flights, and Screams, and Scolding fail.
> Beauties in vain their pretty Eyes may roll;
> Charms strike the Sight, but Merit wins the Soul.
>
> (v 29–34)

In a Dedication that is a perfect example of the virtue he recommends, Pope says to the original Belinda,

It will be in vain to deny that I have some Regard for this Piece, since I Dedicate it to You. Yet You may bear me Witness, it was intended only to divert a few young ladies, who have good Sense and good Humour enough, to laugh not only at their Sex's little unguarded Follies, but at their own.

Through poetic laughter Pope is everywhere urging his readers to view these 'Follies' with the necessary distance, moral and aesthetic. He wins us over to mature 'Good Sense and good Humour' by the art of allusive irony that he had originally learned from Dryden and that he now adapts to suit his own aims and sensibility. He gets his purchase on his larger meanings by skilful handling of various literary traditions, Ovidian, pastoral, and heroic. Pope's keen responsiveness to the society about him is expressed through an equally keen responsiveness to literary modes that had imaged other societies, both human and divine.

While it is true that in its general conception the *Rape of the Lock* derives from the *Battle of the Frogs and Mice*, from Tassoni, and more immediately from Boileau and Garth, the actual style of the poem shows rather how much Pope owed to the tradition of Dryden and how much he still was learning from the first of the Augustans. In details of language, as nearly every page of the Twickenham Edition shows, Pope borrows more often from Dryden than from any other single poet. Even when he is not borrowing directly, he is indebted to the late seventeenth-century heroic style that Dryden had fixed as proper for epic and mock epic.

From early in his career we see Pope imitating Dryden, and yet imparting his own quality to his imitations. The two manners dominant in the older poet, the style of public address and the heroic, have left traces on Pope's earliest poems. Pope had seen Dryden once, and in his uneasy friendship with Wycherley he enjoyed a repeat performance of Restoration literary life in its less elegant form. His first attempt in satire, 'To the Author of a Poem, intitled, Successio' (Settle), has the hearty coarseness and the free-and-easy classical comparisons of Dryden's less-finished prologues, while the lines 'On Dulness' and other additions to Wycherley's poems resemble the heavier attacks on Shadwell in *Absalom and Achitophel*, part ii. The comparison of dullness with 'the Leaden Byass of a Bowl', patterned on the 'bias of the mind' simile in *Mac Flecknoe*, was to find a place in the *Dunciad*, the nearest to Dryden of all Pope's major works. But a lightness and grace of rhythm more characteristic of Pope can be felt in some of these fragments, especially in the '*Similitude*' on 'the Stream of Life'. Note that Pope's rhythm comes out more distinctly in the lines after the triplet (in itself characteristic of Dryden):

> The Stream of Life shou'd more securely flow
> In constant Motion, nor too swift nor slow,
> And neither swell too high, nor sink too low;

> Not always glide thro' gloomy Vales, and rove
> ('Midst Flocks and Shepherds) in the silent Grove;
> But more diffusive in its wand'ring Race;
> Serve peopled Towns, and Stately Cities grace;
> Around in sweet Meanders wildly range,
> Kept fresh by Motion, and unchang'd by Change.
>
> (18–26)

Though these are the lines of a town poet, there is a marked similarity in idiom and descriptive style to the 'retirement' passage in *Windsor Forest* (235–70). His early experiments in the heroic style, such as the 'Episode of Sarpedon' and the 'Gardens of Alcinous', in their choice pictorial details and smoother, more evenly balanced couplets, show a sensibility quite different from Dryden's.

The *Ode for Musick on St Cecilia's Day*, though painfully imitative of Dryden, has one passage that anticipates the romantic mythological style of Collins and the early Keats:

> By the Streams that ever flow,
> By the fragrant Winds that blow
>   O'er th' *Elysian* Flowers,
> By those happy Souls who dwell
> In Yellow Meads of *Asphodel*,
>   Or *Amaranthine* Bowers:
> By the Heroe's armed Shades,
> Glitt'ring thro' the gloomy Glades,
> By the Youths that dy'd for Love,
> Wandring in the Myrtle Grove,
> Restore, restore *Eurydice* to Life . . .   (71–81)

The blend of heroic reminiscence with delicate imagery, the classical elegance of diction and movement, are what we should expect from the future poet of the *Rape of the Lock*. These qualities are combined with Pope's intimacy of address (his *Spectator* tone) in the close of the 'Epistle to Miss Blount, With the Works of Voiture', lines that might have been written to Belinda:

> Now crown'd with Myrtle, on th' *Elysian* Coast,
> Amid those Lovers, joys his gentle Ghost,

Pleas'd while with Smiles his happy Lines you view,
And finds a fairer *Rambouillet* in you.
The brightest Eyes of *France* inspir'd his Muse,
The brightest Eyes of *Britain* now peruse,
And dead as living, 'tis our Author's Pride,
Still to charm those who charm the World beside.

(73–80)

The epistle is a miniature exhibition of what Pope can do at this
point in his career and of what he will do in the *Rape of the Lock*
and in a number of his later satires. In the urbanity of Voiture's
art and personal life he sees an ideal for himself, which he expresses with a lightness and sureness of rhythm that beautifully
symbolise an easy inner poise:

Thus wisely careless, innocently gay,
Chearful, he play'd the Trifle, Life, away,
'Till Fate scarce felt his gentle Breath supprest,
As smiling Infants sport themselves to Rest . . .

(11–14)

Pope offers the lady this image of freedom in contrast with the
formal restraint of custom and a 'successful' marriage. Although
he is charmed by feminine beauty, he sees through the glitter
with the eye of the later satirist and harshly brings out the ugliness
glimpsed 'thro' half-shut eyes' in the *Rape of the Lock*. The lady
is offered the same consolation and defence in both poems:

Trust not too much your now resistless Charms,
Those, Age or Sickness, soon or late, disarms;
Good Humour only teaches Charms to last,
Still makes new Conquests, and maintains the past . . .

(59–62)

In the mastery of a personal attitude and of a corresponding
intimacy of tone and ease of rhythm, Pope sets himself apart
from Dryden while continuing to write within the mode of
Dryden's finest epistolary poems such as the prologue 'To my
Dear Friend Mr. Congreve' or the epistle 'To Sir Godfrey
Kneller'.

It was characteristic of Pope and of his integrity as a poet that the traditional styles with which he had been experimenting should find a place in the work that most surely marks his arrival at maturity. We have seen how he renewed his early pastoral style in the scene of Belinda's journey down the Thames, how he parodied the style without burlesquing it, expressing in this way an awareness of a world where man had once lived in significant and harmonious relationship with Nature. It is not unexpected that his youthful experiments with Ovid also left a mark on the *Rape of the Lock*. In making his versions of the *Metamorphoses* Pope had again been imitating Dryden, and in particular the heroic style of his translations from Ovid. As a result Pope's *Fables* are closer to the heroic than to the implied tone of easy colloquial speech of the original, although his 'Vertumnus and Pomona' has a more Ovidian lightness of touch than his 'Dryope'. But whatever their failings as translations, they gave Pope valuable experience in combining gallantry and heroics in narratives of magical change. Partly owing to this early practice the *Rape of the Lock* is epic 'Ovidianised'. There are the specific borrowings such as the change of the lock into a star, the allusion to Scilla's theft of Nisus' sacred lock, and the comparison of Sir Fopling's death to 'th' expiring Swan' of 'Dido to Aeneas'. (All are discussed in Tillotson's excellent introduction.) But more important proof of Ovid's influence is the total effect of Ovidian transformation, of an imagined region where belles become nymphs and goddesses, playing cards become Homeric heroes, and where the whims and concealed passions of lovers are turned into creatures of the four elements. Significantly enough, Ariel comes from the play of Shakespeare that is most thoroughly permeated by Ovidian metamorphosis. In its union of the comedy of young love with classical myth and fairy lore, the *Rape of the Lock* stands as Pope's *Midsummer Night's Dream*, the last successful work in the Renaissance mythological tradition that includes the tales of Marlowe, Lodge, and Drayton, and the plays of Lyly. Pope's success in this mode, like the Elizabethans', depends less on learning than on a happy gift of mythological invention. As Tillotson finely notes, Pope is being thoroughly Ovidian when he sees among the wonders of the dressing table

> The Tortoise here and Elephant unite,
> Transform'd to *Combs*, the speckled and the white.
>
>   (I 135–6)

And where is there a better piece of mythological 'seeing' than
in the vision of the sylphs, in which the human and the natural
interchange with all the fluidity of metamorphosis?

> He summons strait his Denizens of Air;
> The lucid Squadrons round the Sails repair:
> Soft o'er the Shrouds Aerial Whispers breathe,
> That seem'd but *Zephyrs* to the Train beneath.
> Some to the Sun their Insect-Wings unfold,
> Waft on the Breeze, or sink in Clouds of Gold.
> Transparent Forms, too fine for mortal Sight,
> Their fluid Bodies half dissolv'd in Light.
> Loose to the Wind their airy Garments flew,
> Thin glitt'ring Textures of the filmy Dew;
> Dipt in the richest Tincture of the Skies,
> Where Light disports in ever-mingling Dies,
> While ev'ry Beam new transient Colours flings,
> Colours that change whene'er they wave their Wings.
>
>   (II 55–68)

The sylphs and the heroic actors of the *Rape of the Lock* are
Ovidian in still another way that links Pope's invention with the
Metamorphoses. In his epic of transformations Ovid shocks and
amuses by giving divine and heroic lovers the manners and
attitudes of contemporary Roman society. Although Ovid
knows what real passion is, the talk of love among his heroes and
divinities is full of coquetry and extremely 'wise'. In similar
fashion Pope's spirits are 'Denizens of Air' and of London society,
unsubstantial, but very knowing in all the arts of love. Their
view of beauty is reminiscent of Ovid's *Ars Amatoria*:

> Our humbler Province is to tend the Fair,
> Not a less pleasing, tho' less glorious Care.
> To save the Powder from too rude a Gale,
> Nor let th' imprison'd Essences exhale,
> To draw fresh Colours from the vernal Flow'rs,
> To steal from Rainbows ere they drop in Show'rs

A brighter Wash; to curl their waving Hairs,
Assist their Blushes, and inspire their Airs;
Nay oft, in Dreams, Invention we bestow,
To change a *Flounce*, or add a *Furbelo*.   (II 91–100)

Belinda's charms are the product of magical cosmetic arts over
which the 'busy *Sylphs*' preside, 'And *Betty*'s prais'd for Labours
not her own' (I 148) Pope's refashioning of epic in Ovidian
terms, making it more splendid and more amusing, is one of the
large ways in which he adapted heroic poetry to his purposes in
the *Rape of the Lock*.

But Pope was thoroughly aware that he was writing in an
established genre practised by many poets before him. Besides
being familiar with well-known examples of mock-heroic and
burlesque poetry, he also must have read Dryden's comments on
the relations between satire and heroic poetry, and he was certainly well acquainted with contemporary theories of the epic.
More important, he had first-hand knowledge of Homer, Virgil,
and the English 'heroic' poets. The 1713 revision of the *Rape of
the Lock*, in which the epic machinery was added, was made at
the time when Scriblerus Club was in full swing,[2] in an atmosphere of mockery of solemn learning and literature of all kinds.
Earlier in the same year Pope had published his ironic essay on
pastoral poetry and his prose burlesque, 'A Receit to make an
Epick Poem'. The proposals for the *Iliad* had gone out in 1713,
and by May of 1714 he was surely at work on the translation. He
may have already started to translate before completing the
revision of the *Rape of the Lock* in December 1713. The resemblances between the poem and the translation of the *Iliad*
are at points very close, but as William Frost[3] has shown, it
is impossible to decide whether Pope is parodying his translation
or anticipating it. In a broad sense, Pope had always been a
translator of Homer, from his early experiments in epic and his
translations of passages from the *Iliad* and the *Odyssey*, to the
Rape of the Lock, and the style of his *Iliad* is hardly distinguish-
able from that of the considerably earlier 'Episode of Sarpedon'
and the 'Gardens of Alcinous'. Whether or not he had completed
any part of the translation before revising the *Rape of the Lock*,

the poem is the inevitable example for comparing Pope's heroic and mock-heroic modes.

We have already seen how finely Pope transformed heroic poetry by the beautiful diminution of phrases like 'glitt'ring Forfex' and 'shining Altars'. In general he produces epic effects in the *Rape of the Lock* much as in his translation. Allusive imitation of Virgil or Dryden or Milton is the basis of his heroic style whether he is making a serious translation or writing a parody, and sharpening of visual details is as common in the epithets and scenes of the *Rape of the Lock* as of the *Iliad*. Pope's treatment of the fixed epithet in the *Rape of the Lock* makes clear what happened when he transferred the heroic style to a less serious subject. Exact translations of Homeric or Virgilian expressions are rare, though we do find 'seven-fold fence' for '*sevenfold* shield' and 'Garbs *succinct*' for Virgil's *succinctus*, and a fair number of phrases modelled closely on Virgil or Dryden, such as 'th' Etherial Plain', 'the Purpled Main', 'th' Aerial Kind', 'the wintry Main', and 'the kindly Rain'. By their generalised form and meaning, they give a passing if humorous glance at the great order of Nature 'out there', beyond the doings of Belinda and her friends. 'The gen'ral Fate', like similar phrases in Pope's *Iliad*, conceals the Homeric Moira under Roman solemnity and abstraction. Some of the combinations of epithet and noun – 'th' Etherial Plain', 'th' Aerial Kind', 'the Finny Prey' – have a peculiar quality that makes them perfect for the *Rape of the Lock*. Like certain periphrases in Homer or in Virgil, especially as Englished by Dryden, they are tiny enigmas, some of them almost seventeenth-century scientific jokes, with an allusion to classification by genus and species. The definition of periphrase in the *Art of Sinking* fits precisely both the serious and the comic epic:

Periphrase is another great Aid to *Prolixity*; being a diffus'd circumlocutory Manner of expressing a known Idea, which should be so misteriously couch'd, as to give the Reader the Pleasure of guessing what it is that the Author can possibly mean; and a Surprize when he finds it.

The wit latent in Virgil and apparent in Dryden (as in *volubile buxum*, 'wooden engine', for a top)[4] works with a new force in the context of the *Rape of the Lock*, since the slightly enigmatic flavour and our 'Pleasure of guessing' and finding what 'the Author can possibly mean' are now thoroughly in place.

The use of heroic diction for ridicule might be described simply as bad translation of the kind Pope refers to in the Preface to the *Iliad*. Render literally an epithet like 'ox-eyed Hera' and set it down mechanically in any context, however serious, and in English the result is absurd. (Literal translation of formulas will always seem comic to readers unfamiliar with the conventions of oral epic.) Applying in reverse his principle that the translator should use those phrases that 'agree with the tenor and main intent of the particular passage', Pope gets the desired effect in the *Rape of the Lock*. Part of the fun comes from seeing Pope deliberately use clichés of the type called 'diminishing Figures' in the *Art of Sinking*:

THE EXPLETIVE,

admirably exemplified in the Epithets of many Authors.

> *Th' umbrageous Shadow, and the verdant Green,*
> *The running Current, and odorous Fragrance,*
> *Chear my lone Solitude with joyous Gladness.*

But the effect of even the most commonplace eighteenth-century epithets is often more than comic. When used of the card-table at Hampton Court, 'verdant Field', 'velvet plain', and 'level Green' have their sensuous value renewed, and unexpectedly fresh images come to mind. (The silken surface becomes the smooth and shimmering expanse of an English lawn. We may note again the fine imaginative extensions of the technique in 'glitt'ring Forfex' and similar phrases.) In these expressions and in many others the nice incongruity and the slightly enigmatic quality of epic language blend with lively sense impressions of scene, persons, and artifacts.

In the *Rape of the Lock*, as in the *Iliad* and the *Odyssey*, there is much poetry of luxury and well-made things, of 'glitt'ring Spoil', 'rich Brocade' and 'silver Lamps', of 'rich *China* Vessels' and 'gilded Chariots'. Through many descriptive devices Pope builds up little scenes of 'historic painting' that are the exact complement to the grander pictures of his *Iliad*. But the art and the artist in the epullion and the epic are the same, and positive effects of magnificence and pictorial beauty persist in the *Rape of the Lock* where they 'ought not to'. If we refer to the effects as 'exquisite', or 'charming', or 'Watteauesque', we also want to add something stronger. For through his use of epic style, at once traditional and highly individual, Pope realises more serious meanings. If comparisons with battles, feasts, and sacrifices diminish the importance of the persons and events, they also express values of a world where greatness and ceremony were serious matters, where grace and beauty of manners were an index to civilisation, a world alive in the 'historical present' of the mind of the poet and of readers who have a sense of the past.

Probably the largest single way in which Pope imparted qualities of splendour and wonder to his actors and action was through his brilliant adaptation of epic machinery. His success in producing the 'marvellous' needs little comment. Like Homer's gods, Pope's sylphs move easily in and out of the lower world, they surprise without offending our sense of the probable, and they give ordinary human impulses a sensuous form that makes us see them as they are, and yet as beautiful. What they 'really' stand for – feminine honour, flirtation, courtship, the necessary rivalry of man and woman – is seen in its essence, and a human impulse seen in its essence, as Keats observed of a street quarrel, is beautiful.

By inventing the sylphs Pope solved the almost impossible problem that the theorists set for the heroic poet. He is almost certainly the only modern poet to create a company of believable deities which are not simply the ancient classical divinities in modern dress, and which are not offensive to a Christian audience. As Warburton pronounced with his usual sententiousness:

. . . that sort of Machinery which his judgment taught him was only fit for his use, his admirable invention supplied. There was but one System in all nature which was to his purpose, the *Rosicrucian Philosophy*.

The tact with which Pope combined hints from *Rosicrucian Philosophy* with memories of Shakespeare, Milton, Lucretius, Ovid, and English country lore is finely described by Tillotson in his essay on the *Sylphs*. He brings out two main reasons for Pope's success in pleasing both epic theorists and the common reader: his choice of a mythology known well enough to count as 'established', and his 'grafting the whole heterogeneous system on "all the Nurse and all the Priest have taught" ... By this stroke he connects the machinery with the beliefs of his own country, a connection required of an epic poet'. We may also add that it was Pope's familiarity with Ovid that helped him reach a unifying vision and metaphor (the sense of magical change), and that gave him hints for creating a style in which the marvellous, the socially sophisticated, and the heroic could be successfully combined.

Pope's achievement in introducing the marvellous into a modern poem carried him well beyond mere 'correctness', since he succeeded also in recovering something of Homer's vision of a human drama played in relation to a divine order. (To describe this feat without sinking in prose, we should need Pope's lightness of touch in poetry.) By deftly linking his invented deities with popular country beliefs and with the 'Heathen Mythology' of Fate and Jove, Pope makes us feel the presence of forces greater than Belinda and the Baron and their friends. The dwarfing of the persons, which everyone notices, is one sign that this is so. As unchanging Nature-Moira was implied in the diction and rhythm of Pope's *Iliad*, so in the *Rape of the Lock* a larger natural order is implied through setting or descriptive epithet and playful allusion. In the 'silver Thames' and the 'morning Sun', in 'the Rival of his Beams', and the 'Nymph' with her 'destructive' powers, we feel a link between social and natural worlds, and in the movement of stars and of time, we have an almost Homeric sense of the necessary end of Belinda's beauty and virtue:

> Then cease, bright Nymph! to mourn thy ravish'd Hair
> Which adds new Glory to the shining Sphere!
> Not all the Tresses that fair Head can boast

Shall draw such Envy as the Lock you lost.
For, after all the Murders of your Eye,
When, after Millions slain, your self shall die;
When those fair Suns shall sett, as sett they must,
And all those Tresses shall be laid in Dust;
This Lock, the Muse shall consecrate to Fame,
And mid'st the Stars inscribe *Belinda*'s Name!   (v 141–50)

This is of course elegant spoofing, literary and social. We are
amused by the absurdity of the apotheosis and the analogies to
Daphnis (Caesar) and to Achilles lying 'in the Dust', and also by
the allusion to the *Lock of Berenice*, which was itself a spoof.
(The effect is a kind of double parody.) We are also reminded of
the *Elegy to the Memory of an Unfortunate Lady*:

How lov'd, how honour'd once, avails thee not,
To whom related, or by whom begot;
A heap of dust alone remains of thee;
'Tis all thou art, and all the proud shall be!

(71–4)

But in the *Rape of the Lock* as in the *Elegy* the death of innocence
and beauty are not laughing matters, and the apotheosis offers
serious as well as playful consolation to Belinda and Mrs Arabella
Fermor. With perfect deference to fact and poetic fiction, Pope
has found his equivalent for Homer's Death and Sleep, and it is
hard not to suppose that his sensibility and the internal form of
his poem have been subtly shaped by his familiarity with the
Homeric use of myth. Not only the mock apotheosis and the
sylphs, but the whole drama of the *Rape of the Lock* is a piece of
wonderful myth-making. 'Mythos' as a fable or plot and 'mythos'
as symbol are two growths of the basic process of seeing and
dramatising that can be observed in the *Pastorals*. Pope's
growth as a poet may be seen in his progress from the pictorial
mythologising of the *Pastorals* to the descriptive splendours and
the fully developed symbolism of *Windsor Forest*, to the 'fable'
of Belinda's lock. In the dramatic image of the *Rape of the Lock*
Pope created a native Augustan myth, as later readers have
instinctively and perhaps naïvely demonstrated, by taking the
poem for the stock symbol of the 'Age of Queen Anne'. A not

wholly adequate symbol, to be sure, if we think of the public grandeurs and the common miseries of London life in 1714. For the one, we need something like the Roman-Augustan myth of *Windsor Forest*; for the other, 'The Harlot's Progress' or 'Beer Street' and 'Gin Lane'. But Pope gives at least a hint of the grandeur in 'Where *Thames* with Pride surveys his rising Tow'rs' (III 2) and of the misery in 'Wretches hang that Jury-men may Dine' (III 22). Note that both references are made through epic allusion, that Pope has found in mock-epic a way like Homer's of 'looking out' on another world beyond the scene of his action. Pope uses allusion or parody to give us a glimpse of the great Homeric world, thus imitating Homer's technique while reversing the direction of our view. Similes compare Belinda with Aeneas, 'Not half so fixt the Trojan cou'd remain' (v 5) or the fracas over the lock with the quarrels on Olympus, 'So when bold *Homer* makes the Gods engage' (v 45).

It was between these two heroic comparisons that Pope in 1717 set his '*parody*[5] *of the speech of Sarpedon to Glaucus*' in order to '*open more clearly the* MORAL *of the Poem*'.

> Then grave *Clarissa* graceful wav'd her Fan;
> Silence ensu'd, and thus the Nymph began.
>   Say, why are Beauties prais'd and honour'd most,
> The wise Man's Passion, and the vain Man's Toast?
> Why deck'd with all that Land and Sea afford,
> Why Angels call'd, and Angel-like ador'd?
> Why round our Coaches crowd the white-glov'd Beaus,
> Why bows the Side-box from its inmost Rows?
> How vain are all these Glories, all our Pains,
> Unless good Sense preserve what Beauty gains:
> That Men may say, when we the Front-box grace,
> Behold the first in Virtue, as in Face!
> Oh! if to dance all Night, and dress all Day,
> Charm'd the Small-pox, or chas'd old Age away;
> Who would not scorn what Huswife's Cares produce,
> Or who would learn one earthly Thing of Use?
> To patch, nay ogle, might become a Saint,
> Nor could it sure be such a Sin to paint.
> But since, alas! frail Beauty must decay,

Curl'd or uncurl'd, since Locks will turn to grey,
Since painted, or not painted, all shall fade,
And she who scorns a man, must die a Maid;
What then remains, but well our Pow'r to use,
And keep good Humour still whate'er we lose?
And trust me, Dear! good Humour can prevail,
When Airs, and Flights, and Screams, and Scolding fail.
Beauties in vain their pretty Eyes may roll;
Charms strike the Sight, but Merit wins the Soul.
So spoke the Dame, but no Applause ensu'd . . .

(v 7–35)

Pope's treatment of the passage shows finally and clearly where
the mock-epic of the *Rape of the Lock* stands in relation to Homer
and the English heroic tradition. The main effect of Clarissa's
speech for readers not over-conscious of Homer or Le Bossu
comes from hearing the voice of common sense in the midst of
much ado about nothing. We feel too a fairly hearty amusement
in the obvious parallels to the *Iliad* and a flicker of Walleresque
sentiment, 'But since, alas! frail Beauty must decay'. An eighteenth-century reader would recognise that Pope was now giving
'the moral' demanded by theorists and so anticipating the ob-
jections of Dennis, who had found Pope's purpose not sufficiently
clear. Closer comparison with Homer will show how skilful
parody readjusted Homer's moral to fit the values of Augustan
society.

The parody opens on Dryden's high-heroic level, with an
allusion to one of the most serious speeches in *Absalom and
Achitophel*, the 'temptation' of Monmouth:

Say, why are Beauties prais'd and honour'd most,
The wise Man's Passion, and the vain Man's Toast?

In the Homeric counterpart, Sarpedon cites as proofs of glory
the simple goods of meat and drink, speaking of them with
complete certainty as to their value. In Pope's version, as we
noted in the last chapter, Sarpedon acknowledges these glories,
but they have been raised to a nobler pitch, since they are signs
of a divine blessing. The ultimate value is 'above', not here
below. The translation in effect if not in fact anticipates Clarissa's

attitude. In her appeal 'these Glories' of social success are in themselves 'vain', and the Homeric parallels underline the gap between true and false grandeur. But the superior virtue recommended by Clarissa, the combination of 'good Sense' and 'good Humour', is not quite transcendental and so altogether perfect for the occasion. It is a real virtue, but a 'smiling' one, and attainable within the limits of a worldly society more inclined to trust intelligence than enthusiasm. But it can accomplish some fairly wonderful things: 'Charms strike the Sight, but Merit wins the Soul'. As elsewhere in the poem, Pope attunes his moral sentiments to the mock-heroic by means of his tone,

> And trust me, Dear! good Humour can prevail,
> When Airs, and Flights, and Screams, and Scolding fail.

This is cosily feminine to the point of caricature: Clarissa moralising is very much 'like a woman'.

But in adopting such a tone Pope is edging away from mock-heroic towards burlesque, and at some points in the passage he slips into the kind of 'jest', as Dryden would say, that 'gives us a boyish kind of pleasure'. In serious neo-classical parody ordinary persons and actions are presented in a style so nicely simulating the heroic as to barely break the epic decorum. (This is Dryden's manner at its best in his heroic satires.) In burlesque, by contrast, high-heroic persons are presented in a low style, a travesty of the heroic. We take 'a boyish kind of pleasure', in seeing the style debased, and we laugh less at the person than the language. By Canto v of the *Rape of the Lock* 'grave Clarissa', Belinda, and Thalestris have become surprisingly heroic, hence any descent seems more of a let-down. Set certain lines in the passage beside Homer or beside Pope's translation, and they become in an eighteenth-century sense 'vulgar':

> Oh! if to dance all Night, and dress all Day,
> Charm'd the Small-pox, or chas'd old Age away . . .

> To patch, nay ogle, might become a Saint . . .

> Curl'd or uncurl'd, since Locks will turn to grey,
> Since painted, or not painted, all shall fade . . .

The level of the diction comes perilously near to Swift's *Corinna*
or *The Progress of Beauty*. Dryden will go this far in ridiculing
the most despicable butts of his satire, but not often, and his best
parodies of Virgil have a Latin finesse rarely equalled by Pope
(probably because he was a better Latinist). Pope shows a similar
finesse in parodying English poets, including Dryden himself, but
his occasional coarseness has a value. By this mention of a horrid
disease and the gross deceptions of cosmetics, the ugly realities
of the London world are particularised and brought home to us.
As a result Pope comes closer to Homer's 'ten thousand shapes
of death' in this burlesque than in the bland abstractions of his
translation. The effect is like Gay's in *The Shepherd's Week*,
where Gay recovered some of the healthy charm of Theocritus
by introducing exact if vulgar details. Pope's thrust into realism
in this speech and at other points in the *Rape of the Lock* brings
his trifle nearer to the 'naïve' realism and the inclusiveness of
vision of Homeric poetry.

That some coarsening of mockery appears in a passage added
in the 1717 edition is significant. Pope is no longer quite the
'gayest valetudinaire alive' of his 'Farewell to London', nor the
would-be Voiture of his 'Epistle to Miss Blount'. He has been
through his ugly experience with Curll, and he has suffered more
'contamination' through various Scriblerian projects and his
collaboration with Gay in the *What D'Ye Call It*, a burlesque of
Addison's *Cato*. He is nearer in mood to Swift now that Swift is
no longer near at hand. But he is not ready for a poem combining
this vein of harshness and tougher wit with the surface magnificence of Dryden's heroic style; that is, he is not yet the poet of
the *Dunciad*.

For the *Rape of the Lock* and the world Pope is mocking in
the poem, consistent use of Dryden's tone would of course be
absurd. It was justified in Dryden's own satires because his
victims were elevated by the great public issues in which they
were involved. But Pope at this point in his career has no scene
or historic vision of similar scope. His social scene, in comparison
with Dryden's, is private, and the vices ridiculed and the moral
offered belong to private life. But the more intimate scene

favoured Pope's use of the more personal tone denied to Dryden, and though Pope can allude to the high heroic manner for ridicule or serious placing of his action, he is not bound by it, as he was in translating the *Iliad*. In his translation Pope writes within the limits of proper heroic solemnity, and he cannot allow his Jove and Juno to come down to the comic level of Zeus and Hera. If he had done so, the 'true Heroick' artifice would have collapsed. But in the *Rape of the Lock*, starting from a premise of mockery, Pope is happily free to include ugly and serious implications in a literary and social *divertimento*. Pope, like Horace, can be convincingly serious only when it is certain that no one will take him quite seriously.

NOTES

1. Cf. the use of 'th' ethereal plain' in the conclusion to the *Dunciad*, IV 636, where the Virgilian and Miltonic context makes the phrase perfectly appropriate.

2. For the chronology, see *Memoirs of . . . Martinus Scriblerus*, ed. Charles Kerby-Miller (New Haven, 1950) pp. 14–20, 26–8, 36–9; and also the *Art of Sinking in Poetry*, ed. E. L. Steeves (New York, 1952) pp. xv–xvii. On the 'atmosphere' in which the *Rape of the Lock* was revised, see Kerby-Miller, p. 28.

3. William Frost, '*The Rape of the Lock* and Pope's Homer', in *Modern Language Quarterly*, VIII 352–3.

4. See R. A. Brower, 'Dryden's Poetic Diction and Virgil', in *Philological Quarterly*, XVIII 211–17.

5. Frost, op. cit. p. 344, notes that Pope was not parodying Homer's Greek directly or only, but his own translation and possibly also a number of earlier versions.

Murray Krieger

THE 'FRAIL CHINA JAR' AND
THE RUDE HAND OF CHAOS (1961)

CONTRARY to the usual impression, recent critical approaches
to literature, at their most valuable, need not restrict themselves
to the ivory tower of formalism, in which analytical ingenuity is
paraded for its own sake. Elsewhere, arguing from aesthetic
principles, I have tried to prove that, far from stifling extra-
literary relations, the so-called new criticism can allow literature
to be uniquely revelatory of life, to give us a new rendering of the
stuff of experience. But here I should like to venture even further
in an effort to correct the common misconception that sees
modern criticism as no more than formalistic. For despite the
fact that this criticism grew up largely in opposition to the historical disciplines, I shall here attempt to show how literature –
if it is seen thoroughly and with new-critical care as literature –
can illuminate in a rather special way even so un-new-critical an
area as the history of ideas.

To this end I should like to conduct a somewhat reckless
allegorical excursion in order to assure myself the freedom I
need to explore an extraordinary dramatic relation between
perhaps the two greatest poems of the eighteenth century, *The
Rape of the Lock* and *The Dunciad*. It may be that I shall have to
construct a kind of mythology of idealized generalizations which
are to pass for the psychological history of the tensions of the
eighteenth-century artist by allowing certain ideological commonplaces to bear more weight than the more careful historian
may believe they can sustain. And I may end by doing violence
to other more widely accepted commonplaces of the orthodox
historian. But surely this is one of the chief functions of poetry,
this violation of the commonplace. Finally, my claims may be
seen to ignore the significance of the chronological relations

among *The Rape of the Lock*, *An Essay on Man*, and *The Dunciad* by assuming something like a simultaneity among poems spread among three decades. I hope that the facts of chronology will not be seen to disturb more essential dialectical relations among the works of this single poet. Let me add only this further apology: that I mean to suggest these dramatic and allegorical extensions of the poems no more than tentatively, even hypothetically – hoping only that by being suggestive they may be especially illuminating in a way that a more literal transcription would prefer to ignore, perhaps (let me admit the possibility) because the latter, in its scholarly caution, is more anxious to avoid being wrong. But the extensions that follow – at the worst – would have been nice if they were there to be justly read this way. They do make for an exciting drama of the eighteenth-century mind at work.

I

It is by this late date not at all original to claim that Pope's *The Rape of the Lock* is double-edged throughout, that in it he celebrates the artificial world of eighteenth-century social convention even as he satirizes it. Even Mr Geoffrey Tillotson, the rather orthodox editor of the poem in the Twickenham Edition, acknowledges:

The social mockery of the *Rape of the Lock* is not simple, does not make a pat contribution to single-mindedness. The world of the poem is vast and complicated. It draws no line of cleavage between its 'seriousness' and its mockery. Belinda is not closed up in a rigid coterie which Clarissa and the rest of the poem mock at. Pope, fierce and tender by turns, knows no more than Hazlitt, 'whether to laugh or weep' over the poem. He is aware of values which transcend his satire:

> *Belinda* smil'd, and all the World was gay

and

> If to her share some Female Errors fall,
> Look on her Face, and you'll forget 'em all.

The poem provides a picture rather than a criticism; or, rather, the criticism is so elaborate, shifting, constellated, that the intellect is baffled and demoralized by the emotions. One is left looking at the face of the poem as at Belinda's.

But this is all he has to say. He follows his hunch no further. In a well known essay, Mr Cleanth Brooks argues in a more extensive and highly detailed fashion that our awareness, through Pope's double meanings, of the biological facts that lie just beneath the artful façade of the poem and of the social mannerisms of Belinda's world creates a two-way irony that admires even as it patronizes. Thus for Mr Brooks also the poem does more than mock at a 'tempest in a teapot'. Many of my observations about the poem will be all too obviously related to his. But even he has not quite pursued his approach to this poem to a unified conclusion, resting content – as he all too often does in *The Well Wrought Urn* – with merely complicating the dimensions of the poem and of the irony it exploits and so leaving it, exposed but not regrouped, in all its multiplicity. Mr Allen Tate, in an analysis he has never to my knowledge published, moves from Mr Brooks' scattered insights to an over-all conception of the poem as metonymy and thus as what Mr William Empson has defined as pastoral. It is this notion I should like to develop here.

In so far as we view the poem as a mockery of the selfconscious seriousness displayed by trivial characters over a trivial occurrence, we see them, in their self-importance, indulging the logical fallacy of metonymy: they have mistaken the lock of hair, actually incapable of being violated, for the lady's body – vulnerable, but unassaulted by the baron. Similarly, they have taken their rarefied and pomaded world of conventional play for the great world, that changeable heroic world of princes and states in which rape brings vengeance and catastrophe lurks. Hence the mock-epic. Granted that these are the delusions of the complacency fostered by an artificial society, and that Pope forces us to see them as such. But surely, for all its absurdities, this self-contained and inconsequential 'toyshop' world can manage an aesthetic perfection and (from the standpoint of an ugly, lurking reality) a disinvolvement that allow it a purity along with its thinness.

We may rightly smile – perhaps in envy as well as in disdain –
at the metonymic wigs that are fighting in this world of decorum
instead of the gory, if more glorious, lords of heroic mold; for,
as Pope so brilliantly arranges things, the disembodied wigs
fight, properly, with sword-knots instead of swords ('Where
wigs with wigs, with sword-knots sword-knots strive'). The
'toyshop' society that self-importantly mistakes itself for reality
is defender, too, of 'honor', that fashionable word out of Restoration comedy which so befits this world of fashion. Appearance is all. The lock of hair is to this world what the actual body
is to the real world, except that the former is even more to be
cherished since reputation is the only value in the world of
fashion. So the rape of the lock is more to be avoided in honor's
world than are the more sordid, but less openly proclaimed,
assaults in classical legend and in London back-alleys. Belinda,
perhaps unconsciously, acknowledges as much in her lament to
the baron,

> Oh hadst thou, cruel! been content to seize
> Hairs less in sight, or any hairs but these!

In honor's world the lock *is* the woman as the wig is the man
and the sword-knot his weapon. There simply is no flesh and
blood in these people – or rather in these artificially created
shadows of people – so that, even without looking to John
Milton, we should understand why it is fitting that:

> No common weapons in their hands are found,
> Like Gods they fight, nor dread a mortal wound.

And of course not Belinda herself is flesh and blood – at least
not the artful and perfected abstraction that Belinda creates of
herself in administering 'the sacred rites of pride'. It is a brilliant
stroke in this dressing-table passage that the real Belinda is only
the priestess at the altar, and that the goddess whom she decorates
as she worships is her reflection in the mirror. She worships not
fleshly or cosmic, but 'cosmetic pow'rs' whose kingdom is not of
this world, but of the elegant world of appearance. The Belinda
who, fully created in artifice, is to enter honor's world on the

Thames and in Hampton Court, is not a woman but a goddess, a disembodied image: she is the insubstantial Belinda, composed of smiles that have been repaired and of the 'purer blush'. Deprived of the imperfections that mar – even as they humanize – flesh and blood reality, the painted blush is indeed aesthetically purer than a natural blush, an improvement upon it. And it is morally purer too; for it is caused not by blood – by any natural, unmaidenly immodesty – but by the cool calculations of art. It is far less spontaneous, or suggestive, than the blush earlier induced in her dreams by the disguised Ariel:

> A Youth more glitt'ring than a Birth-night Beau
> (That ev'n in slumber caus'd her cheek to glow).

This world of images, from which – as in Yeats' Byzantium – the fury and the mire of human veins are excluded, is also the world of play, and thus of innocence. And it is the sense of play that justifies Pope's frequent and brilliant use of zeugma in the poem. When Ariel suggests to his 'sylphs and sylphids' what catastrophes may threaten Belinda, he couples[1] 'real' dangers with merely fashionable ones:

> Whether the nymph shall break Diana's law,
> Or some frail China jar receive a flaw;
> Or stain her honour, or her new brocade;
> Forget her pray'rs, or miss a masquerade.

Elsewhere 'the virgin's cheek' pales in a fear that yokes maidenly dishonor to the loss of the card game:

> She sees, and trembles at th'approaching ill,
> Just in the jaws of ruin, and Codille.

Or kings captured in battle are yoked to aging virgins, fierce and unrepentant tyrants to an imperfectly dressed young lady. To be sure, these and similar instances emphasize the triviality of the action and thus the poem's mock-heroic aspect. But given this world where images and wigs and sword-knots replace real men and women, where fashion replaces emotion, where 'honor' replaces moral earnestness, this very triviality should alone be

taken seriously. Utterly inconsequential in contrast to both the
heroic world and the sordid everyday world, the insubstantial
quality of the world in which woman is recognized as woman
only by the clothes she wears and the way her hair is dressed
makes it actually unworldly. As a world of play and of art, it is
utterly self-contained, self-justified. Absurd as it may be from
the standpoint of the heroic and of the everyday world, it is yet
an idyllic world whose very purity gives it a unique value. Thus
Mr Tate's characterization of it as pastoral. Even as Pope con-
descends to its creatures, may he not envy them? May he not be
suggesting his admiration of a world in which dress is more
significant than tyranny, maidenly attitudes more significant
than victories and defeats of princes – and more to the point, the
flawing of a china jar more significant than the violation of a
virgin? How precious and delicate a world, if utterly thin, irresponsible, and unreal! Or should I not say precious and delicate
because utterly thin, irresponsible, and unreal? The price of
substance, responsibility, and reality – of conscientious social
significance – Pope knew only too well, as we do. He computed
it for us in the bitterness of his satire elsewhere, and especially
in *The Dunciad*. It is as if, seeing as Henry James later did that
'life persistently blunders and deviates, loses herself in the sand',
like James the artist Pope wanted to preserve 'his grain of gold'.
And part of him wanted, as a devotee of art for art's sake, or of
the world for art's sake, to salvage the world of fashion as that
grain of gold.

II

We must ask, then, whether the epic tone and machinery are so
easily and so uniformly seen as incongruous as our normal
understanding of the mock-heroic would have us believe. Belinda, seen repeatedly as rival to the sun, is treated throughout
as a goddess. Now of course this is absurd, as it is meant to be.
But is it only absurd? Is it not really, as we have seen, that it is
the image of Belinda that appears as the goddess, a kind of sun-
goddess? And to the extent that we see her as the world of fashion

does – as disembodied and thus not of the dull world of substance and consequence – is she perhaps not in some sense a goddess after all even while she remains the shallow fool of social convention? We have seen already that in a strange sense the terms in which Milton's airy beings do battle are not totally inapplicable here. When early in the poem our humorist asks, 'In tasks so bold, can little men engage?' he may be playing a more complex game than that of mere mockery.

Belinda, of course, is warrior-goddess, too. From the time her 'awful beauty puts on all its arms', we know that the war between the sexes – limited by the rules of the drawing-room rather than of the Geneva convention – is on. All is directed to the final superhuman battle at the end. We learn that her locks of hair are 'nourish'd' and nourished 'to the destruction of mankind'; and we are warned by the general claim:

> Fair tresses man's imperial race ensnare
> And beauty draws us with a single hair.

We begin to suspect that Belinda, Amazon as well as nymph, may be the aggressor as well as the assaulted in the war of love. For after all, the realistic, common-sense view that Pope forces before us, too (and that Clarissa later so painfully represents) makes us recognize that behind the masque of the drawing-room lurk the biological and domestic facts of life. The war is finally but a game that disguises the uninspiring realities of the social and sexual mating urge. Since the war is only symbolic and as innocent as mere war-games, no wonder no one is harmed. In Canto v, when the issue is joined, we see death being scattered around by the eyes of various nymphs with wits dying in metaphor and in song and reviving as the lady's frowns change to smiles. Allusions to the sexual act abound in secondary meanings even as on the surface, in the living deaths and the burnings in the flames of love, the stale love-song clichés – dull remnants of a long-outworn Petrarchan convention – continue the melodramatic pretense on a heroic scale. The players must take the game seriously, play it as war – though happily a war without war's consequences – in order to preserve that artful and idyllic

purity of their innocent make-believe. Yet, of course, this final
battle is not the only one in the poem. To pile absurdity upon
absurdity, Pope prepares us for the war-game at the close with
the 'combat on the velvet plain' – the game of Ombre, that
earlier military maneuver disguising sexual reality, in which
Belinda barely escaped 'the jaws of ruin, and Codille'. The card
game is a symbolic prophecy of the final battle which, ironically,
is itself only symbolic. The earlier battle, symbol behind the
symbol, proves the game-like quality of the later: it establishes
the later one as pure nonsense, as pure as itself, as pure as games
alone are. If all this reminds us of the play-theory of art, it
reminds us also of my earlier claim that Pope loves Belinda's
world as a true aesthete.

Of course, the unaesthetic world of biological and domestic
fact lurks always beneath. Pope is not afraid for us to see it
beneath his language, since he wants us to know that he can
cherish Belinda's world only in continual awareness of its evasions
and delusions: it evades the real world by deluding itself about its
own reality. Indeed, Pope is so anxious for us to be aware of his
awareness of the real world that he forces an explicit representative of it upon us by inserting Clarissa's speech into a later edition
of the poem. But he has shown this awareness to us all along in
the sexual secondary meanings of phrase after phrase and in the
'serious' half of zeugma after zeugma. We must remember also
the suggestion that Belinda after all is the aggressor, and that at
the crucial moment, before the baron acts, Ariel is rendered
powerless by viewing:

> in spite of all her art,
> An earthly Lover lurking at her heart.

Surely this is the baron, so that Pope is suggesting that on one
level – that of flesh-and-blood reality – Belinda is, to say the
least, a willing victim, shrewd enough to know the truth of the
pronouncement later made by 'grave Clarissa': 'she who scorns
a man, must die a maid'. But Belinda also – or at least her painted
image – is dedicated to the game and will play it through at all
costs. So the show of resistance must be maintained, with the

mock-battle of love and its sexually suggestive overtones as its proper consequence.

Once Pope feels secure that he has established Belinda's world as one we can cherish, but always with a chuckle, he dares introduce materials from other and realer worlds more openly as if to prove the power of his delicate creation. Thus the biological realities are paraded in the Cave of Spleen, whose queen, be it noted, rules 'the sex to fifty from fifteen'. Or earlier Pope introduces figures of the great world – 'Britain's statesmen' and 'great Anna' – only to reduce them through zeugma to the pastoral level of his central action, the statesmen foredooming the fall 'Of Foreign Tyrants and of Nymphs at home' and Anne, in the famous line, taking tea as well as counsel. Is the great world being transformed to the petty or the petty to the great? A question appropriate to the double-edged nature of the mock-heroic. Surely it can increase the stature of normally trivial subject-matter by playing up that within it that surprises us with its hidden grandeur. There is also Pope's daring glance at the sordid everyday world in which:

> The hungry Judges soon the sentence sign,
> And wretches hang that jurymen may dine.

But this break into Belinda's world is no defect. It rather reinforces the wonderfully inconsequential pastoralism of that world. This brief, terrorizing glance at the alternative should send us clutching at the innocuous grace of the 'toyshop' where we need fear neither hunger nor execution though we may have the make-believe equivalent of each. And, as if to prove the point, Pope turns almost at once to Belinda, who like the statesman wants victory in war and more important, like the judge, wants to assign her own arbitrary sentence of execution: she will 'foredoom' in her own way.

> Belinda now, whom thirst of fame invites,
> Burns to encounter two advent'rous Knights,
> At Ombre singly to decide their doom.

Of course, it is Clarissa who furnishes the most serious intrusion upon Belinda's world by the alien world of undeluded

common-sense reality. It is she, Pope tells us in his note, who is
'to open more clearly the moral of the poem'. How inspired a
touch that earlier it was Clarissa who perversely furnished the
baron with the scissors he used to commit his assault.[2] By all
means let her be the earlier Clarissa who even then, in her anti-
pastoralism, plotted the downfall of the make-believe world of
artifice. In her speech she breaks all the rules, says all that is
unmentionable, shatters the mirror in order to replace the
painted image with the flesh-and-blood creature of fleeting charms
who marries, breeds, ages, and wears, has all sorts of dire consequences – eventually dust and the grave. Of course, she alone
speaks only the truth. And so she does open the moral, but only
to make us recognize its price. No wonder that 'no applause
ensu'd'. She is intolerable even if she is right. In Belinda's world,
the fancy cheats too well to be abandoned for its grim alternative.

Even the sylphs, Pope's magnificent addition to his heroic
machinery, are implicated, at least by negation, in the quarrel
Belinda's world has with Clarissa. We have seen that Ariel
first appears to Belinda in her dream as so attractive a youth as
to cause in her a blush of desire. And we may see him throughout
the poem as an unearthly rival to the baron, the 'earthly Lover'.
It is Ariel who speaks the magnificent couplet:

> Know further yet; whoever fair and chaste
> Rejects mankind, is by some Sylph embrac'd.

What a stroke to rhyme 'chaste' with 'embrac'd'! Surely the
latter word is to retain its fully sexual flavor here as Ariel is in
effect telling Belinda to save herself for him. And as we turn to
Pope's words in his dedicatory epistle to Arabella Fermor, his
Belinda, we note the different, the more-than-mortal sort of
embrace that sylphs are capable of. How uproariously he toyed
with the poor girl:

For they say, any Mortals may enjoy the most intimate Familiarities with these gentle Spirits, upon a Condition very easie to
all true *Adepts*, an inviolate Preservation of Chastity.

This embrace, then, is the empty equivalent of the sexual act
in that rarefied world of fashion guarded by the decorous sylphs.

Ariel is warning Belinda away from flesh and blood, from yielding to the realistic truths of life and marriage and death attested to by Clarissa. As an image, eternalized in art, dehumanized in perfection, she must remain Ariel's alone. It is he, anxious to protect his own, who keeps her safe from assault and seduction. And so, as he tells Belinda, he comes to represent 'honor', the word used by us 'men below' to characterize the maidenly purity the sylph has ensured. No wonder, then, that he is so solicitous and that, once he spies:

> An earthly Lover lurking at her heart.
> Amaz'd confus'd, he found his pow'r expir'd,
> Resign'd to fate, and with a sigh retir'd.

He must, with Belinda, yield the field to the baron. But she yields only the metonymic symbol rather than the thing itself; and she yields only momentarily, since she returns to Ariel's world of honor by calling for war. The sylphs, then, 'wondrous fond of place', with their innumerable ranks reflecting all the levels of cosmic and human order, are the ideal superhuman attendants of the empty and yet perfect world of fashionable decorum. And they are as ineffectual, their airiness being an extension of the airiness of that disembodied world whose integrity they claim to protect.

As his *Homer* shows Pope to have viewed it, in the old and revered heroic tradition the world of serious significance and consequence and the world of high play and the grand manner were one. Actuality was somehow hospitable to decorum. But in the dwarfed mock-heroic world Pope sees about him, actuality, in becoming sordid, rejects all style: its insolent insistence allows decorum to make only a comic appearance as its pale reflection. Instead of the all-accomplishing homeric heroes, Pope must accept either the jurymen and wretches or the wigs and sword-knots, either Clarissa's breeder or Ariel's nymph of the 'purer blush'.

All this must return us to my earlier insistence that in so far as Pope values Belinda's world, which from the standpoint of reality he must satirize, he values it for an aesthetic purity that frees it from ugliness even as it leaves it utterly insignificant. It is, as I have said, a world created for art's sake, one in which the zeugma can finally create a miraculous inversion, so that the 'frail China jar' becomes more precious than virginity – in effect comes to be not merely a symbol for virginity, but even an artificial substitute for it in this world of artifice.

III

But is there not, in Pope's day, a larger and more important, if equally unreal world, created for art's sake: the world of Epistle I of *An Essay on Man*? (I call a halt after Epistle I, since Pope opens Epistle II with those brilliant and tragic lines on man's middle nature.) Here, the aesthetic perfection of the universe is set forth and adored. In the conclusion to the epistle, we are warned in our blindness not to claim any imperfection in the infallible order that enfolds all. And in these famous lines occur the parallel oppositions that are to fade as we recognize the full and true cosmos:

> All Nature is but Art, unknown to thee;
> All Chance, Direction which thou canst not see;
> All Discord, Harmony not understood;
> All partial Evil, universal Good.

Is not such a universe decorum itself, decorum erected into a cosmic principle, all the spheres and the links in the chain of being taking and keeping their places with a propriety resembling that of the sylphs, and of the drawing-room? And the seeming disturbances within it are seeming only: the discord that is a false front for harmony reminds us of the battles in *The Rape of the Lock* that are only decorous and conventional mock-battles, war-games that secure rather than threaten the world of fashion. The dangerous casualty of flesh and blood gives way to the controlled inevitability of art.

In *An Essay on Man* we are given a kind of *ersatz* and de-capitated replica of the unified, catholic, psychologically and aesthetically soothing thirteenth-century universe. It is a replica

that represents a last, desperate, brilliant postulation in the face
of the devastations of the Renaissance and of modern science
that left the medieval world (or dream-world) a shambles. It
even rationalizes the static generalizations of early modern science
by analogizing them and coming up with the 'Newtonian world-
machine'. It thus represents also a supreme act of human will,
the will to order – and to sanity. It is, finally then, an aesthetic
construct only. Hence Pope's insistence in these final lines of
Epistle I that we leave this delicately created china jar unflawed.
(One can, of course, see the same forces, the same insistence on
order at all costs, reflected in Pope's indiscriminate reduction of
the troublesome dimensions of his world to the uniformity of
his perfected version of the heroic couplet.) As the Humes and
Kants convincingly reveal in shattering the false, dogmatic
security of this world, the price of the construct is a metaphysical
flimsiness – a naïveté, the reverse side of its symmetrical delicacy – that made it easy prey to the rigors of critical philosophy
and the ravages of social-economic revolution.

Is it not, however, rather smug of us to assume that minds
as sensitive and probing as Pope's could believe in their dream-
world so utterly and simply? That they could rest so secure in an
unquestioning acceptance of this architecturally perfect model-
universe? Perhaps at some level of their consciousness they were
alive to the ultimate futility of their desperate postulation. Nevertheless, postulate they had to in western man's final attempt to
resist universal disintegration. But in this last assertion of cosmic
solidarity there may have been the insecurity that was aware of
its vulnerability and of the surrounding hordes of modernism
already closing in. I am here suggesting, of course, that *The Rape
of the Lock* is Pope's testament of the aesthetic universe, one that
reveals a nostalgic yearning for it along with a critical acknow-
ledgment of its impracticability; and that *The Dunciad* is his
bleak acceptance of the chaotic forces he most feared.

One can account in a general way for the enlightenment's
ethic and metaphysic as well as for its aesthetic by treating as
synonyms for what is to be avoided all the first terms in the two
couplets I have quoted from *An Essay on Man*, and as synonyms

for what is to be sought all the second terms. Thus nature, chance, discord, yielding partial evil; and art, direction, harmony, yielding universal good. And it is clear why the unchanging permanence of art must be preferred to the dynamic casualty of history, the china jar to unpredictable flesh and blood. But the spirit of Clarissa has been abroad and it leads away from art to the realities of history. It is ultimately to the last book of *The Dunciad* that she points, to Pope's prophecy of the chaos that modern historical reality brings. Perhaps we can re-interpret a couplet from this last book for our own purposes:

> But sober History restrain'd her rage,
> And promis'd Vengeance on a barb'rous age.

Here in the victory of Dullness is her vengeance, what she has saved for us in the world of jurymen and wretches.

It is clear that *The Dunciad* extends in its satirical range far beyond the literary world to the ethical and metaphysical. It is clear also that to the mock-epic quality of the poem is joined a more serious, a not much less than epic – almost Dantesque – quality. There is nothing slight about the Empire of Dullness. The significance of its action is hardly beneath heroic treatment. For these creatures literally absorb all the world. Unlike the action of *The Rape of the Lock* their action has consequences indeed, woeful ones. Their action is heroic in scope; it is repulsive and base on the very grandest scale. While it reverses all heroic values, it does so in heroic terms.

> Then rose the Seed of Chaos, and of Night,
> To blot out Order, and extinguish Light.

The delicate world for art's sake is overcome by ponderous dullness, by what James termed 'clumsy Life again at her stupid work'. Throughout the last book of *The Dunciad* it is the discord of partiality that acts the role of destroyer: 'Joy to great Chaos! let Division reign.' We find the dunces, like their Laputan cousins in Swift, divorcing words from things and thought, cherishing minute parts for their own sakes, refusing to relate them to any whole. Division indeed, and subdivision. And what is chaos for Pope but the multiplication of parts run wild? Discord is no longer resolvable into harmony, or partial evil into universal good. Pope is looking forward to the destruction of totality, to the destruction of the long vogue of naïve philosophical Realism, by critical philosophy – and ever more critical philosophy even down to our contemporary Oxford school. The increasing attractions of partiality to man's microscopic tendencies and the dogged dedication to immediate truth replace the dream-world with a piecemeal chaos.

In *The Dunciad* Pope sees this infinitely divided world, the modern world, as the one finally suited to man, imperfect and partial as he prefers to be. Pope sees the wholeness and sameness and sanity of the art-world as beyond man, now with the placid classic vision no longer his. Man will prefer to be Clarissa, who would destroy an aesthetically satisfying world for the dull truths of homely reality and utilitarian candor. Perhaps Pope comes to feel that he has hoped for too much from man: the capacity for a wilful naïveté that will leave undisturbed the golden world, well wrought like the china jar. Perhaps this is part of what Pope had in mind in dedicating *The Dunciad* to Swift, who, in a famous letter in 1725, had chided Pope and Bolingbroke for a rationalistic optimism that rated man too high and that could result only in an unreasoning hatred of man for falling short. Swift was ready from the start to settle for less, to acknowledge the sordid, to avoid fabricating a purified, pastoral, anti-Clarissa world, as a comparison of the dressing-rooms of his poetic heroines with that of Belinda will readily testify. Perhaps Pope's dedication was his way of acknowledging that Swift was right and that the poem which was to follow is a testament of hatred to those who have proved him wrong, even as he had always feared himself to be. For the usual picture of Pope as pure rationalist must be balanced by that of the subterranean Pope who is the pure and frightened skeptic. By the time of *The Dunciad*, Book the Fourth, Pope may know the dream is shortly to be smashed for ever. But his was not a dogmatic slumber, or a slumber at all. It was an artful delusion – of himself and of us – by a mind too aesthetically fine to accept the universe as less than a work of art.

He would have the china jar, no matter how frail, although the prophet within forced from him at last the poem that acknowledged its destruction by the rude hands swinging out from the motley mob that clutters *The Dunciad*.

IV

My fullest measure of Pope's utterance, then, would find a voice given to the felt subterranean pressures that moved his age despite his and its overt assurances: pressures generated by the tensions between rationalism and empiricism, between classicism and modernism, between confidence in a mechanism that roots the hospitable universe and anxiety about the unknown alien something or nothing that may finally lurk underneath everything out there. As a poet, through the plasticity of his brilliantly controlled and maneuvered language, Pope reached into the unvoiced capacities for praise and wonder and laughter and lament in his world and surmounted the ideological commonplaces of his time to voice all at once; even, of course, while never yielding his finally classical hold on the things of life, those precious if dainty things that in their arbitrary and nonsensical way order life and preserve sanity – and civilization. For these are the things that shape a culture even as they create its vulnerability, the transience that is built into it as one of its most charming features.

In doing all this, Pope was also proving the role and the power of poetry. He was demonstrating the special privilege of poetry to move beyond those facile propositions – drawn from a few 'spokesmen' in prose and from the most obvious voice extorted from its poets – that supposedly characterize the inner 'spirit of an age'; the privilege of poetry to reveal the more-than-propositional (and less-than-propositional) existential shape, the true inwardness, of that inner spirit. That which makes it of man's spirit rather than of a textbook's logic. Thus to the extent that Pope, through his maneuvers of language, becomes involved, at whatever level of consciousness, in any of the complexities of attitude and value, of hopes and frightening realizations, that I have been claiming to find – and I might call also upon the testimony of his friend Swift to support me – I would want to claim that it is in such as these that the full history of ideas in Pope and in the eighteenth century must be found; that any intellectual history which ignores these dimensions in the interest of lesser men's 'documents' (and Pope himself was frequently a lesser man, as is any poet in his less than most creative moments) has sacrificed adequacy to discursive convenience. It is incomplete, inhumanized, forcing the true 'spirit of the age' into an historian's *a priori* (or at least unexistential, pre-poetic) categories. For the ideas of an age may stem out of the more-than-ideological fullness of the poet rather than make their way into his work as a commonplace element that reduces it to themselves. And, so long as this remains a conceivable hypothesis, the historian of ideas had better worry about whether ideas – the ideas that finally come to found intellectual institutions – may not prior to their formulation as ideas be born, in an existential non-ideological form, in the fullness and the tensions of a poet's work rather than come to die there after a long, dull, existentially unchallenged institutional life of their own.

'Tott'ring . . . without a wind' by virtue of its very delicacy, Pope's aesthetic construct of a universe is unable to withstand the merest touch of the hand of reality. It now lies in the 'glitt'ring dust and painted fragments' of 'rich China vessels fall'n from high'. But it did not *only* crash, though *The Dunciad* chronicles that it did. Thanks to Pope, we can cherish with him the very fragility that assured its perfection even as it guaranteed its destruction. For, like Belinda's lock, even as it ceased being a force down here, the muse 'saw it upward rise'. We have perhaps been too taken with the brilliance of Pope's satire and mock-heroics to sense fully the almost single-minded tribute to the lock and thus to Belinda's world contained in the moving final lines in which Pope enshrines the lock eternally in his heavens. It is, after all, one of the stars the Empire of Dullness threatens with extinction at the apocalyptic close of *The Dunciad*. So Pope's universe, seemingly destroyed, does with Belinda's lock 'upward rise',

> Though mark'd by none but quick, poetic eyes:
> (So Rome's great founder to the heav'ns withdrew,
> To Proculus alone confess'd in view)
> A sudden Star, it shot through liquid air,
> And drew behind a radiant trail of hair.
> Not Berenice's locks first rose so bright,
> The heav'ns bespangling with dishevel'd light.
> The Sylphs behold it kindling as it flies,
> And pleas'd pursue its progress through the skies.
> This the Beau monde shall from the Mall survey,
> And hail with music its propitious ray. . . .
> Then cease, bright Nymph! to mourn thy ravish'd hair,
> Which adds new glory to the shining sphere!
> Not all the tresses that fair head can boast,
> Shall draw such envy as the Lock you lost.
> For, after all the murders of your eye,
> When, after millions slain, yourself shall die;
> When those fair suns shall set, as set they must,
> And all those tresses shall be laid in dust,
> This Lock, the Muse shall consecrate to fame,
> And midst the stars inscribe Belinda's name.

As in *The Dunciad*, Pope acknowledges the death of the art-world he has already immortalized in *The Rape of the Lock*, so here he finally can afford to acknowledge Clarissa's truth about the death of the physical Belinda, but only because he is granting a resurrection to that metonymic lock which has been appropriately hailed by the 'Beau monde' that it symbolizes.

> For, after all the murders of your eye,
> When, after millions slain, yourself shall die;
> When those fair suns shall set, as set they must,
> And all those tresses shall be laid in dust,
> This Lock, the Muse shall consecrate to fame,
> And midst the stars inscribe Belinda's name.

The poem, too, is inscribed there! And with it that illusory universe, like the 'Beau monde' constructed as a work of art, whose very artificiality testifies to the persistence, the indomitable humanity of its creator's classic vision – and to his awareness that the insubstantial nature of this universe could allow it to transcend all that chaos ground into 'glitt'ring dust'. Powerless against chaos – that disintegrating force of historical reality whose 'uncreating word' extinguished 'Art after Art' – the frail universe could win immortality with the very evanescent quality that doomed it: for 'quick, poetic eyes' it glows, gem-like, a sphere beyond the reach of the 'universal Darkness' that buried all.

NOTES

1. I am using the term 'zeugma' in a broader sense than its strict grammatical meaning would permit. For example, in the two couplets I quote in what follows, only the line: 'Or stain her honour, or her new brocade' is an actual instance of it. Obviously it is only a triangular affair, so that the two objects must be yoked by the single, double-visioned verb. In this sense, the other lines are merely antitheses of four distinct parts, with each object controlled by its own verb. My point is, however, that in a rhetorical if not a grammatical sense, there is a similar yoking of two disparate worlds in all these instances. In rare cases this yoking is reflected in the short-circuited perfection of the grammatical device; the other cases are effective, but less complete, and thus less brilliant examples yielding the same rhetorical effect.

2. Although Pope in this note speaks of her as a new character, he must mean, as Mr Tillotson supposes, that she is new as a speaking character.

Aubrey Williams

THE 'FALL' OF CHINA (1962)

IN his *Lectures on the English Poets*, near the beginning of his discussion of *The Rape of the Lock*, William Hazlitt cites a passage from Shakespeare's *Troilus and Cressida*, opposes it to the kind of poetry written by Pope, and remarks that, for the Shakespearean 'earthquakes and tempests', Pope typically gives us the 'breaking of a flower-pot or the fall of a china jar'.[1] Hazlitt's observation is, in its own way, remarkably just – and apt, for Pope does deal, on occasion, in an extravagant amount of crockery in his poems. Yet if we are to compare great things with small, it may be only fair to note that Pope is now and again capable of raising his own kind of tempests, even in his teapots.

In *The Rape of the Lock* a most important pattern of imagery is established by pervasive reference to a wide variety of vessels: vases, bottles, pipkins, pots and China jars are signal and memorable articles of the poem's furniture. There is the array of jars on Belinda's dressing-table, the display of cups and silver pots on the sumptuous buffet, the collection of containers in the lunar limbo, where

> Heroes' Wits are kept in pondrous Vases,
> And Beaus' in *Snuff-boxes* and *Tweezer-Cases*.

In the recesses of Belinda's own psyche, where they exist in almost perfect pre-Freudian propriety, Pope reveals to us those 'Unnumber'd Throngs' of 'Bodies chang'd to various Forms by *Spleen*':

> Here living *Teapots* stand, one Arm held out,
> One bent; the Handle this, and that the Spout:
> A Pipkin there like *Homer's Tripod* walks;
> Here sighs a Jar, and there a Goose-pye talks;

> Men prove with Child, as pow'rful Fancy works,
> And Maids turn'd Bottels, call aloud for Corks.[2]

So much crockery in the poem can scarcely be ignored, and neither should the variety of special effects Pope obtains by its use. More particularly, awareness of the range of this vessel imagery serves to underscore its peculiar importance on three occasions when it relates most directly to the poem's central event. These three occasions, often remarked by critics, are, first, in Canto II, where, in a mood of gloomy anticipation, the sylph Ariel wonders

> Whether the Nymph shall break *Diana*'s Law,
> Or some frail *China* Jar receive a Flaw;

second, in Canto III, where, after the lock has been cut, these lines occur:

> Not louder Shrieks to pitying Heav'n are cast,
> When Husbands or when Lap-dogs breathe their last,
> Or when rich *China* Vessels, fal'n from high,
> In glittring Dust and painted Fragments lie;

and, finally, in Canto IV, where Belinda recalls the morning omens:

> Thrice from my trembling hand the *Patch-box* fell;
> The tott'ring *China* shook without a Wind. . . .

Mr Cleanth Brooks apparently first singled out these three special instances of the poem's vessel imagery, and he observed that at least one of them made a comment on chastity: 'Pope does not say, but he suggests, that chastity is, like the fine porcelain, something brittle, precious, useless, and easily broken.' Shrewd as the observation is, there yet seems to be occasion for amplification of Mr Brooks' insight. For Pope's vessel imagery has a particularly rich background, and the association of 'lasses and glasses' in his poem evidently had precise and subtle significances which must have been widely appreciated in the poet's own time.

I

For a number of years in the early seventeenth century the young
James Howell travelled on the continent as agent for a London
glass factory. In his *Epistolae Ho-Elianae* (1645–55), one of his
letters, written from Venice on 1 June 1621, contains this passage:

When I saw so many sorts of curious glasses made here I
thought upon the compliment which a gentleman put upon a
lady in England, who having five or six comely daughters, said
he never saw in his life such a dainty cupboard of crystal glasses;
the compliment proceeds, it seems, from a saying they have here,
'That the first handsome woman that ever was made, was made
of Venice glass,' (which implies beauty, but brittleness withal. ...

Howell's letter reveals a traditional use of 'glass' imagery to
suggest the lamentable fragility of feminine beauty. He may or
may not be correct in assigning the origin of his particular saying
to Venice, but certainly the general terms of the comparison
itself were part of the poetic and proverbial life of England much
before his time. In *The Passionate Pilgrim* (1599), poem VII,
Shakespeare (if indeed he is the author) has these lines:

Fair is my love, but not so fair as fickle;
Mild as a dove, but neither true nor trusty;
Brighter than glass, and yet as glass is brittle . . .

and George Herbert, in his collection of *Outlandish Proverbs*
(1640), includes this saying (no. 244): 'A woman and a glasse
are ever in danger.' In such passages the implications of 'brittleness' are uncomplimentary ones of weakness and inconstancy. As
John Hall uses the image in his *Paradoxes* (1650), however, the
very fragility of porcelain and feminine beauty serves only to
heighten their value:

And are not I pray you the best things ever in the greatest
danger, *Purselain* and *Venice* Glasses are the most apt to be
broke, the richest flowers are the soonest *pulled*, the goodliest
Stag, wil be soonest *shot*, the best Faces doe the soonest decay. ...

(p. 97)

To the examples given so far there must now be added a special usage in which the implications already noted are usually preserved, and have added to them a specific intensification. In this new usage the breaking or cracking of a glass (sometimes the 'glass' is a mirror, sometimes a goblet) or piece of China becomes specifically symbolic of a loss of virginity or chastity. In Shakespeare's *Pericles*, IV vi 150–2, the bawd (speaking of Marina) says to her man-servant:

Boult, take her away; use her at thy pleasure. Crack the glass of her virginity, and make the rest malleable.[3]

This emphasis of the image also points up clearly the ambiguities residing within Herrick's little poem, 'The broken Christall':

> To Fetch me Wine my *Lucia* went
> Bearing a Christall *continent*:
> And making haste, it came to passe,
> She brake in two the purer Glasse,
> Then smil'd, and sweetly chid her speed;
> So with a blush, beshrew'd the deed.

In his 'Elegie on the Lady Marckham' (41–4) Donne provides a variation on this same theme by his exploitation of the superstition that a glass of purest crystal would not admit poison without cracking:

> Of what small spots pure white complains! Alas,
>   How little poyson cracks a christall glasse!
> She sinn'd, but just enough to let us see
>   That God's word must be true, All, sinners be.

The exact nature of Lady Marckham's small spots of sin, the 'little poyson' in her character, is not entirely clear from Donne's poem. He seems to be referring to some small and inescapable sexual taint[4] (perhaps the Hebrew/Miltonic idea of 'child-bed taint') she must have experienced as a wife and mother. In any event the notion that the utmost purity of glass is flawed by the slightest poison seems to relate clearly to the idea that a loss of chastity can be vividly, and poignantly, expressed by a flaw in a very fine piece of China.

As one might expect, in much of this vessel imagery there is an emphasis on the irreparable nature of any damage done to fine glass or China, and an attendant emphasis on the irreparable nature of a loss of beauty, good name, or virginity. Ovid (*Heroides*, v 103–4) had said, 'By no art may purity once wounded, be made whole; 'tis lost, lost once and for all';[5] and *The Passionate Pilgrim* again, poem xiii, has these lines:

> As broken glass no cement can redress:
> So beauty blemish'd once, for ever lost,
> In spite of physic, painting, pain, and cost.[6]

The passages so far cited help to establish the sense of a line of imagery, mainly in terms of glass mirrors and fine crystal, susceptible of application to feminine beauty and frailty in a variety of ways. Perhaps it was a heightened and growing passion for fine China among women themselves[7] that led writers, in the course of the seventeenth century, to a substitution of China vases for crystal glasses in their imagery. At any rate, citation of a few more passages nearly contemporary with *The Rape of the Lock* may suggest not only that to readers of Pope's time such imagery was of traditional and commonplace import; it may also render more explicit to a modern reader exactly what some of these received implications were.

Near the end of Act i of John Crowne's *Sir Courtly Nice* (1685) there occurs this couplet:

> Women like Cheney shou'd be kept with care,
> One flaw debases her [*sic*] to common ware.

A few years later there occurs this passage in Steele's *The Funeral: or Grief A-La-Mode* (1701), ii iii:

> *Lady Harriot.* The fellow is not to be abhorred, if the forward thing did not think of getting me so easily. Oh! I hate a heart I can't break when I please. What makes the value of dear china, but that 'tis so brittle? Were it not for that, you might as well have stone mugs in your closet.[8]

And during the 1730s this song by Fielding was heard scores of times on the London stage:

> A Woman's Ware like *China*,
>   Now dear, now cheap is bought;
> When whole 'tis worth a Guinea,
>   When broke not worth a Groat.[9]

Perhaps the work most clearly revelatory of some of the nuances to be found in this imagery of China vessels, however, is John Gay's poem, 'To a Lady on her Passion for Old China' (1725). The whole poem provides valuable comment on our theme, and seems peculiarly relevant to *The Rape of the Lock*. These lines are perhaps the most revealing:

> When I some antique Jar behold,
> Or white, or blue, or speck'd with gold,
> Vessels so pure, and so refin'd
> Appear the types of woman-kind:
> Are they not valu'd for their beauty,
> Too fair, too fine for household duty?
> With flowers and gold and azure dy'd,
> Of ev'ry house the grace and pride?
> How white, how polish'd is their skin,
> And valu'd most when only seen!
> She who before was highest priz'd,
> Is for a crack or flaw despis'd;
> I grant they're frail, yet they're so rare,
> The treasure cannot cost too dear!

The poem then concludes with this injunction:

> Love, *Laura*, love, while youth is warm,
> For each new winter breaks a charm;
> And woman's not like *China* sold,
> But cheaper grows in growing old;
> Then quickly chuse the prudent part,
> Or else you break a faithful heart.

Such imagery continued in use throughout the eighteenth century, and survived even into later times.[10] Thus Fanny Burney's *Evelina*, Letter VIII of volume II, contains this passage: 'Remember, my dear Evelina, nothing is so delicate as the reputation of a woman: it is, at once, the most beautiful and most brittle of all things.' The sad fate of Phoebe Dawson, seduced and abandoned by her lover, is pathetically symbolized, in part two of Crabbe's *The Parish Register*, by the 'broken pitcher' she takes to the pool for water. And even Keats' Grecian urn, that 'still unravish'd bride', may be in the same symbolic tradition, though of course it is a symbol of virginity still intact.

The ultimate sources for all this vessel imagery seem undiscoverable: Freud, indeed, sees all imagery of containers to be feminine, and thus attributes archetypal status to it. Yet some possible ancient sources should be noted, principally the general biblical tendency to use vessels as an image of man,[11] and, more particularly, the passage in 1 Peter iii 7, which enjoins husbands to give 'honour unto the wife, as unto the weaker vessel'. The stress of the injunction should be observed: woman is accorded honor *because* she is the weaker vessel, and so the passage suggests that the very fragility of the vessel, as of feminine beauty and character in general, is somehow the source of the value and honor accorded it. And alongside such biblical usage, there is the pagan classical tendency to see women as vessels. Thus Dryden translates Lucretius, III 1008 ff:

> This is the fable's moral, which they tell
> Of fifty foolish virgins damn'd in hell
> To leaky vessels, which the liquor spill;
> To vessels of their sex, which none could ever fill.

But regardless of the ultimate sources for such' imagery, we can now return to one of the crucial instances of its use in *The Rape of the Lock*, these lines,

> Whether the Nymph shall break *Diana*'s Law,
> Or some frail *China* Jar receive a Flaw,

and perhaps more easily describe some of its implications. The first line of the couplet is relatively direct in its implications, and the harshness of 'break' is admirably set off against the more subdued 'receive' in the second line.[12] This second line, on the other hand, seems almost inexhaustible in its range of suggestions. First of all, there is the suggestion, here as in much of the poem's vessel imagery, that Pope is exploiting the biblical image of woman as the weaker vessel, and that he is in some sense doing homage to this vessel: though Pope's view of her is laced with irony, Belinda's beauteous virginity is somehow rendered more precious, and our regard for it somehow more tender, by recognition of how easily it can be marred or shattered. At the same time, Pope's 'frail' and brittle China jar humorously recalls the general view of women exemplified by Hamlet's exclamation, 'Frailty, thy name is woman', or by George Herbert's saying that 'A woman and a glasse are ever in danger'. There is the hint of mortality inherent in all the imagery which likens women to something so frangible as fine glass or China: existing in a state of tremulous instability and inconstancy, the vessels seem to lean of themselves towards disaster. Made of the dust and clay of the earth, they seem destined for a shocking reversion to 'glitt'ring Dust and painted Fragments'. Too, there are also all those inherent, as well as inherited, suggestions of loss – loss of perfection, beauty and virginity – so wittily engaged by the course of the poem and its central event. All three of the poem's crucial images of the 'fall' of China, indeed, gather to themselves, and impart to the meaning of the poem at large, all of these suggestions, along with one more. This is the suggestion, made with varying degrees of emphasis by the three images, of the utter finality of the loss involved in the breaking of fine China, or of the frail bond of chastity.

II

Criticism of *The Rape of the Lock* in recent years has moved far from the nineteenth- and early twentieth-century tendencies to approach the poem as a marvelous, but ultimately inconsequential, bit of filigree. The critical mood of our day will not suffer the poem to be 'admirable in proportion as it is made of nothing',[13] nor can it now be said that the poem has 'no substance at all', that it is 'nothing but grace; the astral body of an heroic poem, pure form, an echo of divine music . . . thin and clear!'[14] But in contrast to the mode of critical address represented by such declarations as these, yet another effort to describe the more melancholy

undercurrents of Pope's wit and humor in *The Rape of the Lock*
may well seem to wear a lamentable air of too high seriousness.
Still, there seems to be as much danger in taking the poem too
lightly as there is in taking it too seriously: the poem seems able
to tease us into thought, as well as out of it.

Recent discussions of *The Rape of the Lock* have been very
successful in focusing attention on some of the more ritualistic
aspects of the 'war of the sexes' in the poem. Even so, some of
the emphases in these discussions seem to require adjustment.
Mr Brooks, for example, seems to insist too much that the 'issues
in Pope's poem are matters of taste' and that 'matters of morality
. . . are never raised'. In effect, he does not seem to face directly
enough the ultimate implications of the imagery he explores so
well: Belinda, after all, does undergo a kind of 'fall' in the poem;
her 'perfection' is shattered, and she does lose her 'chastity', in
so far as chastity can be understood, however teasingly, as a
condition of the spirit. Mrs Rebecca Price Parkin mainly follows
Mr Brooks, but in addition she regards Clarissa's speech as
largely hypocritical, and as essentially irrelevant to Belinda's
situation.[15] And Mr Hugo Reichard, who establishes a number
of valuable contexts for events in the poem,[16] may encase Belinda
too rigidly in an iron maidenliness of 'coquetry', with the result
that she, and the experience she undergoes, seem deprived of
general significance.

Belinda's central experience can be approached by a wide
variety of ways, but there are two ways especially prepared for
by the foregoing discussion of the poem's vessel imagery. These
are provided, first, by the parallels to *Paradise Lost*, and second,
by the parody of Sarpedon's speech in the *Iliad*. The ethical
discriminations insinuated by these two realms of reference are
intimately related to, and strengthened by, the implications of the
vessel imagery. Both realms of reference insist that Belinda
undergoes one or another fall from 'perfection', and to these
other 'falls' in the poem there are added the special heightenings
furnished by Pope's imagery of the 'fall' of China.

The parallels to *Paradise Lost* in *The Rape of the Lock* are
numerous, and not all of them seem to have been remarked in

print. But the main direction and force of the Miltonic references can be illustrated by the sequence of three major parallels alone. First, there is the dream of pride and vain-glory insinuated into Belinda's ear, which recalls the dream insinuated into Eve's ear in books v and vi of *Paradise Lost*. Second, there is the parody of the Mass at Belinda's dressing-table, where Belinda worships herself and which vividly recalls, as Mr Reichard has noted, the new-born Eve's admiration of herself as mirrored in the pool of Eden (*PL*, iv 460 ff). But perhaps the crucial parallel is the third, which occurs just before the cutting of the lock, when Ariel searches out the 'close Recesses of the Virgin's Thought'. There he finds an 'Earthly Lover lurking at her Heart', and Pope writes:

> Amaz'd, confus'd, he found his Pow'r expir'd,
> Resign'd to Fate, and with a Sigh retir'd.

The situation seems to echo clearly, as Mr Reichard again has noted, the moment in *Paradise Lost* when, after the fall of Adam and Eve, the angelic hosts retire, 'mute and sad', to Heaven. The angels could have protected Adam and Eve from any force attempted by Satan, but against man's own free choice of evil they are as helpless as Ariel and his cohorts are in the presence of Belinda's free choice of an earthly lover.

The course of the Miltonic parallels makes it clear that Belinda undergoes a 'fall', at least in the eyes of Ariel. Yet this fall is only a fall from the narcissistic self-love and arid virginity which the sylphs, in one of their aspects, both represent and seek to pre-serve (this accounts for Pope's ability to merge, in his parody, the actions of both Satan and the good angels), and so in one sense it is merely a fall into a more natural human condition and one best regarded, perhaps, as a kind of 'fortunate fall'. Belinda simply falls in love, and thus a situation is created whereby she can escape from the meaningless virginity and honor represented, on the poem's most serious level, by the sylphs. Here Pope further intensifies the issues (and the element of free choice) by his hints, delicate though they be, that Belinda actually acquiesces, how-ever faintly, in the 'rape'. The sylphs warn her of the Baron's approach by blowing back her hair and by thrice twitching 'the

Diamond in her Ear'. Thrice she looks back to the Baron, and it
is noticeable that only after the warnings have been ignored does
Ariel search her heart. What he finds there (and the poem gives
us no reason to suspect that the 'Earthly Lover' is anyone but
the Baron) suggests that Belinda is in some sense aware of the
Baron's attempt on her, and that she does not turn from it.

Even so, Belinda's response to the rape is, from the viewpoint
of her society (and perhaps of any society), perfectly natural: as
critics have not tired of noting, the Baron's act is a rude violation
of the rules of courtship. Too, Belinda does well to remember
that, in John Gay's words, 'She who before was highest priz'd, /
Is for a crack or flaw despis'd'. Yet the main point to be stressed
is the fact that, after the rape and her immediate response to it
(her tantrum), Belinda is faced now with the necessity of making
a much more serious and deliberate decision: her immediate
response, whatever its justification, had been marked, as the
Cave of Spleen episode insists, by prudery, hypocrisy, and
affectation, but she may now choose a course other than that
which had placed her under the dominion of the gnome Umbriel.
To make the alternatives before her emphatically clear, Pope
presents her, and the reader, with the two points of view represented in the speeches of Thalestris and Clarissa. Thalestris,
significantly given the name of an Amazonian queen, represents
a kind of empty and vicious principle of female victory and
dominance at all costs, and she also gives perfect expression to
the prevailing moral chaos of the poem's world:

> *Honour* forbid! at whose unrival'd Shrine
> Ease, Pleasure, Virtue, All, our Sex resign.

But placed against the viewpoint of Thalestris, and her society,
is the set of values voiced by Clarissa (the clarifier) and re-
enforced by the whole weight of Sarpedon's speech in Book XII
of the *Iliad*. Pope's translation of this speech, it should be
remembered, was among the very first of his works to be published, for it appeared in 1709 in *Poetical Miscellanies: The
Sixth Part*. This early translation of Sarpedon's speech passed,
with only trivial revision, into Pope's full translation of the

Iliad. Volume III of Pope's *Iliad*, containing book XII, appeared in 1717, and in the same year Pope worked the speech of Clarissa into *The Rape of the Lock*, with the design, as he later noted, of opening 'more clearly the Moral of the Poem'.[17] Pope's own translation of the speech (exemplifying, one must suppose, his own best understanding of Sarpedon's character) provides, therefore, the best background against which to view Clarissa's words. There is no need to cite here the full text of Sarpedon's speech, but there is need perhaps to emphasize its two concluding couplets, and to stress their relevance to Belinda's situation:

> The Life which others pay, let us bestow,
> And give to Fame what we to Nature owe;
> Brave tho' we fall, and honour'd if we live,
> Or let us Glory gain, or Glory give!

Sarpedon's words are a glorious enunciation of the spirit of magnanimity (in the Preface to his *Iliad*, Pope distinguishes Sarpedon as 'gallant and generous'). The admiration his speech elicits is the direct result of the utter generosity of spirit, the supreme magnanimity of attitude, with which he faces the loss of his life.

Pope's parody of his own translation of Sarpedon's speech invokes an epic context which, from one point of view, may be said to 'trivialize' the mighty pother kept over the loss of a lock. At the same time, it must also be recognized that Clarissa's speech offers to Belinda the possibility of adopting an attitude toward her loss quite at variance with the ugliness of attitude endorsed by Thalestris. And in so far as the attitude offered by Clarissa is at variance with the surrounding moral chaos of the poem's world, this attitude is supported, even corroborated and verified, by its Homeric antecedent. Moreover, Pope makes us aware of the fundamental validity of Clarissa's attitude by the grave and sobering currents in her speech: the melancholy reminders of small-pox, housewifery and old age, while perfectly subdued to the poem's gloss of wit, yet give the whole speech a momentary air of mournful sobriety. At the very least, Clarissa's speech opens up the possibility that Belinda may choose an attitude towards her loss in some way fully analogous (however vastly different their spheres of experience and action) to the attitude adopted by Sarpedon towards his loss.

One may well shrink from explicit exposition of the analogy Pope has so discreetly and delicately imparted to his poem. Baldly and briefly, however, the terms of the analogy would seem to be something as follows: Sarpedon and Belinda enter into different kinds of 'war', and each kind of war imposes its attendant consequences. The consequence on the epic level of war between heroes is loss of life; on the level of war between the sexes it is loss of virginal innocence. Both Sarpedon and Belinda experience moments of victory, and both are called upon to face their moments of defeat and loss. The main difference between them (other than the extreme disparateness of contexts) is the difference in attitude with which loss is faced. A volunteer (like Sarpedon) in the lists, with the earlier victory over the Baron at Ombre (as well as countless other victories) under her belt, and with the 'Earthly Lover' in her heart, Belinda is called upon to acknowledge and accept her defeat on one level, and yet, by virtue of the 'good Humour' of such an acceptance, gain a different kind of victory on another level. For 'good Humour' is here the perfectly appropriate analogy to the magnanimity of spirit displayed by Sarpedon, and when Clarissa says that

> good Humour can prevail,
> When Airs, and Flights, and Screams and Scolding fail,

she means essentially that the only victory possible to Belinda is that victory which gallantry and generosity of spirit in the face of defeat or loss always gain, whatever the level of experience. Having in some sense admitted an earthly lover to her heart and already separated herself from the virginal purity symbolized by the sylphs, Belinda is asked (and here we should recall the particular emphases in the last lines of Sarpedon's speech) to be 'brave' though she 'fall', that is, to 'keep good Humour still whate'er . . . [she] . . . lose'. Only thus might she be truly 'Mistress of herself, tho' China fall'.[18]

This interpretation of the purport of Clarissa's speech is

confirmed, perhaps, by what may be another of the analogies to
Paradise Lost in the poem. Here we are again indebted to Mr
Brooks, who suggested, though with quite another emphasis,
that the advice offered to Belinda by Clarissa is analogous to
that offered to Adam and Eve by Michael after their fall: 'Michael
promises that Adam can create within his own breast "A Paradise
. . . happier farr" ', and 'Clarissa's advice to Belinda makes the
same point'.[19] Separated from her state of innocence, no longer
may Belinda enjoy familiar intimacy with her guardian sylphs,
just as Adam may no longer, after his loss, expect to enjoy the
familiar intimacy of 'God or Angel Guest': now Belinda must
rely, says Clarissa, on the support of a true and inner virtue, not
the mere face of virtue.

But Belinda, as the course of the game of Ombre had already
implied and foretold, is not a good loser, and she does not rise
to the occasion afforded by her loss here. Instead, she ratifies
the course of prudery delineated earlier in the Cave of Spleen
episode, and persists in the ways of Ill-Nature and Affectation.
This is her real fall in the poem, and in this fall the richest and
fairest of the poem's many vessels is irreparably shattered.

Given the world of Hampton Court, any attitude other than
that actually adopted by Belinda would have seemed to be a
violation of the poem's decorum. Yet it should also be recognized
that, on the level of the poem where the humor becomes a little
stern and the examination of manners edges into an examination
of morals,[20] an opportunity is given to Belinda to transcend the
limitations of a world where 'honor' and 'virtue' are equated
with 'reputation' and 'appearance'. Pope maintains the decorum
of his poem, but this should not obscure the fact that Belinda
fails to meet the test of her spirit proposed by Clarissa.

Of course, as many critics have stressed, Pope's attitude
toward Belinda is very mixed and complicated: mocking and yet
tender, admiring and yet critical. This mixed and complicated
attitude, however, is at least partly the product of Pope's concern
with a 'type' of human experience which simultaneously involves
both loss and gain, one in which loss must be suffered if the gain
is to be at all achieved. The paradoxical nature of Pope's attitude

is thus intimately related to the paradox of Belinda's situation, and to the sexual terms of that situation: if Belinda is to find her role of woman, she must lose the role of virgin, and the more graceful her acceptance of loss the greater victory she achieves through it. Because Pope is dealing with this paradox, his attitude must be mixed and complicated. He can appreciate virginal perfection, however narcissistic, and 'mourn' its loss; yet he can also give final honor to a kind of perfection achieved on another level.

The loss of perfection and the marring of beauty, imaged by the fall and shattering of rich China vessels, is seen in the poem as an inevitable part of human experience. But in recompence for her particular losses, Belinda is offered the gain of a different kind of beauty and perfection: the kind Sarpedon achieved through simple generosity of spirit in the face of his loss, the kind Adam and Eve were offered after their loss, or the kind John Donne had in mind when, in the refrain to his 'Epithalamion made at Lincolnes Inne', he wrote of another maiden who, through loss of virginity, 'To day puts on perfection, and a womans name'.

Blinded by a false sense of shame and thinking only of reputation, Belinda can scarcely be expected to transcend the values of her society, but this does not mean that the reader, whatever his anxiety not to spoil the hilarious mockery of the occasion, is to ignore the ignominy of her real defeat, or the sadnesses of the poem at large. For amidst all the glitter and gaiety and irony, amidst all the shimmering brightness and lightness and sheer fun of the poem, there are insistent reminders of the shades just beneath and beyond the pale of paint and light. It is with such a reminder, indeed, that the poem approaches its close. There, in lines which recall other rich vessels which had fallen to lie in their own glittering dust, Pope looks forward, in a final suggestion of defloration, to the time when Belinda's eyes,

> those fair Suns shall sett, as sett they must,
> And all those Tresses shall be laid in Dust.

The awareness of these sadnesses in the poem, along with an

awareness of Belinda's inability to turn defeat into victory, perhaps justifies the repetition again of another, the finest, of Hazlitt's responses to Pope's art: 'You hardly know whether to laugh or weep.'

NOTES

1. See supra, pp. 92–3.
2. Even the 'Painted Vessel' of Canto II 47 may glance at Belinda.
3. See also *The Winter's Tale*, I ii 321–2, and *Cymbeline*, v v 206–7.
4. Cf. 'An Anatomie of the World: The first Anniversary', 177–82. I owe the example in Donne to Professor Robert Bryan.
5. Loeb translation. The original reads: 'nulla reparabilis arte / laesa pudicitia est; deperit illa semel'.
6. Cf. Robert Sanderson, *Twenty Sermons* (1656) p. 21: 'I have sometimes . . . likened a flaw in the *Conscience*, and a flaw in the *good name*, to the breaking . . . of a *Chrystal glass* or *China dish* . . . no art can piece them so as they shall be either sightly or serviceable. . . .' Cf. Franklin, *Poor Richard's Almanack* (1750): 'Glass, China and Reputation, are easily crack'd and never well mended.'
7. The famous 'China scene' in Wycherley's *The Country Wife* provides eloquent testimony for this passion.
8. Cf. this earlier passage in the same play (I i): 'We run, we strive, and purchase things with our blood and money, quite foreign to our intrinsic real happiness, and which have a being in imagination only, as you may see by the pudder that is made about precedence, titles, court favour, maidenheads, and china-ware.'
9. The *Welsh Opera* (1731) Air XVII. The song also appears, with slight modifications, in *The Grub-Street Opera* (1731) Air XIX, and in *The Mock Doctor* (1732) Air VI. I owe these examples from Fielding, and the one from John Gay, to Professor Charles B. Woods.
10. The image survives into the twentieth century. See the expression 'crack a Judy's tea-cup' in Eric Partridge, *A Dictionary of Slang and Unconventional English*, 3rd ed. (1949) p. 187.
11. For a burlesque of the biblical usage, see the sermon on 'The Dignity, Use and Abuse of Glass-Bottles', in *The Prose Works of Alexander Pope*, ed. Norman Ault (Oxford, 1936) I 203 ff.
12. For other discussion of these lines, see W. K. Wimsatt, 'One Relation of Rhyme to Reason', in *The Verbal Icon* (University of Kentucky, Lexington, 1954) p. 162.
13. See supra, p. 93.

14. W. P. Ker, 'Pope', in *English Critical Essays: Twentieth Century* (World's Classics ed.: Oxford, 1947) p. 112.

15. *The Poetic Workmanship of Alexander Pope*, pp. 126–7, 171–2.

16. 'The Love Affair in Pope's *Rape of the Lock*', supra, pp. 158 ff.

17. Pope's 'Epistle to Miss Blount, With the Works of Voiture' (1712) also has relevance to Clarissa's speech.

18. See 'Of the Characters of Women', 268.

19. *The Well Wrought Urn* (New York, 1947) pp. 98–9 (a passage omitted in the version included in this volume).

20. See the discussion of the poem by Maynard Mack, supra, pp. 154 ff.

Martin Price

THE PROBLEM OF SCALE:
THE GAME OF ART (1964)

IN *The Rape of the Lock* we move from the nature-become-art of the pastoral to the heroic-turned-artful. The world of Belinda is a world of triviality measured against the epic scale; it is also a world of grace and delicacy, a second-best world, but not at all a contemptible one. Here Pope has built upon a theme that plays against the epic tradition: the mock-heroic world (in Dryden's version) of Virgil's bees is a world that has some real, if extravagant, claim to the epic style. The *Georgics* celebrate a mundane heroism and place it against the special virtues of the martial hero.

The emphasis of the epic had, moreover, moved by Pope's day – through Spenser and Milton – further and further toward spiritual conflict. In *The Rape of the Lock* the primary quality of Belinda is spiritual shallowness, an incapacity for moral awareness. She has transformed all spiritual exercises and emblems into a coquette's self-display and self-adoration. All of it is done with a frivolous heedlessness; she is not quite a hypocrite.

> Fair nymphs, and well-drest youths around her shone,
> But ev'ry eye was fix'd on her alone.
> On her white breast a sparkling cross she wore,
> Which Jews might kiss, and Infidels adore.   (II 5–8)

Our perspective closes more and more sharply, upon Belinda as cynosure, and upon the sparkling cross that fixes attention upon her beauty. The cross is a religious symbol turned to the uses of ornament, and by the rules of the little world of the poem it gains new power through this translation. At every point in the poem grace and charm supplant depth of feeling or heroic action; the only direct survivors of the old heroic virtues are the miniature playing-cards. Here Pope's play with scale becomes most fascinating. Within the heroic frame of the mock-epic language we have the miniature world of belles and beaux who live by an elaborate and formal set of rules. Within that small world is framed in turn the card game (with its further formalization of rules), where kings and queens, mortal battles and shameful seductions, still survive as a game within a game.

The principal symbol of the triviality of Belinda's world is the machinery of sylphs and gnomes. The 'light militia of the lower sky' are a travesty of both Homeric deities and Miltonic guardian angels. Like their originals, they have an ambiguous status: they exist within and without the characters. They are, in their diminutive operation, like those small but constant self-regarding gestures we may associate with a lady conscious of her charms. The sylphs who protect Belinda are also her acceptance of the rules of social convention, which presume that a coquette's life is pure game. The central action of the poem is Belinda's descent from coquette to prude, from the dazzling rival of the sun ('Belinda smil'd, and all the world was gay') to the rancorous Amazon who shrieks in self-righteous anger. It is Clarissa who vainly points to the loss. Her speech in the last canto is a parody, as Pope reminds us, of Sarpedon's speech to Glaucus in book XII of the *Iliad*. For 'the utter generosity of spirit, the supreme magnanimity of attitude' with which Sarpedon faces the loss of life, Clarissa offers to Belinda a substitute that is analogous: within the scale of the playground world of the coquette there is the selflessness of 'good humor', the ability to place value rightly and accept the conditions of life. This will permit Belinda to retain the radiance that has warmed and illumined her world.

Pope's use of scale has set up a double view of this play-world. It has the smallness of scale and fineness of organization of the work of art, yet like a game, it is temporary and threatens to break down. 'At any moment "ordinary life" may reassert its rights either by an impact from without, which interrupts the game, or by an offense against the rules, or else from within, by a collapse of the play spirit, a sobering, a disenchantment'.[1] Clarissa's speech offers a view of life as it must be when the playing has to stop. Thalestris offers the outrage of the spoilsport. 'By withdrawing from the game [the spoilsport] reveals the relativity and fragility of the play-world in which he had temporarily shut himself with others. He robs play of its *illusion* – a pregnant word which means literally "in-play" (from *inlusio, illudere,* or *inludere*)'.[2] Pope's play-world in *The Rape of the Lock* hovers between the trivial fragility of mere play (with its obliviousness to the possibilities of mature life) and the preciousness of a life ordered with grace, however minute its scale or limited its values.

In the dressing-table scene at the close of Canto I we see Belinda's beauty both as mere ornamentation governed by pride and as the realization of a genuine aesthetic ordering. The worship before the mirror of the 'cosmetic powers' produces the appearance Belinda wishes to have and which she further adorns, her maid attending 'the sacred Rites of Pride'. With that word, the world pours in, diminished in scale:

> Unnumber'd treasures ope at once, and here
> The various off'rings of the world appear. . . .
> This casket India's glowing gems unlocks,
> And all Arabia breathes from yonder box.
> The tortoise here and elephant unite,
> Transform'd to combs, the speckled and the white.

> (129–30, 133–6)

The spacious world can enter Belinda's dressing-room only in a serviceable and diminished form. Arabia is compressed into its perfume; the unwieldly elephant and tortoise are transformed into the elegance of shells and ivory combs. The universe, the Indian philosopher tells us, is a great elephant standing on the back of a tortoise. John Locke had made much of the fable in his treatment of substance (*Essay of Human Understanding,* II ch. 23, para. 2). This condensation of the vast into the small is at once reversed: the pins extend into 'shining rows' or 'files' of soldiers, and Belinda becomes the epic hero investing himself in armor as well as the godlike 'awful Beauty'. Here is the triumph of art: Belinda 'calls forth all the wonders of her face' and gives them realization with her cosmetic skill. She is the mistress of the 'bidden blush', but also the culmination of nature. Her art trembles on the precipice of mere artifice, but it retains its poise. We can say, then, that the world of Belinda is once more a pastoral world, the world of the 'town-eclogue'. But it is filled with omens: balanced against Belinda's rites of pride are the Baron's prayers at another altar; balanced against Belinda's generous smiles are the labyrinths of her hair. As she descends the Thames, the 'painted vessel' is the literal craft on which she sails and also Belinda herself – perhaps reminiscent of the 'stately Ship / of Tarsus . . . With all her bravery on, and tackle trim, / Sails filled, and streamers waving, / Courted by all the winds that hold them play' – the Dalila of Milton's *Samson Agonistes*. Belinda is at once the pastoral mistress ('Where'er you walk, cool gales shall fan the glade'), the power of harmony, and the imminent temptress and sower of discord. But her greatest power arises from the fact that she is not really aware of what she is leading the Baron to do or of what disaster may befall herself. Like Eve's, her very weakness increases her power for destruction, and the sylphs, lovely but variable, express her ambiguous selfconsciousness – the sense of disaster that is also a sense of her power to call forth violence.

With the fall of her coquette's world, as the Baron snips her lock, we descend to the realm of anarchy, the Cave of Spleen, with its surrealistic atmosphere of fantasy and compulsions. Spleen is the anti-goddess; as Dulness is opposed to Light, so here the vindictive and self-pitying passions are opposed to good humor and good sense. This is surely one of the great cave or underworld passages, and we must call to mind the caves of Error and Despair or the dwelling of Night in Spenser to see its full value. Pope's special contribution is closer to the late medieval landscapes of Hieronymus Bosch: an erotic nightmare of exploding libidinous drives. The passions repressed by prudes find neurotic expression in mincing languor or prurient reproach; they scrawl, as it were, those graffiti that are a nasty travesty of love. The Cave of Spleen is one of the strongest pictures of disorder in the age: it gives us the measure of order, a sense of the strength of the forces that social decorum controls and of the savage distortion of feeling that it prevents.

The first effect of the entrance of spleen into the upper world is Thalestris' skeptical questioning of the art Belinda has lavished upon herself:

> Was it for this you took such constant care
> The bodkin, comb, and essence to prepare?
> For this your locks in paper-durance bound,
> For this with tort'ring irons wreath'd around?
>
> (IV 97–100)

If we compare these harsh lines with the reverential rites of pride, we can see how false are the doubts cast upon the art of the dressing-table under the strain of injured pride. The creative skill that brought nature to its full realization becomes for the prude and spoilsport a torturing of nature by a strained and cruel art. And Belinda herself becomes, in turn, like Lady Wishfort and Mrs Marwood in Congreve's *The Way of the World*, or even Alceste in Molière's *The Misanthrope*, an affected and pharisaical 'primitivist':

> Oh had I rather unadmir'd remain'd
> In some lone isle, or distant northern land . . .
> There kept my charms conceal'd from mortal eye,
> Like roses, that in deserts bloom and die.
>
> (IV 153–4, 157–8)

Belinda is not unmindful of the fragrance she might have wasted, but she is professedly ready to renounce the whole game.

The game is, of course, in her world everything; we need not be put off by an effusion like, 'O had I stay'd, and said my pray'rs at home!' (IV 160). What Belinda renounces and seeks to destroy, in her spleen, is the pattern of order by which she has lived and of which she was the moving force. It is always someone like Belinda who gives style and grace to a social pattern. If the heroic overtones of the poem constantly insist upon the comparative triviality of this pattern, they serve also to glorify it. Just as the brilliant detail of the Flemish painters gave a heightened reality to those bourgeois subjects that pre-empted the space of the saints, so Pope's almost dazzling particularity – in each case woven out of generalities of heroic splendor – insists upon the

intense if miniature order of his society. The heroic virtues are
transposed to the scale of charm, and one cannot resist quoting
Burke's famous phrases about another such order:

It is gone, that sensibility of principle, that chastity of honor,
which felt a stain like a wound, which inspired courage whilst it
mitigated ferocity, which ennobled whatever it touched, and
under which vice itself lost half its evil, by losing all its grossness.

(*Reflections on the French Revolution*, 1790)

These words define what a code of civilized life must do. *The
Rape of the Lock* leaves its moral judgments implicit in its double
mock-heroic scale, but it makes of that scale an illuminating
vision of art as a sustaining pattern of order. It is an art of 'good
humor', of tact and charm, and its symbol is the delicate beauty
of a frail China jar. The metamorphosis at the close, in which
the lock rises above the splenetic battle and becomes an enduring
source of light, is more than a wry joke. Pope has shown in small
scale the ferocities that such an order can mitigate. And if it is
not the stain upon honor but upon brocade that is felt like a
wound, there is at least a real correspondence between those
worlds of transposed scale. The players of ombre are themselves
not unlike the playing-card kings and queens, and their battles
and intrigues are formalized into a pattern that is more real than
the actors.

The incongruity of the mock heroic is dissolved in its even
more surprising congruity, in its creation of an unheroic world
of art and grace where the relative proportions are retained even
as the total scale is sharply reduced. The poem does not rise to
the elevation of *Windsor Forest*, for it does not seek to reconcile
the least order with the highest. Instead it carries to new intensity
the double vision that sees both the fragility and strength, the
triviality and dignity, of art. (The elevated lock is, in a sense, the
poem, shining upon beaux and sparks, but upon all others who
will see it, too.) If this order remains an aesthetic one, below or
beyond morality, it none the less insists upon the formal delight
that is a dimension of all stable structures, whether cosmic
harmonies or heroic codes, poems or patterns of civility. And it

looks toward those more inclusive and morally significant visions of order that give weight to Pope's later work.

NOTES

1. J. Huizinga, *Homo Ludens: A Study of the Play Element in Culture* (Boston, 1955) p. 21.
2. Ibid. p. 11.

J. S. Cunningham

AN INTRODUCTION TO
THE RAPE OF THE LOCK (1966)

I

THE reader of Steele's periodical *The Guardian* on 10 June 1713 found himself offered a recipe or 'receit' for concocting an epic poem which would satisfy the requirements of the best critical theorists. The bland anonymous voice proposed '(for the Benefit of my Countrymen) to make it manifest, that Epick Poems may be made *without a Genius*, nay without Learning or much Reading'. Choose an old story which would allow scope for long passages of Homeric-Virgilian description, and a hero on whom you could heap all the best qualities to be found in 'the best celebrated Heroes of Antiquity'. To supply the traditional epic set-pieces, adopt 'a large quantity of Images and Descriptions from Homer's Iliads, with a Spice or two of Virgil'. As for the 'Machines', the obligatory Gods and Goddesses, 'the wisest way is to reserve them for your greatest Necessities' – they were invaluable for rescuing the hero from awkward situations if you could think of no more plausible way of contriving the plot.

The recipe was set out in a manner 'intelligible to ordinary Readers' – by which a Queen Anne essayist often meant chiefly his growing female audience – who could be similarly diverted a year later by the tone of mischievous flattery in the dedicatory letter prefacing the revised version of a notorious poem:

The Machinery, Madam, is a term invented by the Critics, to signify that part which the Deities, Angels, or Dæmons are made to act in a Poem: For the ancient Poets are in one respect like many modern Ladies; let an action be never so trivial in itself, they always make it appear of the utmost importance.

The letter went on to explain the unusual, indeed unique, celestial and infernal agents which had been added since the poem first appeared: interfering deities, malignant or benign, the most flimsy of which assist the heroine's coquetry, and reflect her beauty, in an environment of intrigue and malicious gossip. With this addition of 'Machinery', the poem satisfies in miniature the whole epic recipe, and does so with a self-delighting thoroughness which is hilariously misapplied, given the unvenerable subject, but at the same time marvellously apt. The pretentious vanity of the heroine and the beau-monde is mocked, but their intricate beauty and style simultaneously celebrated.

The title-page description of the poem is 'heroi-comical', following the example of Boileau's *Le Lutrin*. It is of some interest to look at such earlier mock epics as Boileau's poem and *The Dispensary* by Sir Samuel Garth. Pope knew both poems well, and may be tracked now and then in their snow. They set his wit playing on the heroic conventions, and he parodies similar passages and sometimes takes up a phrase or a cadence. However, it is plain that these debts by no means amount to inert imitation. *The Rape of the Lock* has an altogether distinctive imaginative coherence. A reader of an annotated edition of the poem might be forgiven for thinking the converse – namely, that it is merely an exercise of parody and ironic allusion, drawing on previous mock epics, and on the classics and their translators, with a familiarity we might despair of matching. But if we think of ancient and modern, or epic and contemporary, as the opposite poles of the poem's satiric wit, we have to go on to remark the complexity of the field set up between them – each has power to attract and to repel. And the whole design is governed by Pope's perception of non-satiric aptness in using the heroic idiom on an occasion ostensibly so slight. The epic rhetoric of transience seems to fit one girl's tribulations and future old age as properly as it suited Troy or Dido or Hector.

This is to say that *The Rape of the Lock* bears to classical epic not merely a parody relation. It has a truer relatedness to Homer and Virgil than had the poetasters who, as Pope saw, seriously set out to write epic 'without a Genius'. The poem called for both the witty irreverence of Pope's recipe for cooking up an epic and the deep-seated respect which sustained him through years of labour in translating Homer into English heroic couplets. The first four books of his *Iliad* were published in 1715. The author of the 'Receit' and *The Rape of the Lock* was then only twenty-seven years old.

II

A 'universal genius', no less, and 'universal learning', had been required of the intending epic poet by John Dryden:

he must have exactly studied Homer and Virgil as his patterns; Aristotle and Horace as his guides; Vida and Bossu as their commentators; with many others, both Italian and French critics, which I want leisure here to recommend.[1]

The requirement was daunting, and fortified dauntingly by Milton's example of deliberate scholarly preparation reflected in the complex allusiveness of the epic poem itself. Pope had proved on his own pulse very early in his career how easily such a project could turn into glorified plagiarism. He describes with characteristically lucid self-criticism his own juvenile attempt at writing an epic:

I endeavoured in this poem to collect all the beauties of the great epic writers into one piece: there was Milton's style in one part, and Cowley's in another; here the style of Spenser imitated, and there of Statius; here Homer and Virgil, and there Ovid and Claudian. . . . It was better planned than Blackmore's *Prince Arthur*; but as slavish an imitation of the ancients.[2]

From as late in his career as 1743, the year in which *The Dunciad* reached its final form, a very Drydenesque-Virgilian eight lines survive of Pope's project of writing an epic about Brutus. The ambition had persisted, unfulfilled, alongside the writing of mock epic, and together with the rebuking of those who debased the tradition unwittingly by letting 'Farce and Epic get a jumbled race'.[3]

In this obviously complicated situation, translation of the

classics was one way in which an English poet could honour traditions he felt to be exemplary, while avoiding mere pastiche. Since *Paradise Lost*, and partly dependent on it, there had emerged an epic idiom in English, tailored to the heroic couplet, and owing most to the robust genius of Dryden himself. Dryden's heroic satire and, above all, his great verse translation of Virgil's *Aeneid*, ring in Pope's mind as he in turn translates Homer. Dryden had brought Virgil 'to speak such *English*, as I could teach him'.[4] This 'heroick' idiom was vigorous, orotund, masculine, capable of many disciplined rhetorical effects and a powerful overt trenchancy: Pope's word for such a style is 'copious'. It was also, as a grand manner, suitably distanced from usages which might be felt to be provincial by virtue of their colloquialism or their limited contemporary reference. A heroic idiom should, it was felt, be 'judiciously antiquated'. On this principle Pope found fault with Dryden's own use of jargon in his Virgil, asserting that 'no Terms of Art, or Cant-Words, suit with the Majesty & Dignity which Epic Poetry requires'.[5] By contrast, Pope indicates how easily 'heroick' could be made *injudiciously* antiquated, when he ironically suggests 'darkening it up and down with *Old English*'.[6]

The recent translations by Dryden and others offered on the whole a model for fresh attempts – and, for the mock-heroic poet, a conveniently established currency for the practice of ironic fraudulence. In *The Rape of the Lock*, Pope adopts or adapts whole lines and phrases and rhetorical figures from the translators, sometimes with minimal verbal alteration, but always, of course, with the sea-change caused by the difference of context. Frequently there are exact or close equivalents to be found in Pope's own translation of Homer – the occurrence of a heroic word in mock epic did not blacklist it for the translator. In Dryden's poetry, which Pope 'searched for happy combinations of heroic diction', he found grandiloquence put to the service of heroic values. Phrases like 'the dire Event', 'th'unequal Fight', 'glitt'ring Spoil', 'rebounding Cries', seemed almost definitive as the language of extreme and glorious conflict. Here were ways of conveying as roundly in English as in Latin the stresses of noble character: 'But doubtful thoughts the hero's heart divide', or 'The dark recesses of his inmost mind', or, signicantly for *The Rape*, the 'secret springs of women's passions'. Ceremonious rhetoric gave order and dignity to oath and anger and lament. Words like 'mystick', 'thrice', 'sev'nfold', and 'Honour', carried a weight of suggestion deriving from the epic traditions of heroic devoutness and observance of the martial code. The 'Force or Fraud' choice, which had exercised Milton's fallen angels, occurred repeatedly in Dryden's Virgil. A sense of mutability, 'the slippry state of Humane-kind, And fickle Fortune', was fortified by resounding sententious commentary:

> O Mortals! blind in Fate, who never know
> To bear high Fortune, or endure the low!

And the superintending 'Machinery' – Jove, Juno, Fate – gave a long perspective to human endeavour, at once dwarfing and ennobling. But the question stood: was 'heroick', in 1710 or so, as academic as it was authoritative, as constricting to the inventive faculty as it was inviting to the imitative?

Mock epic allowed Pope to mimic and even emulate true epic without being subject to the rather oppressive prohibition of contemporary idiomatic usage and contemporary unheroic subject.

> Pretty! in Amber to observe the forms
> Of hairs, or straws, or dirt, or grubs, or worms;
> The things, we know, are neither rich nor rare,
> But wonder how the devil they got there?[7]

In the amber of the epic idiom are caught, in *The Rape of the Lock*, cant-words ('Wounds, Charms, and Ardors'), current slang ('Plague on't! 'tis past a jest – nay prithee, Pox!'), the very form and pressure of intimate contemporary speech ('trust me, dear', 'the horrid things they say'). Playing cat and mouse with epic etiquette, Pope is free to make transitions from heroic to topical, from sublime to ridiculous, in ways that are sometimes glaringly absurd, sometimes subtly masked and graded, but surprisingly often with a real enhancing effect. His repertory of comic effects runs from broad farce to the most sly innuendo. He found in *Tatler* and *Spectator* essays contemporary follies anatomized and banteringly rebuked in the name of a civilized sense of proportion. Beau and fopling, prude and flirt, had been decisively focused, with their wardrobe of gestures and their comic armoury of properties – fan, snuff-box, lap-dog, cane. But the essayists' irony is often too plain, and their material sometimes idly repetitive. Given Pope's shifting perspectives and spirited duplicity, we can 'feel all the appetite of curiosity', as Dr Johnson put it, 'for that from which we have a thousand times turned fastidiously away'.[8]

III

As early as 1714 Pope was collecting instances of involuntary absurdity where poetry aimed at grandeur and fell into bathos. Eventually, this material would be put to use by Pope, with the help of others, in *The Art of Sinking in Poetry* (1728). This ironic inversion of Longinus's treatise *Of the Sublime* included, among its sixteen chapters of mock advice, the 'Receit to make an Epick Poem' in a slightly altered version. It also carried instructions on how to *achieve* unholy mingles of heroic and contemporary, startling descents from exalted to vulgar. There is a difficult art, Pope argues tongue-in-cheek, in 'Modernizing and Adapting to the Taste of the times the works of the ancients'. By this means you could aspire to the 'Alamode' style, or the 'Pert' style, so contriving things that

Tacitus talks like a *Coffee-House Politician*, *Josephus* like the *British Gazetteer*, *Tully* is as short and smart as *Seneca* or Mr. *Asgill*, *Marcus Aurelius* is excellent at *Snipsnap*, and honest *Thomas a Kempis* as *Prim* and *Polite* as any Preacher at Court.[9]

The smart world of repartee ('*Snipsnap*'), of

> Coffee, (which makes the politician wise,
> And see thro' all things with his half-shut eyes)
>
> (III 117–18)

of 'singing, laughing, ogling, and all that' (III 18) was too delicate, to Pope's delighted amusement, for a particular preacher at
Court to mention Hell, 'a place which he thought it not decent
to name in so polite an assembly'.[10] In *The Rape of the Lock*,
'Modernizing and Adapting' the epic visit to the Underworld,
Pope is able to show the hells of hypochondria and worry that
lay just beneath the polite veneer.

The Art of Sinking carries many examples of unwitting bathos
from the works of Sir Richard Blackmore, a writer of slavishly
imitative epics who could be mockingly saluted as 'our English
Homer'. Pope quotes him when he comes to recommend the
use of 'Technical Terms'

which estrange your Stile from the great and general Ideas of
Nature: And the higher your Subject is, the lower should you
search into Mechanicks for your Expression. If you describe the
Garment of an Angel, say that his *Linnen* was *finely spun*, and
bleach'd on the happy Plains. Call an Army of Angels, *Angelic
Cuirassiers*, and if you have Occasion to mention a Number of
Misfortunes, stile them

>   *Fresh* Troops *of Pains, and* regimented *Woes*.[11]

When Pope himself describes the sylphs as 'The light Militia
of the lower sky', he is inviting mirth at the cost of inept English
Homerics, and at the cost of the sylphs, and also at the cost of the
epic convention of ranked quasi-military deities. But this difficult
art of calculated bathos is also, in Pope, a matter of affectionate
scaling-down, of 'beautiful diminution'.[12] There is a level of
delighted half-seriousness on which the sylphs are seen as marvellous, ephemeral images of the precarious loveliness of a young
girl in a corrupt but brilliant society, among the '*Ladies, Whis-
perers, and Backbiters*'.[13]

The 'Machines' of Homer and Virgil were, after all, part of an
obsolete mythology – if we can speak of obsolete myths. Dryden
had conceded the need for supernatural agents in epic, but had
reflected discouragingly on the feebleness of 'the machines of our
Christian religion' for this purpose.[14] The serious use of pagan
mythology by modern poets could even, Addison thought,

amount to 'downright puerility'.[15] Pope himself came to think that 'Jupiter, Juno, etc.' were not any longer 'open enough to the understanding'.[16] Dr Johnson finally asserts quite roundly that 'heathen deities can no longer gain attention'.[17] Using 'the Rosicrucian doctrine of Spirits', Pope in *The Rape of the Lock* avoids both embarrassments – that over paganism and that with the pale Christian alternatives. Here were, in words he would use later about a Voltaire poem, 'allegorical persons . . . equally proper to ancient and modern subjects and to all religions and times'.[16] It is as true of mock epics as of epic that 'the pains and diligence of ill Poets is but thrown away, when they want the Genius to invent and feign agreeably'; and Dryden has apt words again when we reflect that Pope in feigning the sylphs was able 'to draw Truth out of Fiction'.[18]

However, these Augustan discussions of the use of supernatural agents in poetry feel ponderous beside Pope's beautiful and mostly ineffectual angels (and devils). Taking up the Rosicrucian immortals is essentially a witty joke edged with irony. However, a seriously disposed reader of the expanded 1714 version of the poem could buy, in the same year, *The Count of Gabalis. Very necessary for the Readers of Mr Pope's Rape of the Lock*. Pope's own dedicatory letter to the poem is entertainingly terse about this French source of his 'Machines'. *Le Comte de Gabalis*, by the Abbé de Montfaucon de Villars, had appeared in 1671, and was available in two English versions some ten years later. One version, Pope remarks, looked 'so like a Novel, that many of the Fair Sex have read it for one by mistake'. The book presents the mysterious Count, an amateur Mephistophilis, seeking to bring his hearer to a belief in the four 'Elementary Nations' – sylphs (air), nymphs (water), gnomes (earth), and salamanders (fire). If belief were accompanied by the renunciation of all interest in the opposite sex, untold mysteries would be made clear, and even a full love partnership with spirits could be achieved.

There was much in this to amuse and stimulate the author of the first version of *The Rape*. The darling lap-dogs and pet monkeys of society ladies, said the Count, might be sylph-lovers in disguise. Sylphs, he agreed, were responsible for oracles, and 'still give them every Day in Drinking-Glasses or Looking-Glasses'. But Pope transforms the source-material, and by virtue of it transforms the poem. Mischievous analogies and satiric applications spring to his mind. The apparition of a sylph prompts the recall of sombre epic visitations; the properties of Milton's angels are hilariously at hand to describe these worldly butterflies. Gnomes are made practical jokers and associated with prudish spinsterdom, and sylphs are nervously virginal, with a generous allowance of coquetry. The dark mysteries of cabalistic lore are mockingly exploited to evoke the mystique of feminine beauty and the puzzles of feminine conduct. The injunction to be chaste is transformed through association with the coquette's teasing flirtatiousness, which lures men on only to refuse. In the sylphs, satire on women and the apotheosis of women are indivisible. With the gnomes we enter the world of spleen, where tantrum and nightmare, hypochondria and genuine melancholy, shadow each other in a world of moral disarray: society ladies modelled on Burton's *Anatomy of Melancholy*, their heads full of 'absurd, vain, foolish toys', lacking all sense of self-control and relative value – 'with every small cross again, bad news, misconceived injury, loss, danger, afflicted beyond measure, in great agony, perplexed, dejected, astonished, impatient, utterly undone' (1 iii 1(2)). Pope correlates inventiveness and moral point, and all without losing control of his blend of gravity and play.

IV

On the authority of Dryden among many others, and by common consent, epic was 'the greatest Work which the Soul of Man is capable to perform'. Not only was it an exacting test of creative stamina. It had honoured the human being by inventing and then sustaining and enriching a poetic language and a set of traditional observances in which man's highest aspirations and noblest energies could be mirrored and upheld. To catch fire from the classics was therefore, in an invigorating way, to 'follow Nature'. Of particular importance for *The Rape of the Lock* was the presence in classical epic of a rhetoric of fortitude in the face of Fate, threat, omen, defeat, and death. Pope had translated perhaps the most sonorous single passage of such rhetoric as early as 1707, five years before the first version of *The Rape* was published. It is the stirring rallying cry of Sarpedon to Glaucus in the hard-pressed Trojan ranks. Its closing lines run in Pope's version as follows:

> But since, alas, ignoble Age must come,
> Disease, and Death's inexorable Doom;
> The Life which others pay, let Us bestow,
> And give to Fame what we to Nature owe;
> Brave, tho' we fall; and honour'd, if we live;
> Or let us Glory gain, or Glory give.

The couplets balance the heroic alternatives in a formal discipline which readily conveys both inexorability and a hard lucid stoicism.

Critics had come to agree that the first obligation for a writer of epic was 'to make the moral of the work'.[19] Here, as with the 'Machines', there were embarrassments for an eighteenth-century Englishman in coming to terms with classical epic. It could be said that Homer wrote of times 'when a Spirit of Revenge and Cruelty reign'd thro' the World, when no Mercy was shown but for the sake of Lucre, when the greatest Princes were put to the Sword, and their Wives and Daughters made Slaves and Concubines'.[20] Homer might be excused such barbarity, Pope argued, on the grounds of historical accuracy – he reflected savagery, but did not condone it. But this argument had a make-shift look. Besides, Pope could see very well the demerits of the dry itemisation of the characteristics of epic: the Fable, the Machines, the Descriptions, the Hero, the Moral. There had been a plethora of critics who strained interpretation in the service of these abstractions, writing dull prescriptive advice for active poets:

> Some on the leaves of ancient authors play,
> Nor Time nor moths e'er spoil'd so much as they:
> Some dryly plain, without Invention's Aid,
> Write dull Receits how Poems may be made:

These leave the Sense, their Learning to display,
And those explain the Meaning quite away.[21]

Pope's mock 'Receit' is casually terse on the subject of 'the Moral
and Allegory' of epic: 'These you may Extract out of the Fable
afterwards at your leisure: Be sure you strain them sufficiently.'
   Nevertheless, the moral authority of epic was very strongly
felt, and Pope saw that this could, at least hypothetically,
encourage the modern poet who sought to convey 'noble morals
in a new Variety of Accidents'. In that *The Rape* is as much epic
scaled down as epic parodied, the obligation to 'make the moral'
could be felt to apply here too. And the poem had originally a
direct moral motive – the reconciliation through laughter of two
estranged families. Pope's dedicatory letter to the 'heroine',
Arabella Fermor, made the essential reference to good sense and
good humour and good nature. But Pope continued to feel that
the moral needed explicit reinforcement, until in 1717 he hit upon
the expedient of adding a speech closely modelled on Sarpedon's,
designed 'to open more clearly the MORAL of the Poem'. This is
the final major revision of the poem, and itself a triumphant
demonstration of Pope's tact and inventive duplicity. Clarissa's
speech cheapens Sarpedon's rhetoric so as to show up, without
her quite realizing it, the self-seeking materialism, the vanity
and the shallowness of those who are engaged in this other kind
of battle, the sex war. But she also adjusts both the fears and the
ethic of Sarpedon so as to convey a moral which is realistic and
enlightened for its own context and at its own level. Masculine
and militant is transposed into pacific and feminine.
   Dr Johnson was disposed to take the 'moral' of *The Rape*
rather too seriously, or with too plain a seriousness:

The freaks, and humours, and spleen, and vanity of women, as
they embroil families in discord and fill houses with disquiet, do
more to obstruct the happiness of life in a year than the ambition
of the clergy in many centuries.[22]

We may put it less austerely, but the Cave of Spleen, the tan-
trums of Thalestris, and Belinda's love of her own reflection,
lend support to Johnson's case. A poem Pope contributed to the

1712 *Miscellany*, in which *The Rape of the Lock* first appeared, reflects on the spoilt society lady who

> glares in *Balls*, *Front-boxes*, and the *Ring*,
> A vain, unquiet, glitt'ring, wretched Thing!

The poem goes on to announce the morality of grace and balance and lucid contentment in much the same terms as are later given to Clarissa in her speech:

> Trust not too much your now resistless Charms,
> Those, Age or Sickness, soon or late, disarms;
> *Good Humour* only teaches Charms to last,
> Still makes new Conquests, and maintains the past:
> Love, rais'd on Beauty, will like That decay,
> Our Hearts may bear its slender Chains a Day,
> As flow'ry Bands in Wantonness are worn;
> A Morning's Pleasure, and at Evening torn.[23]

More than twenty years later, Pope will recall this poem and *The Rape* in once more addressing to Martha Blount lines on this ideal of feminine character, which

> Lets Fops or Fortune fly which way they will;
> Disdains all loss of Tickets, or Codille;
> Spleen, Vapours, or Small-pox, above them all,
> And Mistress of herself, tho' China fall.[24]

The relevance of such sentiments to *The Rape of the Lock* may be seen from another angle if we turn back to Pope's letter to 'Belinda' on the subject of her marriage in 1714:

It was but just, that the same Virtues which gave you reputation, should give you happiness; and I can wish you no greater, than that you may receive it in as high a degree your self, as so much good humour must infallibly give it to your husband. . . . Besides, you are now a married woman, and in a way to be a great many better things than a fine Lady; such as an excellent wife, a faithful friend, a tender parent, and at last as the consequence of them all, a saint in heaven.[25]

One model for this letter's graceful ease and temperate morality was the published correspondence of Vincent de Voiture. Greatly

in vogue at the time, Voiture's letters had been translated by
Dryden and others, and the 1712 *Miscellany* poem I have mentioned, although it was later addressed to Martha Blount, originally carried the title 'To a Young Lady. With the Works of
Voiture'. Elegant, courtly, suave, tender, the letters as a whole
brought together romantic compliment and a smiling practical
wisdom. They commend 'good Nature', 'the Rule of Moderation', and 'that Greatness of Mind by which you are rais'd so
far above Crowns and Scepters', combining praise and reasonableness as Pope would to Martha Blount or Arabella Fermor:
'Nor indeed, Madam, is it any more than just, that a Person so
cœlestially Bright as you are, should comply with the Will of
Heaven; and having received so much from it, be content it
shou'd take something from you'.[26] The contrast is the world of
spleen, that vexatious ill-nature which treats misfortune as
calamity, and a prank as an outrage.

Voiture had also become a model for the billet-doux:

it is now a whole Day, since I have sigh'd, and look'd silly, and
languish'd, and dy'd, and all that for you. Without having even
seen your Face, I am taken with its Beauty; and am charm'd with
your Wit, tho' I never have heard one Syllable of it. I am ravish'd
with my every Action, and I fancy in you a kind of I know not
what, that makes me passionately in Love with I know not
whom.[27]

When we read in Voiture such protestations as 'I am more
apprehensive of Death from your Eyes, than your Hands', or
'whatsoever Mortal Wounds I have, I believe, my Soul cannot
detach itself from my Heart, because it sees your Image there',
we meet an idiom Pope both mocks and sustains. Vulgarized,
this style had declined into the 'Wounds, Charms, and Ardors'
of the courtly love-letter Belinda reads when she wakes; its
operatic equivalent on the London stage at the time, 'Those
Eyes are made so killing', turned farcical at a touch. That Pope
should mock such flights as affectation is not surprising. Yet he
can do so and still engage our sympathetic respect for romantic
hyperbole:

> For, after all the murders of your eye,
> When, after millions slain, yourself shall die;
> When those fair suns shall set, as set they must,
> And all those tresses shall be laid in dust . . .

That Pope is able to both mock and enhance such material may remind us that although we can be quite specific about the poem's *moral*, we should not seek to reduce its *morality* to the merely didactic. The life and validity of the poem's moral point can be realized only by way of a full response to the living text. Its resilience, its delicate but energetic balance, its civilized tempering of seriousness with levity – such are the artistic correlatives of the morality of good humour and nurtured ease.

v

Pope's dedicatory letter, we have seen, offered a mischievous comparison of ancient poets and modern ladies: they were both apt to exaggerate, as if the fall of a vase were as catastrophic as the crash of an empire. The hint is useful, and the comparison broadens readily for a reader of *The Rape of the Lock*. On the one hand, there is the heroic code of behaviour, with its own imperatives, its own stresses, gestures, rituals, portents. The code is mirrored in the traditional observances of epic, which had obvious authority but degenerated in time and in the wrong hands into empty routines:

> If *Ulysses* visit the Shades, the *Æneas* of *Virgil* and *Scipio* of *Silius* are sent after him. If he be detain'd from his Return by the Allurements of *Calypso*, so is *Æneas* by *Dido*, and *Rinaldo* by *Armida*. If *Achilles* be absent from the *Army* on the Score of a Quarrel thro' half the Poem, *Rinaldo* must absent himself just as long, on the like account.[28]

The modern ladies, for their part, have their own priorities, gestures, and rituals, and these can also become vacuous conventions easily. They are partly social – dressing-table, tea-table, card-game – and the epic analogues for these – hero arming,

epic feast, pitched battle – mimic the inflated seriousness with
which the ladies (and the fops) engage in them. They have a
strong literary element: love-letter jargon, operatic song, the
reading of romantic novels as fantasy models of behaviour. In
this respect, Pope's use of obsolescent literary conventions to
describe the ladies and the fops has a direct aptness.

The historical link with classical epic is through romance,
which Dryden had ruled out of place in epic poems:

Even the least portions of them must be of the Epick kind; all
things must be Grave, Majestical, and Sublime: Nothing of a
Foreign Nature, like the trifling *Novels*, which *Ariosto* and other
have inserted in their Poems.[29]

Pope has his eyes on Ariosto more than once in *The Rape of the
Lock*, most notably in the catalogue in Canto v of things lost in
the lunar sphere. He makes a generalized allusion to romance at
the moment when Clarissa produces the fateful scissors:

> So Ladies in Romance assist their Knight,
> Present the spear, and arm him for the fight.

Mock epic may stoop to the trifling. At the same time, we should
remember that classical epic itself is not devoid of 'am'rous
causes'. The seizure of Briseis by Agamemnon is the immediate
cause of the wrath of Achilles:

> no more Achilles draws
> His conquering sword in any woman's cause.[30]

The Rape of the Lock frequently insinuates the love of Dido and
Aeneas as a mock analogue of the affair of Belinda and the Baron.
Part of the point of the poem's opening couplet is that it could
stand unaltered as a comment from one viewpoint (one that
Shakespeare, for example, had entertained in *Troilus and Cressida*)
on the Trojan war:

> What dire offence from am'rous causes springs,
> What mighty contests rise from trivial things

We may make this point in another way if we ask Yeats's

question: 'What theme had Homer but original sin?' In his
poem 'To Belinda on the Rape of the Lock', Pope is not merely
flattering her in moving from her misfortune to

> Thus *Helens* Rape and *Menelaus'* wrong
> Became the Subject of great *Homer*'s song.

In the main, however, *The Rape of the Lock* is matching artificiality with artifice, pretentiousness with pretence – satirically,
but with a mitigating gaiety and lightness of touch. The vanity
of belle and beau meet the aptest of poetic justice in being presented, as their own wishful mirrors reflect them, as hero and
heroine (Thalestris a 'fierce virago', but Belinda – except in the
first version – consistently a 'nymph'). There is another satiric
aptness in this: remote from Troy, the fashionable are engaged
in their own intriguing conflict. Nearly all the initiative and the
weapons lie with the ladies – killing glance, ogle, 'Puffs, Powders, Patches', 'sighs, sobs, and passions'. The traditional sexual
pun on 'die' permits Pope a wickedly minute correspondence
between the two sorts of warfare:

> See fierce *Belinda* on the Baron flies,
> With more than usual lightning in her eyes:
> Nor fear'd the Chief th'unequal fight to try,
> Who sought no more than on his foe to die.

Both sides manœuvre for high stakes, but the poem exacts
admiration and sympathy for the belle's beauty and her predica-
ment, consigning the beaus and fops to mockery. Pope repeatedly
insinuates the fragility ('glittering' celebrates and places her) of
her moment of eminence – adored, envied, named in every toast.
Knowing that 'she who scorns a man must die a maid', she is also
beset by prurient scandal-mongers ready to interpret love-
trophies in the worst of lights. To them, the 'raped' lock of hair
would be the welcome token of a worse violation. Virginity is
lost as easily as a 'frail China jar' is broken; but more important,
in the social ethos of the poem, is the loss of 'Honour', which has
dwindled to mean little more than mere reputation. Thalestris

even implies, unperturbed, an opposition between 'Honour' and
'Virtue':

> Gods! shall the ravisher display your hair,
> While the Fops envy, and the Ladies stare!
> *Honour* forbid! at whose unrival'd shrine
> Ease, pleasure, virtue, all, our sex resign.

It is characteristic of the poem that even this speech, urging
Belinda to avenge the theft of the lock, allows us to sense real
calamity behind the worldly estimate of lost reputation:

> Methinks already I your tears survey,
> Already hear the horrid things they say,
> Already see you a degraded toast,
> And all your honour in a whisper lost!

These lines are a miniature demonstration of the poem's tonal
resilience, moving from an echo of epic (Hecuba foreseeing
Hector's death) through 'contemporary' (with a cheapness that
contrives to be touching) to the stealthy eloquence of the fourth
line. If the term 'mock epic' suggests a mere contrast of opposites,
it will hinder more readers than it will help. There are, after all,
genuine distresses in Belinda's world: besides notoriety, there is
bitter, virginal old age, and the murderous small-pox. All three
might be mitigated, as Clarissa argues, by self-possession and a
lucid stoicism. But Belinda herself – 'ev'n Belinda' – will die in
course of time. The sun in the poem both rises on her and,
prospectively, sets.

VI

In one of his own notes to the poem (III 122), Pope refers us to
Ovid's *Metamorphoses* to explain his allusion to the myth of
Scylla, who was changed into a bird after stealing a magical lock
of her father's hair in a vain attempt to win the love of Minos.
In the wake of Dryden once again, Pope had translated a few
stories from Ovid's comprehensive collection of transformations
while still a very young poet. One of them was published in the
1712 *Miscellany* along with *The Rape of the Lock*. To convey in

formal verse the subtle declension of one thing into another is a taxing proposition, carrying all the fascination of what's difficult. Pope tried it again in *Windsor Forest*: in some rudimentary Ovidian mythologizing of his own, he describes how the nymph Lodona, chased by Pan like Syrinx before her, is magically transformed into the river Loddon:

> The silver stream her virgin coldness keeps,
> For ever murmurs, and for ever weeps;
> Still bears the name the hapless virgin bore,
> And bathes the forest where she rang'd before.
>
> (205–8)

Accomplished, but essentially academic, myth-making. The important thing is that Ovid had helped to alert Pope to metamorphosis both as a topic in poetry and as something poetry might astonishingly accomplish. His imagination and moral sensibility are very decidedly polarized towards effects of change – for instance, the distortions brought about by mist and fog, images of moral and intellectual delusion. In *The Dunciad*, Dulness is 'cloud-compelling' in a sense never intended for Zeus; she looks through fogs, and can flatter folly by spreading 'a healing mist before the mind'. Under her regime, crowds 'turn coxcombs', bards assume (like Ovid's Proteus) the shapes of monsters, cooks turn hares into larks, and Order is transformed back into Chaos:

> The Forests dance, the rivers upward rise,
> Whales sport in woods, and dolphins in the skies.[31]

Such a nightmare of degree untuned, identity sliding out of itself, relates back from *The Dunciad* to the Cave of Spleen in *The Rape of the Lock*. Here, in a parody Underworld itself indebted to Ovid's Cave of Envy, the fashionable hypochondria of the privileged classes spawns its fantasy brood. Pope echoes Dryden's translation of Ovid closely in offering to describe these infernal transformations:

> Unnumber'd throngs on ev'ry side are seen,
> Of bodies chang'd to various forms by Spleen.

Ill-nature, migraine, sickly affectation, inhabit the Cave. It is a limbo of social frustration and attitudinizing and petulance, with a strong and comic sexual element:

> Men prove with child, as pow'rful fancy works,
> And maids turn'd bottles, call aloud for corks.

By contrast, Belinda's day is patrolled by the spirits of women metamorphosed after death in accordance with the chief element in their nature – fire, water, earth, or air – 'by soft Transition'. Her guardian is a sylph (a metamorphosed coquette) whose duty is to guide her intricate attractive waywardness. Rejecting 'Mankind', she is inconsistently steeped in worldly vanity, and yet tantalizes men's affections with a marvellous innocence and grace. Cleopatra-like, she is herself metamorphosed from moment to moment, a miracle she assists at the dressing-table mirror. For the daily cosmetic ritual,

> The Tortoise here and Elephant unite,
> Transform'd to combs, the speckled, and the white.
>
> (I 135–6)

In '*China*'s earth receives the smoking tyde', the pouring of tea meets not merely an ironic aggrandizement – a familiar thing has been made new. Belinda's fated lock, like that of Catullus's Berenice, is itself transformed into a new star in the last of the poem's many metamorphoses.

Words like 'soft' and 'melting' and 'transient' carry through in the poem, from the imaging of metamorphosis to Pope's insistence on feminine changeableness. But this insistence is as varied in tone as its subject is: the moral point does not eclipse, but is sustained by, the sense of a perpetual miracle of ephemeral grace and momentary beauty. In the contrast with fixed heroic will, femininity emerges now deplorably capricious, now radiantly pliant and even partly wise. Dryden had made Virgil speak 'such *English*, as I could teach him'. Pope's translation of Homer, intended 'to revive the old of past ages to the present', spoke a civilized, formal, elegant English with a Roman and Drydenesque cast. In *The Rape of the Lock* the metamorphosis of epic gains a full creative freedom that was denied even to so decidedly un-Greek a translator, in the shifting lights of a spirited sympathetic mockery.

NOTES

1. *Essays*, ed. W. P. Ker (Oxford, 1900) II 43.
2. See Joseph Spence, *Observations, Anecdotes, and Characters of Books and Men*, 1820 ed. pp. 47–8, 50.
3. *The Dunciad*, IV 70.
4. 'The Dedication of the Æneis', in *Poems*, ed. James Kinsley (Oxford, 1958) p. 1055.
5. Letter to Henry Cromwell, 28 Oct. 1710, in *The Correspondence of Alexander Pope*, ed. G. Sherburn (Oxford, 1956) I 101.
6. See supra, p. 29.
7. 'Epistle to Dr Arbuthnot', 169 ff.
8. *Lives of the Poets*, ed. G. B. Hill (1905) III 339.
9. *Art of Sinking*, ed. E. L. Steeves (New York, 1952) p. 66.
10. See *Moral Essay IV*, 149 ff and Pope's note.
11. *Art of Sinking*, ed. Steeves, p. 62.
12. Cf. R. A. Brower, *Alexander Pope* (Oxford, 1959) p. 144.
13. *Art of Sinking*, ed. Steeves, p. 73.
14. *Essays*, II 32.
15. *Spectator*, no. 523, of 30 Oct. 1712.
16. Letter to Bolingbroke, 9 April 1724, in *Correspondence*, II 228.
17. *Lives*, III 233.
18. 'The Dedication of the Æneis', in *Poems*, ed. Kinsley, p. 1031.
19. Dryden, *Essays*, I 213.
20. Pope's Preface to *The Iliad of Homer*.
21. *Essay on Criticism*, 112–17.
22. See supra, p. 69.
23. 'Epistle to Miss Blount, With the Works of Voiture', 58–66. Originally addressed 'To a Young Lady'.
24. *Moral Essay II*, 265–8.
25. *Correspondence*, I 272.
26. *Familiar and Courtly Letters*, trans. Dryden and others, 3rd ed. (1701) II 21. Voiture is consoling the Duchess of Longueville on the death of her father.
27. Ibid. I 21. Letter 'To his unknown Mistress'.
28. *The Iliad of Homer*, Preface.
29. 'The Dedication of the Æneis', in *Poems*, ed. Kinsley, p. 1003.
30. *The Iliad of Homer*, I 395 ff.
31. *The Dunciad*, III 245 ff.

QUESTIONS

1. 'For even satire is a form of sympathy' (D. H. Lawrence). How are Pope's sympathies made apparent in *The Rape of the Lock*?

2. What allusions are made to other literature in *The Rape of the Lock*? How do they affect your reading of the poem?

3. Compare the 1712 and 1714 versions of the poem. What has Pope gained by his additions? Similarly, what is added to the poem in the 1717 version by the insertion of Clarissa's speech?

4. 'The little is made great, and the great little' (Hazlitt). How does this happen in the poem? Why is it done?

5. How would you explain the *seriousness* of the poem?

6. Is the machinery superfluous, as Dennis says?

7. Pope 'correlates inventiveness and moral point' (Cunningham). How does he do this?

8. What meaning do you attach to the description of *The Rape of the Lock* as 'mock-heroic'?

9. What comments does the poem make either directly or indirectly on Queen Anne Society?

10. How would you describe some of the niceties of *tone* that control the poem and their activity in the poetry?

11. How far does the following passage from W. B. Yeats's 'A Prayer for My Daughter' represent the moral of Pope's poem?

> May she be granted beauty and yet not
> Beauty to make a stranger's eye distraught,
> Or hers before a looking-glass, for such,
> Being made beautiful overmuch,
> Consider beauty a sufficient end,
> Lose natural kindness and maybe
> The heart-revealing intimacy
> That chooses right . . .

SELECT BIBLIOGRAPHY

1. There is really only one regrettable omission from this volume, namely, J. S. Cunningham, *Pope's 'The Rape of the Lock'* (Studies in English Literature 2: Arnold, 1961), which proved rather too compact for extracting something meaningful from it. Its intricate and informed reading of the poem should not be missed.

2. Also interesting for its discussion of the relationship of *The Rape of the Lock* to Pope's translations is William Frost, 'The Rape of the Lock and Pope's Homer', in *Modern Language Quarterly*, VIII (1947) 342–54; it is also included in *Essential Articles* (see below, under 5).

3. No student of the poem would fail to derive assistance from either of the two modern editions of the poem: Geoffrey Tillotson edits volume II of the Twickenham Edition of the poems of Alexander Pope, 3rd ed. (Methuen, Yale U.P., 1962), which contains *The Rape of the Lock*. There is also *The Rape of the Lock*, ed. J. S. Cunningham (O.U.P., 1966), which has notes that are helpful, for instance, in spelling out some of the allusions that the poem makes.

4. Some other pieces may be helpful: Lawrence Babb, 'The Cave of Spleen', in *Review of English Studies*, XII (1936) 165–76, and Ian Jack, *Augustan Satire. Intention and Idiom in English Poetry 1660–1750* (O.U.P., 1952; paperback 1966), where the chapter on the 'complex mock-heroic' of *The Rape of the Lock* has some useful material on the Rosicrucian spirits. See also Rebecca P. Parkin, 'Mythopoeic Activity in *The Rape of the Lock*' in *Journal of English Literary History* XXI (1954) 30–8; Earl R. Wasserman, 'The Limits of Allusion in *The Rape of the Lock*', in *Journal of English and Germanic Philology*, LXV (1966)

425–44; and W. K. Wimsatt, Jr, 'The Game of Ombre in *The Rape of the Lock*', in *Review of English Studies*, NS I (1950) 136–43.

5. Otherwise it is a question of suggesting material that will place the poem in fuller historical and critical perspective: Maynard Mack, ' "Wit and Poetry and Pope": Some Observations on his Imagery', in *Pope and his Contemporaries*, ed. J. L. Clifford and L. A. Landa (O.U.P., 1949); Douglas Knight, *Pope and the Heroic Tradition* (Yale U.P., 1951); Reuben A. Brower, *Alexander Pope: The Poetry of Allusion* (O.U.P., 1959), from which the chapter on *The Rape of the Lock* in this volume has been taken; George Sherburn, *The Early Career of Alexander Pope* (Princeton U.P., 1934; Russell & Russell, 1963); Thomas R. Edwards, Jr, *This Dark Estate: A Reading of Pope* (Perspectives in Criticism 11: California U.P., 1963); finally an excellent selection of criticism on Pope is available in *Essential Articles for the Study of Alexander Pope*, ed. Maynard Mack (Frank Cass, 1964).

NOTES ON CONTRIBUTORS

WILLIAM L. BOWLES (1762–1850) is chiefly remembered for his sonnets, which stimulated Coleridge, and for his edition of Pope, which drew him into controversy with Byron.

CLEANTH BROOKS, formerly Professor of English at Yale University, is the author of *Modern Poetry and the Tradition* and *The Well Wrought Urn*, both important books in the history of the American 'New Criticism'.

REUBEN A. BROWER was Professor of English at Harvard University. Besides his book on Pope, his writings include *The Fields of Light. An Experiment in Critical Reading*. He died in 1975.

GEORGE G. N. BYRON, 6th Baron Byron (1788–1824): poet and political liberationist.

THOMAS CAMPBELL (1777–1844) was a poet, principally remembered for such war-songs as 'Ye Mariners of England' and 'The Battle of the Baltic'.

J. S. CUNNINGHAM is Professor of English at the University of Leicester.

JOHN DENNIS (1657–1734) was satirised for his bombast by Pope in the *Essay on Criticism*; he wrote tragedies and was best known for his critical essays.

WILLIAM HAZLITT (1778–1830) was a prolific journalist and essayist, best remembered now for his *Lectures on the English Poets*, *Characters of Shakespeare's Plays* and *The Spirit of the Age*.

JOHN DIXON HUNT has taught in the Universities of York and London. In 1983 he was appointed Professor of English Literature in the University of Leiden. His publications include *The Pre-Raphaelite Imagination, 1848–1900*, *The Figure in the Landscape: Poetry, Painting and Gardens in the Eighteenth Century*, the 'Macmillan Critical Commentary' on *The Tempest* and the Casebook on Tennyson's *In Memoriam*.

SAMUEL JOHNSON (1709–84) was a poet (*London,* and *The Vanity of Human Wishes*), editor (*The Rambler*), literary critic and personality.

G. WILSON KNIGHT is Emeritus Professor of English Literature at the University of Leeds and is the author of many books on Shakespeare, such as *The Wheel of Fire* and *Principles of Shakespearean Production.*

MURRAY KRIEGER formerly at the University of Iowa, is Unversity Professor of English, University of California at Irvine.

MAYNARD MACK is Professor of English at Yale University and is the author of some excellent articles on Pope and the eighteenth century.

MARTIN PRICE is Professor of English at Yale University and is the author of *Swift's Rhetorical Art* and *To the Palace of Wisdom: Studies in order and energy from Dryden to Blake.*

HUGO M. REICHARD is Professor of English at Purdue University, Indiana.

GEOFFREY TILLOTSON (1905–69) was Professor of English Literature at Birkbeck College in the University of London and the author of *On the Poetry of Pope* and *Pope and Human Nature.*

JOSEPH WARTON (1722–1800) was a (very unsuccessful) headmaster of Winchester and a literary critic.

AUBREY WILLIAMS, Professor of English at the University of Florida, is the author of *Pope's 'Dunciad': A Study of its Meaning* and joint editor of the first volume of the *Twickenham Edition* of Pope's poetry.

Index